cross *the* bridge Every Day

DAVID McGEE

xulon PRESS

Design Director: Mike Crump
Cover design by: Mike Crump
Editing, compilation by: Bob Bennett, Shawn Bumpers, Mike Crump, Irene DeArmond, Leigh Ann Proctor, Angela Short and Jody Stowman.

www.xulonpress.com

❖

To God and His continuing work in my life and yours.
To my family—Nora, Ashli and her husband, John, John David and Benjamin Aaron—who have given and sacrificed much in this journey. Thanks to the staff and volunteers at the Bridge and Cross the Bridge (past, present and future). Thank you for all your hard work. Thank you to all those who support the work of the ministry financially, you make so much possible. Especially to you, dear reader, who helped make this a labor of love. May you discover your adventurous life every day as you walk with Him.

TABLE of CONTENTS

❖

YOU CAN KNOW YOU ARE FORGIVEN!

We all need forgiveness.

Romans 3:10 "As it is written: 'There is none righteous, no, not one.'" **NKJV**

Romans 3:23-24 "for all have sinned and fall short of the glory of God," **NKJV**

God wants to forgive us.

Romans 5:8 "But God demonstrates His own love toward us, in that while we were still sinners, Christ died for us." **NKJV**

Romans 5:12 "Therefore, just as through one man sin entered the world, and death through sin, and thus death spread to all men, because all sinned — " **NKJV**

Jesus died to offer us the gift of forgiveness.

Romans 6:23 "For the wages of sin is death, but the gift of God is eternal life in Christ Jesus our Lord." **NKJV**

We can ask and receive this forgiveness from God.

Romans 10:9-10 'that if you confess with your mouth the Lord Jesus and believe in your heart that God has raised Him from the dead, you will be saved. For with the heart one believes unto righteousness, and with the mouth confession is made unto salvation." **NKJV**

Romans 10:13 "For 'whoever calls on the name of the Lord shall be saved.'" **NKJV**

Please pray a simple prayer like this with me right now.

Dear Jesus,

I believe that You died for me so that I could be forgiven. I believe You were raised from the dead so that I could have a new life. I admit that I have done wrong things, and I am sorry. Please forgive me of all of those things. Please give me Your power to live for You the rest of my life. In Jesus' name, Amen.

If you prayed that prayer, please call us at 877.458.5508, write us or email me at pastordavid@ crossthebridge.com

I want to encourage you in your life. You just made the greatest decision ever.

Introduction

The Bible is such an incredible book. I have dedicated my life to understanding it and sharing it with people just like you. With this devotional, I will walk with you every day and guide you through this incredible, life-changing book. It is important we read and apply the Bible every day.

Hebrews 2:1 "So we must listen very carefully to the truth we have heard, or we may drift away from it." **NLT**

I want you to not just read a verse, but I want you to think about it and turn those thoughts into actions.

Joshua 1:8 "Study this Book of Instruction continually. Meditate on it day and night so you will be sure to obey everything written in it. Only then will you prosper and succeed in all you do." **NLT**

Every devotional has a scripture or scriptures, a life lesson, a directed prayer and some thoughts. Life often gives you the pain and then the lesson. I want to give you the life lesson so you can often avoid the pain. It is the product of many hours of study, preparation and most importantly hearing from God. I know this book can help you find the life that God wants to give you.

John 10:10b "…My purpose is to give them a rich and satisfying life."**NLT**

Please take the time to read this book every day. It has made a difference in many individual lives and it will help you. If you happen to miss a day, jump right back and continue reading. It is especially important to read it on the days you don't feel like it or when you mess up the day before. Just like walking somewhere, you grow in your faith step by step. If someone you know is hurting, please give them a copy of this book. Give a copy to family, friends or co-workers. Take copies to hospitals, prisons, rehab centers, retirement homes or other places where people may recognize their need for God. If we can help you in anyway, please just give us a call or send an email.

I am living to tell what He died to say,

Pastor David McGee

Pastor David McGee
Cross the Bridge Ministries
The Bridge Christian Fellowship
crossthebridge.com
aboutthebridge.com

JANUARY 1
FRESH

Revelation 21:5a

"Then He who sat on the throne said, "Behold, I make all things new.""..."
NKJV

How timely it is to stop and consider this verse today. As we have a New Year starting, in like manner we have a fresh new start in our life for the Lord. What does the year hold for you? Well I can assure you that the Lord has some awesome things prepared for each of us individually and as a church. This past year the Lord did some incredible things and I look forward to a new year filled with family and friends coming to know the Lord. We will see multitudes moved forward in the spiritual journey from discovery to discipleship. What awwwn adventure! It is all made possible by a fresh start ... Thanks Lord for new beginnings!

Life Lesson: Jesus makes all things new... including you.

Dear Father,
Thank You for new beginnings. What an incredible day this is with a fresh year's potential stretched out before me. I want to be found faithful this year in each and every opportunity you bring to me. Thank You, Lord, for new beginnings. I pray this in Jesus' name, Amen.

JANUARY 2
IT'S ALL ABOUT JESUS

John 3:30
"He must increase, but I must decrease."
NKJV

This saying was true for John the Baptist when speaking of Jesus and it is true for us today. As Christians, we should be learning about the Lord. What does the Lord want? What does He desire and how can I serve Him? Instead we often think: 'What can God do for me?' We ask, 'What can the church do for me?' or 'Why don't they understand it's all about me?'

When we gaze at our wounds, our pains and our needs, we delay and may even prevent our healing. The spiritual things of life - Love, joy, peace, patience, kindness, goodness, faithfulness, gentleness, self-control and the practical things of life... If we take time to really focus on the Lord, then all these things will be added unto us. We will receive our healing, our forgiveness, the joy unspeakable and the peace that passes all understanding. It's all about Jesus.

Life Lesson: It's all about Jesus.

Dear Father,
Thank You for loving me so much You sent Jesus to die on the cross for my sins. Forgive me for times when I've lost focus and become self absorbed. Empower me to let go of my own will and seek Yours. I pray this in Jesus' name, Amen.

JANUARY 3
VESSELS FOR GOD'S GRACE

John 4:10
"....He would have given you living water."
NKJV

Jesus desires to give living water. After all of our mistakes and all of our failures, He still desires to give mankind life eternal. He wants to give it to the atheists and those who defraud and defame His glorious name. He wants to give it to those who try to silence the Good News by false interpretations of church and state. He wants to give it to Muslims, to New Age gurus, to those who say He was married to Mary Magdalene. If only they would ask for it.

He gave it to a woman with a sordid past. He gives it to those who do not deserve it. He gave it to you and to me. Now Jesus wants to use us as earthen vessels to distribute this 'living water' into a world that is dying of thirst.

Life Lesson: We should be vessels for God's grace to others.

Dear Father,
Thank You for the grace You have so abundantly heaped onto my head. I want to be established each morning in Your new mercies and I am ever dependent on Your grace and love. Let me be a light of Your grace to all who I come across today. I pray this in Jesus' name, Amen.

JANUARY 4
GIVE ME SOME WATER

John 4:15
"Please, sir," the woman said, "give me some of that water! Then I'll never be thirsty again, and I won't have to come here to haul water."
NLT

The Israelites and Samaritans lived in a dry, thirsty land; in a desert. It is hard for many of us to imagine how valuable water is in such a desperate place. Yet, we live in a spiritually dry and thirsty land; we are often oblivious to the lack. I wonder how many times a day someone tells us they are thirsty. Perhaps not, 'please give me some of that water', but they put it another way. When they speak of problems with their children, troubles in their marriage and trials in their life, they are really saying, "I am thirsty." When they are short tempered, worn out and angry, they are saying they don't know how to quench their thirst. I also wonder how many times we don't really understand their plea and their thirst. How many times we walk past opportunities to minister to them. Be filled up this morning and go give it away. Look for the thirsty and look for the dry. Hear their cries and offer them living water.

Life Lesson: We should be pouring out to the world what God has poured into us.

Dear Father,
Thank You for loving me so much that You allow me to serve You. Lord, I lift this land up to You and ask You to raise up workers for the harvest. You offer the water that completely quenches our need and You offer it abundantly and freely. Open the hearts of this world to Your gift and allow me to play a part in the quenching of this thirsty world. I thank You that the results are in Your almighty hands. I pray this in Jesus' name, Amen.

JANUARY 5
WHY SALVATION?

John 4:35-36
"Do you not say, 'There are still four months and then comes the harvest'? Behold, I say to you, lift up your eyes and look at the fields, for they are already white for harvest! And he who reaps receives wages, and gathers fruit for eternal life, that both he who sows and he who reaps may rejoice together."
NKJV

We talk about the importance of people hearing the Gospel, but it is not enough to just talk about it. No, it must be our desire to see people get saved and become Talmudim (disciples). Here, we do a lot of things in order to reach the lost. Our Cross the Bridge Outreaches, our Tell the World gatherings, the support we give to missionaries - these are just a few of the many ways we are reaching the lost. In order to do this, the whole church chips in and, quite frankly, I am amazed at the tremendous giving nature of The Bridge and our Bridge Builders (Cross the Bridge Partners).

Because of your generosity and desire to see the lost reached, we are able to take the resources that God has provided through you and use them prayerfully and wisely to speak the Gospel into millions of ears. The wise use of these resources advance the kingdom of God. I want to encourage you in joining with us to reach the world. Be committed to this work that God is doing. This ministry is reaping an incredible harvest that is clearly of God. As you sow into this ministry and this ministry reaps the harvest, we have formed a partnership that is providing eternal rewards. Let's reach the world for Jesus and not stop until the whole world hears. May God bless you for your faithfulness.

Life Lesson: Be committed to God's work.

Dear Father,
Thank You for those who give so generously to see others blessed by the life-giving Gospel of Jesus Christ. I ask You to bless these precious providers even as they selflessly bless others. I ask that You continue to open doors of opportunity for Cross the Bridge Ministries and The Bridge and our supporters because we want the whole world to hear. I pray this in Jesus' name, Amen.

JANUARY 6
GOT TROUBLE?

John 4:50
"So the man believed the word that Jesus spoke to him,"
NKJV

How much trouble could we avoid if we simply did what the nobleman in John chapter 4 did? What if we stopped in the middle of crummy circumstances and sticky situations and chose to believe the Word that Jesus has spoken to us? We read the newspaper and believe it. We read stuff on the Internet and believe it. We read the Bible and sometimes we think, "Well, that doesn't apply to me or my situation."

Sometimes we believe our emotions, fickle though they are, over the Word of God. We listen to the skeptics and the naysayers. We listen to our experiences as well as our faulty interpretation of events. Of all the things that we can listen to and believe, the Word of God is the most reliable. It has proven its sturdiness many times through the centuries. It has outlasted all of its critics and still stands ever faithful and true. Many voices are calling out for your attention. Which one will you choose to act on and believe? I choose to believe Jesus and the Word He has spoken to me.

Life Lesson: We should believe the Bible.

Dear Father,
Thank You for Your steadfast love. Thank You that Your Word has stood the test of time and remains the source of truth and light for every situation in our lives. Please continue this work of opening my heart up to the amazing faithfulness of your Bible. I pray this in Jesus' name, Amen.

JANUARY 7
WOULD YOU LIKE TO GET WELL?

John 5:6
"When Jesus saw him and knew how long he had been ill, He asked him, 'Would you like to get well?'"
NLT

What an awesome question! The Lord Jesus has such a way with words! No mincing or dancing around the issue. No, He cuts right to the heart of the matter. Would you like to get well? Would you? That is His question to you today. That is His question to your neighbors and to your friends and family who do not know Him. That is His question to those who ridicule Him in the media and the press. That is His question to those who speak out against Him and even persecute those who believe in Him. That is His question to all of humanity.

He is not just talking about physical wellness here. Jesus is talking about our very soul being cleansed, our guilt being purged and our sins forgiven. He is talking about wellness of the mind, soul and the spirit in addition to wellness of the body. There is nothing wrong with you that He cannot fix. His death on the cross offers these benefits. The amazing thing is that no matter what you've done, how you've done it or who you've been... the offer stands as firm today as it stood yesterday and the day before. The question... Would you like to get well? Your response....

If you would like to accept Jesus as your Lord and Savior ...

Dear Lord Jesus,
I believe in You. I believe You died on the cross for my sins and rose again in three days defeating death. I have sinned. I am a sinner. Please forgive me for my sins. Please give me the power to live for You all the days of my life. Thank You for forgiving me. In Jesus' name, Amen.

Life Lesson: There is nothing wrong with us that Jesus cannot fix.

Dear Father,
Thank You for Your love, grace and mercy. Thank You for the forgiveness of my sins, an internal and external cleansing of all my failures and mistakes. How beautiful is this clean... so much more than any I can earn or manufacture. Thank You for Your healing of my life; all of it. I give it to You. Use my life for Your glory. I pray this in Jesus' name, Amen.

JANUARY 8
WHY COMPLICATE THINGS?

John 5:15
"The man departed and told the Jews that it was Jesus who had made him well."
NKJV

How quickly this man was turned into a witness for the Lord; it was the same day! Sure, he still had problems in his life, but he didn't let those things hinder his witness. He began to tell people about Jesus who had healed him and made him whole. He was very sincere, very simple and unhindered by problems of the past.

I think sometimes we try to complicate things when it comes to telling people about Jesus when it's really very simple. One of the most powerful tools we have in sharing our faith is simply telling people what Jesus has done in our own lives - the simple yet compelling testimony of God's goodness toward you. We should tell everyone what God has done in our lives and we should begin to do it one by one. Let us not stop until the whole world hears.

Life Lesson: We should tell others what Jesus has done in our lives.

Dear Father,
Thank You for saving me. Empower me to be a witness to the ends of the world, starting in my home, my neighborhood and my work. I once was blind and now I see. Help me to keep it simple. I pray this in Jesus' name, Amen.

JANUARY 9
GOT LIFE?

John 5:24
"I assure you, those who listen to my message and believe in God who sent me have eternal life. They will never be condemned for their sins, but they have already passed from death into life." NLT

What an awesome scripture. If we listen and believe we can receive eternal life. If we listen and respond to the message of Jesus, that grand message of salvation and forgiveness, then we have passed from death to life. As I look around this church and see the people, the reality of this passage quickens within me. Why? Because the people here are so filled with life! Not filled with their life ... no that is commonplace. They are filled with the life of Christ. Jesus told us that He came to give us life that is abundant, vibrant and abounding; generous with the joy of the Father.

Are you experiencing this life? Are you walking in the fullness of joy of knowing Him and walking with Him and serving Him? Listen to His message and believe. Experience the kind of life God intended for you to live. I will be faithful to proclaim His message. Grab a hold of God and believe, then watch what He does. Join me on this adventure of faith here with The Bridge and Cross the Bridge Ministries. One questions remains ... got life?

Life Lesson: Christians have passed from death into life.

Dear Father,
Thank You for this new life You have given me. Thank you for the joy of being immersed in Your grace. Thank You for the fountain of mercy you pour out on me every day. Make my life vibrant to the eyes of others so that they may see the joy of salvation within me each and every day. Give me Your words of love, grace and mercy that my speech and my actions might draw people to Jesus. I pray this in Jesus' name, Amen.

JANUARY 10
TELLING

John 5:34

"Yet I do not receive testimony from man, but I say these things that you may be saved."
NKJV

This is the reason Jesus says these things to us. That we may be saved and to give us the opportunity to respond to Him. The word Sozo, translated "save" here from the original Greek means to heal, deliver, protect or to make whole or well. In Webster's dictionary, to save means to rescue from danger, harm, or to keep from being lost. This is what Jesus desires for us. He did not come so that we could find our purpose or direction or that we might find personal fulfillment. He came that we might be saved and to keep us from being lost.

His Words were recorded in the Bible that we could be saved. Jesus not only provides the way to the Father and to heaven but He explains the way to be saved. Aren't you thankful for this simple truth? We can be saved. Two questions then, first, are you saved? The second question is, who are you telling that they may be saved? Feel free to say that to people ... "I tell you these things that you may be saved."

Life Lesson: Jesus came that we might be saved and to keep us from being lost.

Dear Father,
Thank You for Your healing in my life. Thank You for saving me. Please bring me opportunity after opportunity to tell others that they may be saved as well. Your healing is available to all ... that this world may be made well just as You have made me well. I want to play a part. I pray this in Jesus' name. Amen.

JANUARY 11
TRUSTING GOD

John 6:6
"But this He said to test him, for He Himself knew what He would do."
NKJV

Praise the Lord that we don't know everything that is going to happen because that keeps life fragrant. Uncertainty can also be frustrating, because we want to know everything but we can't. There are things we go through that surprise us and catch us off guard. There is, however, nothing in your life that catches God off guard or surprises Him. The things you are dealing with right now, at this moment, God knew before we even came on the scene. That's pretty mind blowing, but here is the kicker.... He also knows how you are going to get out of your tough situations. He saw the curve coming long before you did and He prepared you for what He already saw coming. He knows what fruit this trial is going to produce in your life. For your benefit He allows this trial or that test to proceed. Oh but take heart saints and be strong. While we may wonder how it works out and what happens next, we can trust in our God because He knows all along what He is going to do.

Life Lesson: We don't know everything, but God does.

Dear Father,
Thank You for your provision of growth in our lives. You love me so much that You do not want me to remain who I am but to grow in your good gifts. What an incredible comfort it is to know that my Father in Heaven knows who I am and who I will be and will see me through the changes. Thank You. I pray this in Jesus' name, Amen.

JANUARY 12
COURAGE?

John 6:20
"But He said to them, "It is I; do not be afraid.""
NKJV

How awesome are these words! As we attempt impossible feats the Lord sets before us, we gain courage through these words. We can step out in boldness of faith whether it is missions work in a third world country or stepping out to teach in the children's ministry.

What about you? Have you stepped out in faith to serve the Lord? Have you begun to commit yourself to a church fellowship as your home? The Lord has called you to valiant action. With that charge you must be dedicated to both serving and giving.

The Lord and the Bible are very plain about belonging to a local fellowship. I would encourage you to take that step of faith. As you follow Jesus, hear His words echo in your heart and in our ears. "It is I; do not be afraid."

Life Lesson: We should be committed to serving and giving.

Dear Father,
Thank You for this call to courageous action in the face of a downward spiraling world. I want to be a catalyst for action in my church home. I will walk through your open doors of opportunity to serve and love others. This is my commitment to you, my Lord. I pray this in Jesus' name, Amen.

JANUARY 13
WHICH TREE?

John 6:29
"Jesus answered and said to them, "This is the work of God, that you believe in Him whom He sent."
NKJV

Have you ever sat and thought about how simple and straightforward salvation is? To be born again we simply choose and believe. There are many times where we must make a hard choice to believe and that is when our belief turns into real faith. God has done His part (by far the hardest part). He simply asks us to make our choice.

God won't force you to make the right decision. He allowed Judas to make the wrong election and He allowed Peter to make the right one; each after their own crisis of faith. Judas made the wrong decision. He chose to end his life by hanging from a tree.

It is interesting to note that Jesus made the same type of choice. Jesus chose to end His life by hanging on a tree. Judas could have known the Lord's forgiveness by believing in Jesus as his personal Savior. Judas could have dropped his burden by believing in the work of God, but he chose the wrong tree. Which tree will you chose? Your own tree or the tree of life, the cross of Jesus?

Life Lesson: The choices we make are important.

Dear Father,
Thank You for Your free gift of salvation through Jesus Christ. Thank you that You love me so much that You allow me to make my own choice, yet pursue me as a loving Father desperately seeking his lost child. Your arms are open and I'm running to them, my Father. Home. I pray this in Jesus' name, Amen.

JANUARY 14
LIVING WORDS

John 6:68

"Simon Peter replied, 'Lord, to whom would we go? You alone have the words that give eternal life.'"

NLT

Words are interesting things. Some are long and complicated and some are short and sweet. Some encourage and some discourage. Sometimes you can receive the most encouraging words from some of the least likely sources. The Lord seems to be able to use anyone at anytime to speak to us wherever we are.

It is amazing. There is only one place to receive the words, or the Word, that gives eternal life and that is from Jesus. There have been many clever men over the years who have said many astute things but no one has ever uttered words with such power and wisdom as Jesus. No one has ever given us the words to know how to receive eternal life other than Jesus. That is why we are here, listening to Jesus, learning about His words. Lord, we agree with Peter, you alone have the words that give eternal life.

Life Lesson: We should be reading and listening to the words of Jesus.

Dear Father,

Thank You for words of eternal life. They are just that... the only words that offer true life. Open my ears to your instruction and give me feet that move swiftly to your paths. Search me and know my heart. Lead me in Your way everlasting. I pray this in Jesus' name, Amen.

JANUARY 15
SIDELINE LIVING

Acts 2:42

"They joined with the other believers and devoted themselves to the apostles' teaching and fellowship, sharing in the Lord's Supper and in prayer."
NLT

I have often thought about the early church and how it must have appeared. There was a dynamic move of the Lord and the people responded. The verse here says they devoted themselves. In my estimation, we need to consider that devotion ... what did it look like and how was it expressed? Once again, we look at this scripture for our answer. These early Christians were devoted to teaching, to fellowship and to one another.

Commitment and devotion to a local church body is more important than we might appreciate. When we read the book of Acts we discover that there were heated disagreements and that they were not always in unity. Yet this devotion they had to one another preserved the relationship. There is a powerful move of the Lord going on here at The Bridge. If the Lord has lain it on your heart to call this your church home, then respond to that call. If it is another local fellowship then make it your church home, but do not get caught up in a never ending loop of hopping, bopping, and shopping for a church home. If you do that, my friend, you will miss out on incredible things. Make a commitment and devote yourself to the very same things we see the early church devoting themselves to: teaching, fellowship, sharing in the Lord's Supper and prayer. I promise you, it will be a life changing experience.

Life Lesson: We should be devoted to a local church body.

Dear Father,
Thank You for teaching and showing me how to live my life in order to receive blessings from You. I want to be a part of what You are doing in the world and not just a spectator. Please use me. If I have been living on the sidelines, please forgive me and lead me to the church that is my home. I pray this in Jesus' name. Amen.

JANUARY 16
SUCCESSFUL CHURCH

Joshua 1:8
"This Book of the Law shall not depart from your mouth, but you shall meditate in it day and night, that you may observe to do according to all that is written in it. For then you will make your way prosperous, and then you will have good success."
NKJV

How do we as a church view success? If success is an imposing cathedral filled with lavish decor and luxurious fixtures, then we are not successful. We meet in what used to be a warehouse. If, on the one hand, success is defined by communicating God's Word to God's people then we are very successful. And, if, on the other hand, you view success as lives eternally altered, well, we have hit it out of the ball park. I firmly believe this is, in part, how God views success. We are not finished, we have just begun. Months ago I encouraged you to pray 'Lord give us the Triad.' It appears the Lord is doing just that. I ask you to commit yourself and prayerfully consider joining us on this God sized adventure we call The Bridge.

Life Lesson: God's view of success and man's view of success are two different things.

Dear Father,
Thank You for this incredible move of Your Spirit that is The Bridge. Thank You for the lives that are being eternally changed whether it's through knowing Jesus as Lord and Savior or learning how to follow Him. I thank You in advance for all that You are going to do in this world through The Bridge and Cross the Bridge Ministries. I pray this in Jesus' name. Amen.

JANUARY 17
LIVING OUT POWER

Ephesians 2:10
"For we are God's masterpiece. He has created us anew in Christ Jesus, so that we can do the good things he planned for us long ago."
NLT

What an awesome thing that God says we are His masterpiece. This verse says God has planned long ago that we would do good things and serve Him. The question here is... are we walking in those works? God never intended that we live life as stagnant Christians. James tells us that faith without works is dead. The only real faith is a living faith. The Lord intended that we should serve in the body of Christ. We have been set free to use our freedom to serve God and others. Is your faith living or dead; in bondage or set free? Is it real? How can you tell if your faith is a living faith? Well let me ask the question another way... Are you a functioning and active member of the body of Christ? If not, ask your pastor how you can become involved. If you attend here, we would love to help you find a place where you can show your faith real. We want to encourage you in becoming a follower of Jesus with a living kind of faith. We look forward to helping you in this journey that each follower of Jesus needs to make.

Life Lesson: Our faith should be alive and active.

Dear Father,
Thank You for loving me. Thank You for creating me and giving me purpose and ability. Forgive me for times when I have not lived for You. Please place before me opportunities to show my faith alive. I pray this in Jesus' name. Amen.

JANUARY 18
A SIMPLE PLAN

Luke 19:10
"…for the Son of Man has come to seek and to save that which was lost."
NKJV

Lost people are very precious to God. He was willing to give His very life to save them. He was willing to leave the 99 and seek the one lost. He was willing to go through shame, pain and agony to find the wandering and the wayward. He had an incredible burden, purpose and plan for redeeming people. If we are supposed to be like Jesus, we should be passionate about seeking and saving the lost.

Do you have a burden for the lost, unsaved and unbelieving; the invisible and the irretrievable - the cast away? Or are you much more comfortable condemning them while another one slips off into an eternity without Jesus. Through The Bridge and Cross the Bridge Ministries, the lost can hear a clear explanation of the Gospel, the Good News. We want to partner with you to reach people. We ask you, in the name of Jesus and with all that He held precious, to bring your unbelieving friends, family members and co-workers to this fellowship, the television show, the radio program or to the website. In all of these places they will hear a clear and simple explanation of the Good News of Jesus Christ. It is a simple plan that has worked over and over . You invite them here, and I promise to you, I will invite them to Jesus. Let's partner together to win the world.

Life Lesson: If we are followers of Jesus, we should be acting more and more like Him.

Dear Father,
Thank You for the simple plan of the Gospel. I want to see the lost and dying come to know Jesus as their Lord and Savior. Please provide me with opportunities to show people Jesus. I pray this in Jesus' name. Amen.

JANUARY 19
HEED THE SEED

Hebrews 2:1
"Therefore we must give the more earnest heed to the things we have heard, lest we drift away."
NKJV

At The Bridge, every week we open a precious gift. We open our Bibles to the treasure and wisdom of God's Word. This incredible gift is an eternal present, bearing eternal rewards. The Word of God is pictured as seed in the parable of the sower and other places in the Bible. The question is what are you doing with the seed?

Is it taking root in your life through care and attention and application? Is your faith invading every area of your life? The Egyptians used to bury wheat and other seeds with their dead. I hope that does not describe what you do with the seed incorruptible. We have been saved to live for Him and to be a blessing to others. We have received the Word of God that we might become more and more like Him who saved us and forgave us from our sins. As you hear the Word of God, act on the Word of God and you will be amazed at the spiritual harvest that will happen in your life. In short...heed the Seed.

Life Lesson: It is very important for every Christian to be Bible readers and Bible doers.

Dear Father,
Thank You for the blessing of Your Bible. Thank you for that eternal gift of Your Word that I can study and learn from. Please teach me to be a good steward of this seed that you have invested in me. I pray this in Jesus' name. Amen.

JANUARY 20
TWENTY-FOUR-SEVEN

Acts 2:47
"…praising God and having favor with all the people. And the Lord added to the church daily those who were being saved."
NKJV

What an awesome verse! It is even more awesome when you consider this is happening right here and right now here at The Bridge and through Cross the Bridge Ministries. This is going on day in and day out and according to Acts 2:47, people are coming to know the Lord 24-hours a day, 7-days a week. People are being saved continually, and I am so grateful for what the Lord is doing. I am encouraged at all the people serving and for all those who are giving. Your faithfulness makes this all possible. I consider it an honor to serve Him alongside of you. I like the saying "without Him we can't, without us He won't." Thank you for joining with me in living to tell what He died to say, 24/7.

Life Lesson: Live to tell what He died to say.

Dear Father,
Thank You for saving me. I want to see others saved as well. Give me abundant opportunities to share the Gospel message with others. Thank You for The Bridge and Cross the Bridge Ministries. Thank You for the harvest of souls we are seeing day in and day out. Please continue to reach the lost through our efforts. I pray this in Jesus' name. Amen.

JANUARY 21
TODAY WILL BE AWESOME

Colossians 3:16
"Let the words of Christ, in all their richness, live in your hearts and make you wise. Use his words to teach and counsel each other. Sing psalms and hymns and spiritual songs to God with thankful hearts."
NLT

What an awesome day. Rejoice and be glad for this is the day that the Lord has made. The church has been out of the house for seven years now. It is amazing and miraculous what has happened in those seven years. Not just the growth in number of people that call this home but the personal growth of each individual person. We have laughed together and cried together but through it all we have grown together. I give thanks to God every time I think of the people here. I also want to give my thanks to those who have served so faithfully in this church; to express my heartfelt appreciation to those who serve in the various ministries, those who give of their resources and those who pray for this church. In just a few short years God has knit our hearts into one and we have pulled off an incredible endeavor. I can only imagine what the Lord will do in the next few years. I look forward to walking with you and serving along side of you in whatever God has next.

Today is going to be an incredible day. Not because of anything that I or you can do of our own but because this is the day that the Lord has made. This is the day that the Lord created for us to demonstrate His goodness to everyone we will meet. Let's remember that God will work through me and through you to make His day – this day - incredible for someone else. As we bless others, we will also partake in being blessed. Today will be awesome!

Life Lesson: Rejoice and be glad for this is the day that the Lord has made.

Dear Father,
Thank You for pulling together this rag-tag group of Christians to accomplish together what one man could not accomplish alone. That is to reach not just this community, but the whole world with Your life-changing Word. We look forward to the continuation of Your work in this church and commit to serving and loving each person You bring through these doors. I pray this in Jesus' name. Amen.

JANUARY 22
NEIGHBORHOOD WATCH

Galatians 5:13-14

For you have been called to live in freedom—not freedom to satisfy your sinful nature, but freedom to serve one another in love. For the whole law can be summed up in this one command: "Love your neighbor as yourself."
NLT

My friends, I urge you to live in this freedom Jesus has called you to! Love your neighbor as yourself. Serve your neighbor. Do you know if your neighbor has a relationship with Jesus? Do you know if they are active in their faith? Perhaps get to know your neighbor. Pray for your neighbor. Care for your neighbor. If they are not saved, begin to pray for them to come to know Jesus. As you care for them and pray for them, the Lord will give you a burden for them. Invite them to come to church with you. When they see people worshiping the Lord and hear about the love God has for them, they will be drawn to Him. I have seen it happen time and time again. When you have done this, then you have truly loved your neighbor. Keep loving, praying, and inviting until every neighbor hears.

Life Lesson: Jesus has called you to live in freedom to serve one another in love.

Dear Father,

Thank You for those you have placed around me that I can be a witness to. Please give me opportunities to love them and to talk to them about Jesus. I ask that You would prepare their hearts beforehand that when I invite them to church they will go with me. I also ask that You would give me a desire to see my whole neighborhood come to know Jesus as Lord and Savior. I pray this in Jesus' name, Amen.

JANUARY 23
LET'S CELEBRATE

Luke 15:10
Likewise, I say to you, there is joy in the presence of the angels of God over one sinner who repents. NKJV

Can you just imagine the heavenly scene? Untold scores of angels look on as a man or woman begins to ponder the Good News of Jesus Christ. He considers the wrong he has done and the unbelievable offer of forgiveness set before him. As her heart begins to soften and perhaps... just perhaps a tear forms in her eye, the host of heaven holds its breath in anticipation. Perhaps a few friends are in prayer, joining others, maybe even strangers, who are asking God to draw these precious people to Him. Then when they look up with a new purpose and light in their eye, the angels lean forward to better their view. This isn't the first time they have seen that look; the look of burdens lifted, the past forgiven and the future being secured. It is the look of a decision. As the person makes their way into the aisle and down front to give their life to the Lord, all of heaven breaks out in joy-shouts... and so should we. There is cause for celebration today.

Life Lesson: There is cause for celebration!

Dear Father,
Thank You for miracles. Thank You for the miracle of salvation. Remind me, Lord, to pray for those who don't know Jesus. Remind me to pray in church before and during the altar call. Remind me to pray every day for friends, family and even those I do not know to receive Jesus. I pray this in Jesus' name, Amen.

JANUARY 24
GOD SMACK?

Luke 15:4-5

"What man of you, having a hundred sheep, if he loses one of them, does not leave the ninety-nine in the wilderness, and go after the one which is lost until he finds it? And when he has found it, he lays it on his shoulders, rejoicing."
NKJV

What is your impression of God? Do you believe that He is biding His time - just waiting to strike the moment you step out of line? Is He lurking around the corner readying His 'smite bat' in anticipation of your next mistake? It's the ultimate smack down; He wants to pound you back into submission, right?

Sadly, this is the picture that was painted to many of us in our youth and well into adulthood. While if we continually reject God, we will receive judgment, just taking a good look at that reveals His mercy. God is chasing after us, desiring us to come to repentance. This verse shows that when we are lost, God is looking for us. He is searching and calling out your name. He is not sitting back thinking, 'I'm glad I got rid of that one.'

This is the heart of God. When we stumble, He wants to lift us up. When we are in bondage, He wants to set us free. When we are lost, He is searching for us. If this scriptural picture is different than the picture of God you have, then throw away the old picture because it was not painted by the Master Himself. See Him as He truly is and you will experience incredible joy in what you discover.

Life Lesson: When we are lost, God is looking for us.

Dear Father,
Thank You for Your shepherd's heart. Thank You for searching me out so that You can save me from a life leading to destruction. Truly, You are the Good Shepherd who loves His sheep, of which I am one. You are so good. Please keep me from straying. I pray this in Jesus' name. Amen.

JANUARY 25
DO YOU BELIEVE?

Genesis 1:1
"In the beginning God created the heavens and the earth."
NKJV

This is the first verse of the Bible. It has long been the plan of the enemy to plant doubt about God's Word in our minds. If the enemy can cause doubt about verse one, then obviously the whole book is left in question. That is exactly what the enemy has done with evolution. For a believer this is mission critical. The choice is to believe God or call Him a liar. There is no middle ground. The Lord has not placed before us a cosmic salad bar where we pick and choose what we like or don't like. I choose to believe the Book and its Author. It is important we do that. It is also important that we understand the scientific reasons we can believe God with an assurance of faith.

Life Lesson: It is important that we believe the Bible and its Author.

Dear Father,
Thank You for the truth of Your Word. Thank You that I can believe what the world finds unbelievable. Your creation abounds with evidence of Your wisdom and creativity as well as Your grace and mercy. I thank You for it all. I pray this in Jesus' name, Amen.

JANUARY 26
WHERE IS LOVE?

1 John 4:19
"We love Him because He first loved us."
NKJV

Do you understand what this means? While we did not love God, He loved us. While we did not look for God, He looked for us. The love of God is an active and seeking kind of love. His love is looking for ways to express itself toward us. When He paints a beautiful sunset, He is expressing His love toward us. When He speaks through the pages of His Word, that is His love toward us. When He was dying on the cross, He was proclaiming to a lost and dying world that He had a very real and undying love for us. For God so Loved the world... it doesn't get any better than this.

Life Lesson: God loves us.

Dear Father,
Thank You for the beauty of Your creation and the way You express Your love for me through it. Thank You for searching for me. Thank You for finding me and for speaking to me. Thank You, my Savior, for saving me. I pray this in Jesus' name, Amen.

JANUARY 27
LOVE LESSON

1 John 4:11
"Beloved, if God so loved us, we also ought to love one another."
NKJV

We know that God loves us and because He loves us we should love others. This is how people will recognize us as Christians, by our love. We know we ought to love one another. So, what does that look like? Often we base love on our feelings. Love certainly can be a feeling but it is much more than that. Love is a commitment. At times we act not because of our feelings but in spite of them. At times I may not feel like correcting my children but love (and the Bible) demands that I do. One way we show our love is through serving each other. I am deeply moved by all the people serving one another here at The Bridge. They clean the building; keep the facilities and the grounds ship-shape. They prepare coffee and get the media working as the worship team rehearses. Teachers prayerfully prepare children's lessons. The whole body working together here at The Bridge says, 'I love you.'

Life Lesson: Love should be a commitment in spite of our feelings.

Dear Father,
Thank You for teaching us how to express the love You so bountifully heap on us to others. Lord, I pray that my life would be a reflection of Your love to those who are lost or hurting. Please give me opportunity after opportunity to love others. Lord, please continue to teach me how to love. I pray this in Jesus' name, Amen.

JANUARY 28
BRIGHT LIGHT

John 9:5
As long as I am in the world, I am the light of the world."
NKJV

Matthew 5:14
"You are the light of the world. A city that is set on a hill cannot be hidden."
NKJV

Read these two verses together and you see an incredible thing. Jesus says as long as He is in the world, He is the light of the world. Jesus later says He is leaving and will leave the Comforter. He also left us here with instructions to go and tell people about Him. We are now His lights in this world. Wow! And the city...well, I believe that this church, The Bridge, and Cross the Bridge Ministries is that city on a hill. People are being drawn to Jesus. We cannot be hidden nor do we want to be. Let your light shine bright my friends, because that is the Jesus in you shining forth to a dark and hurting world.

Life Lesson: Let your light shine bright.

Dear Father,
Thank You for the opportunity to be a light to the world. Not just any light, but a light that cannot be hidden. Please continue to bless this ministry so that more and more people will be reached with the gospel of Jesus Christ. Allow me to be a conduit of Your love to this hurting world. I pray this in Jesus' name. Amen.

JANUARY 29
GOD REJOICES IN YOU

Zephaniah 3:17
The LORD your God in your midst,
The Mighty one, will save;
He will rejoice over you with gladness,
He will quiet you with His love,
He will rejoice over you with singing."
NKJV

We often rejoice over the Lord with singing. Now, stop and consider that He rejoices over us with singing; it is incredible to think about. To consider that the Lord rejoices over us as we praise and sing to Him is beyond words. We often imagine an angry God, choosing and grooming a switch with which to beat us up for all our wrongdoing. It just shows that we really don't understand the love of God. Today, let Him quiet you with His love as you realize that He rejoices over you with singing. God is chasing us for sure, but He is chasing us to give us forgiveness of our sins, to give us beauty for ashes and gladness for mourning. Spend some time with the Lord this week and listen quietly for His voice and don't be surprised if you hear singing...

Life Lesson: God rejoices over you.

Dear Father,
The depth of Your love sets me to amazement. I wonder how love can be so incredible and I want to be able to show that love to others. Lord, give me quiet moments this week ... moments when I can just listen to You. I want to understand Your love and I want to learn from You how I can love others straight into Your arms. I pray this in Jesus' name. Amen.

JANUARY 30
WORLD CHANGERS

Matthew 28:19-20

"Go therefore and make disciples of all the nations, baptizing them in the name of the Father and of the Son and of the Holy Spirit, teaching them to observe all things that I have commanded you; and lo, I am with you always, even to the end of the age. Amen."
NKJV

These scriptures are often called The Great Commission. Jesus is telling us what we should be doing. He mentions baptizing which means we should be playing a part of seeing unbelievers becoming believers. If you are a believer, have you been baptized? If you have been saved you should be baptized. Jesus also mentions teaching and making disciples. I want to encourage you in following Jesus. I know that it can be overwhelming at times and I want to help you along the way. Be encouraged you have a church that wants to help you. Together we can change the world one life at a time. Starting with yours.

Life Lesson: We should be living the Great Commission.

Dear Father,
You have given me a commission and I want to live by it. I want to be a part of people coming to know Jesus as Lord and Savior. I want to continue to grow in my faith. Thank You for providing a church and a pastor that will come along side me in this. I pray this in Jesus' name. Amen.

JANUARY 31
ALONE?

1 Thessalonians 3:2b
"...to establish you and encourage you concerning your faith,"
NKJV

This is our hope for everyone who attends The Bridge, who watches the podcast, the live stream, HisChannel.com, the Cross the Bridge television program or who listens to the radio program. That you would find the help you need to be grounded in God's Word, established by His love and grace and grow in your faith. We want to help you in any way we can. I want to personally encourage you, as your pastor, to get involved with one of the many Real Life Groups we are offering now. These groups are designed to help you do just that. If you do not attend The Bridge, then ask someone in your church about its small group ministry and get plugged in. We all need encouragement and direction. We want to provide that for you here at The Bridge. I want you to know that you have someone that is with you and that will pray for you and pray with you. You have a staff and a pastor that loves you and wants to encourage you. Take heart loved ones, you are not alone.

Life Lesson: You are not alone.

Dear Father,
Thank You for Your provision in my life. Lord, create in me a desire to have fellowship with my brothers and sisters in Christ. I know that I need the accountability of others in my life to encourage me and come along side me as I live out my faith in this world. I pray this in Jesus' name. Amen

FEBRUARY 1
APART

John 17:17
"Sanctify them by Your truth. Your word is truth."
NKJV

We are sanctified not only by truth or a truth but by His truth.

Sanctified means set apart for special use. The Bible sets us apart for special use. I want to encourage you to read your Bible. It is so simple that we sometimes overlook the profound impact it will have on our lives. It is one of the simplest acts that can have the deepest results. Don't have the time? May I suggest you make the time? At the end of the day, nothing can help you get perspective like looking at a devotion, with a verse or two. Nothing can prepare you for the day like digging into the treasure of God's Word in the morning. My challenge to you, in love and care, is for you to try to spend a few minutes in the morning and in the evening looking into God's Word. It will bless you. I promise you and more importantly God promises.

"This book contains the mind of God, the state of man, the way of salvation, the doom of sinners, and the happiness of believers. Its doctrines are holy, its precepts binding, its histories are true and its decisions are immutable. Read it to be wise, believe it to be safe, and practice it to be holy. It contains light to direct you, food to support you, and comfort to cheer you. It is the traveler's map, the pilgrim's staff, the pilot's compass, the soldier's sword, and the Christian's character. Here paradise is restored, heaven opened, and the gates of hell disclosed. Christ is its grand subject, our good its design, and the glory of God its end. It should fill the memory, test the heart, and guide the feet.

Read it slowly, frequently, prayerfully. It is a mine of wealth, a paradise of glory and a river of pleasure. It is given you in life, it will be opened at the judgment, and be remembered forever. It involves the highest responsibility, rewards the greatest labor and condemns all who will trifle with its sacred contents."
(From The Doctrine of the Bible Authors Unknown)

Life Lesson: Take the time to read because He took the time to bleed.

Dear Father,

Thank You for the gift of your Bible. Please forgive me when I have made more time in my life for the wrong things while my Bible gathered dust on the shelf. I ask You to open my heart to your Word as I diligently read and study it and open my ears to hear just what You want me to do. I want to be a doer of Your Word. I pray this in Jesus' name, Amen.

FEBRUARY 2
ROLE MODEL

John 18:10
"Then Simon Peter, having a sword, drew it and struck the high priest's servant, and cut off his right ear. The servant's name was Malchus."
NKJV

Sometimes in life, we face challenging moments. This moment was a summons to contest for Peter. Even with all that Jesus had taught him and with all that he had learned, he still had to make personal application. In the heart of the matter, Peter had to learn how to do it God's way and not his own. Do not lean to your own understanding. (Proverbs 3:5, 6) I think that is something all of us have to learn. We would like to learn it all at once or all in one sitting, but that's not the way it happens. Most of us will have many opportunities, in some, we will succeed beautifully and in others, we will fail miserably. Each day that we awake; however, brings us the glorious chance for a fresh start and a new beginning. It is important to remember that and, in that process, please be careful of the ears.

Life Lesson: The Lord wants to direct us in our daily activities.

Dear Father,
Thank You for growing me. Thank You for not being content to leave me as I am because what I am is not as good as what You want me to be. Lord, I may squirm and protest against the process but please continue to conform me to the image of Your Son. I pray this in Jesus' name. Amen.

FEBRUARY 3
ENDURING GRACE

1 John 1:8-10
"If we say that we have no sin, we deceive ourselves, and the truth is not in us. If we confess our sins, He is faithful and just to forgive us our sins and to cleanse us from all unrighteousness. If we say that we have not sinned, we make Him a liar, and His word is not in us."
NKJV

We tend to think about grace pouring down over us as a onetime event. If it was a onetime event, we would be in trouble. You see the grace of God is something that we need every day. We are told that the mercy of the Lord endures forever. That means it will never grow too small or be worn out. As we look at the life of Peter, we see a man who fell and then got up. There is a lesson in that for us. We often count ourselves out when the Lord has not counted us out. There is no one beyond the reach of His grace. If this includes Peter and his denials, it includes us and our misbehaviors. Though we struggle and though we sometimes fail, we can live in this knowledge. We have 24/7 access to His love and forgiveness. We live in the grip of His grace.

1 John 1:8-10 "If we say that we have no sin, we deceive ourselves, and the truth is not in us. If we confess our sins, He is faithful and just to forgive us our sins and to cleanse us from all unrighteousness. If we say that we have not sinned, we make Him a liar, and His word is not in us." NKJV

Isa 1:18 "Come now, and let us reason together," says the LORD, "Though your sins are like scarlet, They shall be as white as snow; Though they are red like crimson, They shall be as wool." NKJV

Life Lesson: As followers of Jesus we can be forgiven of all our mistakes.

Dear Father,
Thank You for Your grace. May we run often to the throne of grace that we may be forgiven of everything that hinders us in running the race. I pray this in Jesus' name, Amen.

FEBRUARY 4
LAY IT ALL DOWN

Romans 6:23
"For the wages of sin is death, but the gift of God is eternal life in Christ Jesus our Lord."
NKJV

Barabbas was guilty. Jesus took his place. We, like Barabbas, stand guilty by the things we have done wrong. We often think of Jesus dying for our past sins but it is much more than that. The Bible says His mercies are new every morning. Jesus died for our sins of the past but He also died for our sins of today and tomorrow. Sometimes we try to carry around the sins He paid for.

How about you right now? Are you carrying a past sin or a past failure or even a recent one around like some twisted badge of courage? Then right now, not 5 minutes from now, I encourage you to lay it all down. Jesus died that you would not have to live under condemnation. You are trying to carry something you were not meant or even designed to carry. Jesus is willing and able to carry it for you. This changes everything.

Life Lesson: Jesus paid a debt He did not owe because we owed a debt we could not pay.

Dear Father,
Thank You that forgiveness of my sins has been granted and I no longer have to carry their burden. Lord, whatever chain of burden I am carrying I lay it all down at the foot of the cross. It is no longer mine to carry. I thank You for that. I pray this in Jesus' name. Amen.

FEBRUARY 5
BIBLE STUDY THAT LEADS TO BIBLE ACTION

John 19:4
"Pilate then went out again, and said to them, 'Behold, I am bringing Him out to you, that you may know that I find no fault in Him.'"
NKJV

John 19:12
"From then on Pilate sought to release Him, but the Jews cried out, saying, 'If you let this Man go, you are not Caesar's friend. Whoever makes himself a king speaks against Caesar.'"
NKJV

John 19:16
"Then he delivered Him to them to be crucified. Then they took Jesus and led Him away."
NKJV

Sometimes we are unsure of what to do. That is why Bible study is so important. It helps us to know right from wrong and to realize God's purpose and direction for our lives. Pilate knew what was right and he did not do it. I think we can all relate to that in our own lives. Sometimes we know what to do, but we just don't do it. That is where Bible action (Bible application) comes into play. The Bible encourages us to be Bible doers, not just hearers. I often encourage the people of The Bridge to be Bible doers. That is why we offer School of Discipleship, Crown Financial and Life Groups.

The church has long been accused of believing, but not doing. May that be different here in this place we call The Bridge. May our Bible study lead us to Bible action as we seek to step out in faith and do all God has called us to do. The Lord who calls us is also faithful to equip us to be doers of His Word.

Life Lesson: Our beliefs should lead us to action. What we say we believe should impact the way we live. Bible study should lead to Bible action.

Dear Father,
You created me to uniquely serve You. I want to serve You well. Search me and know my heart. Test me and know my anxious thoughts. See if there is any offensive way in me and lead me in Your way everlasting. I pray this in Jesus' name, Amen.

FEBRUARY 6
BE

John 19:17-18

"And He, bearing His cross, went out to a place called the Place of a Skull, which is called in Hebrew, Golgotha, where they crucified Him, and two others with Him, one on either side, and Jesus in the center."
NKJV

It is painful to consider what Jesus went through for us and to think about what He endured on our behalf. The remarkable truth I keep coming back to time and time again is... it was His decision. He decided to endure these things... the suffering, the beatings and the crucifixion. It is convicting because I know how little in comparison it has taken to rattle my endurance at times. I have never been beaten for Jesus much less crucified.

It comes down to each and every one of us making a commitment to Jesus. How far will you follow Jesus? Until it gets inconvenient... uncomfortable... what about when it becomes painful? Are you willing to follow Him all the way? Let us follow our Jesus, who is so worthy, all the way until the end. Until we hear the words "well done, good and faithful servant." God bless you as you follow Jesus.

Life Lesson: Make a commitment to follow Jesus.

Dear Father,
You have called me to a disciple's life. I want to embrace that life and yet there are times when I look back. I am Your disciple. I will go where You lead me. Please help my faith. I pray this in Jesus' name, Amen.

FEBRUARY 7
FORGOTTEN

John 19:31-42
"Therefore, because it was the Preparation Day, that the bodies should not remain on the cross on the Sabbath (for that Sabbath was a high day), the Jews asked Pilate that their legs might be broken, and that they might be taken away. Then the soldiers came and broke the legs of the first and of the other who was crucified with Him. But when they came to Jesus and saw that He was already dead, they did not break His legs. But one of the soldiers pierced His side with a spear, and immediately blood and water came out. And he who has seen has testified, and his testimony is true; and he knows that he is telling the truth, so that you may believe. For these things were done that the Scripture should be fulfilled, 'Not one of His bones shall be broken.' And again another Scripture says, 'They shall look on Him whom they pierced.' After this, Joseph of Arimathea, being a disciple of Jesus, but secretly, for fear of the Jews, asked Pilate that he might take away the body of Jesus; and Pilate gave him permission. So he came and took the body of Jesus. And Nicodemus, who at first came to Jesus by night, also came, bringing a mixture of myrrh and aloes, about a hundred pounds. Then they took the body of Jesus, and bound it in strips of linen with the spices, as the custom of the Jews is to bury. Now in the place where He was crucified there was a garden, and in the garden a new tomb in which no one had yet been laid. So there they laid Jesus, because of the Jews' Preparation Day, for the tomb was nearby." NKJV

Not only should we realize what Jesus did, but we should also remember. We are so quick and easy to forget, but Jesus knows how we are created and how we are wired. Some of this forgetfulness is an instrument of God's healing. But we tend to forget (or not think about) the most important thing event of all…the crucifixion.

Communion is a time of remembering what He did for us. He bled. He died. He took it when He did not have to. Celebrate communion often. Do it at home, do it at work, do it with your parents and do it with your kids; and remember Jesus.

1 Corinthians 11:23-26 "For I received from the Lord that which I also delivered to you: that the Lord Jesus on the same night in which He was betrayed took bread; and when He had given thanks, He broke it and said, 'Take, eat; this is My body which is broken for you; do this in remembrance of Me.' In the same manner He also took the cup after supper, saying, 'This cup is the new covenant in My blood. This do, as often as you drink it, in remembrance of Me.' For as often as you eat this bread and drink this cup, you proclaim the Lord's death till He comes." NKJV

Life Lesson: We need to realize what Jesus did for us on the cross.

Dear Father,

Let me never forget what Jesus did for me. I thank You for providing a means of forgiveness so that we can know the fullness of Your grace. Help me not only to remember, but to share and not only to share but to show. I pray this in Jesus' name, Amen.

FEBRUARY 8
FRIENDSHIP

John 20:1-8

"Early Sunday morning, while it was still dark, Mary Magdalene came to the tomb and found that the stone had been rolled away from the entrance. She ran and found Simon Peter and the other disciple, the one whom Jesus loved. She said, "They have taken the Lord's body out of the tomb, and I don't know where they have put him!" Peter and the other disciple ran to the tomb to **see**. The other disciple outran Peter and got there first. He stooped and looked in and **saw** the linen cloth lying there, but he didn't go in. Then Simon Peter arrived and went inside. He also noticed the linen wrappings lying there, while the cloth that had covered Jesus' head was folded up and lying to the side. Then the other disciple also went in, and he **saw** and believed—"
NLT

You see.

You understand.

You know.

Something that stands out in this scripture is the different words used for "saw". The first Greek word *"blepo"* used in verse five means *to see*. The second word for saw in verse seven is *"theoreo"* which means *to understand*. It is where we get our word for theory. The third word for saw used in verse eight is *"eido"* which means *to know*. Where are you on this path? Do you know yet? Not just know in your heart, but are you living it out? Another important lesson from this passage is that John is hanging out with Peter ... after Peter's denial of Jesus.

If someone decides they are no longer going to follow Jesus, or they no longer care about Jesus then the fellowship is broken. But, what if when someone slips and falls? What about when someone makes a mistake and they, like Peter, are sorry it happened? Sometimes the shame, guilt and condemnation come in like crashing waves; fracturing and wearing us down. We no longer feel like fellowshipping with other believers. I do not think it is happenstance that the very thing that will probably be used to restore us (fellowship and encouragement with other believers) is the last thing we feel like doing. Do you know of someone that is going through a hard time right now? Do you know someone that is struggling and having a hard time getting to their feet? Then this week send an email, make a phone call and pray for that person. You may be the instrument of God's grace that will call the prodigal back home. Are you glad someone called you? Care for one another because God cares for you. God loves you and so do we!

Life Lesson: Be a friend during a hard time not just in the good times.

Dear Father,

Thank You for the friends that I have. Help me to be a source of encouragement and love to them. Give me many opportunities to show them Your love, Your grace and Your mercy. I pray this in Jesus' name. Amen.

FEBRUARY 9
OUT OF THE MIRE

John 20:15
"Jesus said to her, 'Woman, why are you weeping? Whom are you seeking?'"
NKJV

Jesus asked two very insightful questions of Mary at this point: "Why are you weeping?" and "Whom are you seeking?" Often in life we find ourselves in a place where we feel like crying and other times find ourselves in tears. Jesus sees those tears and wants to dry them ... if we will let Him.

We need to allow Jesus, through the hands and wisdom of others, to tend to our tears. Sometimes, though, we become strangely comfortable with pain and sadness. They become almost like old familiar friends. Jesus wants to be the better friend. For some it may mean breaking a cycle long established, for others it may mean coming out of a short season of pain.

Seek Jesus. Realize that in the midst of trial, trouble, turmoil and temptation, He is there with you. You may need to turn around to face Him. He wants to pull you out of your problems and liberate you from sadness but before He does He wants to walk with you through the valley. Even when you are in the valley of the shadow of death, He is there. May you know He is there to dry your tears, lighten your load and be a closer friend than any you have ever known. Loved one, right now take a few minutes out of your busy day and turn to Him. You will be glad you did. And so will He.

Life Lesson: Seek Jesus.

Dear Father,
Thank You for sticking by me through good times and bad times. You are the true friend. Sometimes I become content to wallow in self pity. Please forgive me for that and humble me to allow You, through the hands of others, to comfort and even challenge me to step out of the mire. I pray this in Jesus' name, Amen.

FEBRUARY 10
SHALOM-ALEICHEM

John 20:19
"Then, the same day at evening, being the first day of the week, when the doors were shut where the disciples were assembled, for fear of the Jews, Jesus came and stood in the midst, and said to them, "Peace be with you."
NKJV

John 20:21
So Jesus said to them again, "Peace to you! As the Father has sent Me, I also send you."
NKJV

Philippians 4:7
"...and the peace of God, which surpasses all understanding, will guard your hearts and minds through Christ Jesus."
NKJV

The issue of peace seems to be very important to God. Real peace is more than just the 'absence of war'. Real peace is *Shalom* (shal-lom) - a Hebrew word meaning justice, prosperity, good fellowship and health ... a blessed and fulfilled life by the gracious hand of God. People the world over strive and churn, hunting for emotional peace, financial peace or spiritual peace. We spend so much energy trying to find something God wants to give us for free.

How about you, do you have *shalom*? What does it take to 'derail' your peace? A small thing, a big thing or do you have the peace of God that stays with you even in the most trying situations? That is the peace God offers, a peace that surpasses all understanding. In other words, even in the midst of trial or temptation, when you shouldn't have peace, you have it. What a gift from God. Turn off the TV, cell phone, log off of the internet and spend a few minutes with the God that offers you more lasting peace than anyone or anything else. In that time, may the Lord lift up His countenance upon you and give you His peace. *Shalom Aleichem* means "may you be well", so Shalom Aleichem to you, my friend in this New Year.

Life Lesson: We can have peace with God.

Dear Father,

Thank You for Your peace which allows me to press forward in Your call even when the days appear fearsome. Lord, please forgive me for times when I have wandered from Your peace or allowed circumstances to rule over me. I am Your child and as such I have no person, place or thing to fear. Give me the power to live for You in every moment of my life. I pray this in Jesus' name, Amen.

FEBRUARY 11
BFFL

John 20:26-27

"And after eight days His disciples were again inside, and Thomas with them. Jesus came, the doors being shut, and stood in the midst, and said, 'Peace to you!' Then He said to Thomas, 'Reach your finger here, and look at My hands; and reach your hand here, and put it into My side. Do not be unbelieving, but believing.'"
NKJV

We have all heard the comments, "get it together," "straighten up," or the ever classic, "as the good book says, the Lord helps them that help themselves." Sometime later we heard it enough that we believed it. First, I have read the good book from cover to cover several times and let me assure you, it does not say that. Second, the Lord helps those *that ask for His help*.

If you are still determined to make it on your own, or get yourself cleaned up, or fly right or whatever term you want to use, the Lord will let you try. The moment you realize you need the Lord's help, He will be there to help, though not when you are over the trial, but while you are in the trial. To think that He comes to us after we get through the tough stuff is to paint Him as a fair weather friend. Beloved of God, it is you that the Lord longs to walk with through the storms of life. Call out to Him right where you are, just as you are and He will become even more real to you. The Lord loves you enough to take you just as you are, and thankfully He loves you too much to let you stay that way.

Life Lesson: Jesus will come to us right where we are and as we are.

Dear Father,
I've tried it my way and my way doesn't work. I need Your help in my life. Whatever things I'm trying to do on my own outside of You I surrender to You. Please help me. Thank You for being the best Friend forever. I pray this in Jesus' name, Amen.

FEBRUARY 12
DIVINE INTERRUPTION

John 21:3-6

"Simon Peter said to them, 'I am going fishing.' They said to him, 'We are going with you also.' They went out and immediately got into the boat, and that night they caught nothing. But when the morning had now come, Jesus stood on the shore; yet the disciples did not know that it was Jesus. Then Jesus said to them, 'Children, have you any food?' They answered Him, 'No.' And He said to them, 'Cast the net on the right side of the boat, and you will find some.' So they cast, and now they were not able to draw it in because of the multitude of fish."
NKJV

God wants to take an active role in our lives. We all get busy - too busy with what we want instead of what He asked us to do. The Lord has told us to love one another. The Lord has told us to serve one another. That takes a challenging commitment to the physical and spiritual well being of one another. Can helping one another out for a few hours each week really change our lives? My challenge to you is... try it and see. Seeking after empty promises of fulfillment, 'looking out for number one', will rot your soul in the way candy rots your teeth. Jesus tells us to give our life away so that we may find it. Throw your net on the other side and see what happens. Be what you believe. You may find your life divinely interrupted, and you will never, ever be the same again.

Life Lesson: God wants to divinely interrupt our lives.

Dear Father,
Thank You for Your love, Your grace and Your mercy. Just as You are active in my life, I want to play an active role in the lives of others by encouraging them; loving them and serving them. Let my eyes not be blind to the needs of others but grant me dim vision of my own wants. I pray this in Jesus' name, Amen.

FEBRUARY 13
TURN YOUR EYES UPON JESUS

John 21:12
"Jesus said to them, 'Come and eat breakfast.'"
NKJV

What made this moment special? Was it the fish? Was it the fire? Or... was it Jesus? We often get so distracted with things in life that we misplace Jesus. I don't mean we literally stick Him in the wrong drawer or drop Him under the car seat. What I mean is He loses that place of prominence He should have in our lives... our priorities get out of whack.

Our God loves us so much that He wants to bless us. He also wants to rescue us out of our selfish thinking. When you begin to sit in His presence and follow Him, well... as the song says 'the things of this world will grow strangely dim, in the light of His glory and grace.' Beloved, may you never again be cheaply satisfied. May the things of this world never satisfy your spiritual hunger. May you be content with no less than following the King of Kings. May you only be satisfied with serving Him who served us first. May you show forth the love and grace you have received and present it to a world without hope, until the whole world hears.

Life Lesson: The best things in life aren't things.

Dear Father,
You are the Lord of my life. Please forgive me for times when I have allowed other things to take the place of Your Lordship in my life. Please rescue me out of my selfish thinking and allow me to present Your love and grace to the world. I pray this in Jesus' name, Amen.

FEBRUARY 14
LOVE

Jonah 1:5b
"But Jonah had gone down into the lowest parts of the ship, had lain down, and was fast asleep."
NKJV

Valentine's Day is designated as a special day of love. Greeting card company conspiracy or not, most married men have learned that on that day with their wives, actions matter. Some days, you might be able to slide by on words alone but not that day. That's a day where, quite literally, actions carry a bullhorn. But why is that? Shouldn't every day call for a special demonstration of love? Absolutely! I am sure that most people reading this, in some way, demonstrate love for someone else daily.

Revelation 2:4 Nevertheless, I have this against you, that you have left your first love. NKJV

Are you forgetting someone? God expects us to express our love for Jesus by doing the things Jesus asked us to do. Yet, so many Christians are asleep on the job. Fall asleep at work and what happens? You get fired. God knows who is faithful and who is not. But God is a God of second chances; even third, fourth and fifth. Wake up and show Jesus you love Him. How many days have passed without a demonstration of love for your spouse or loved one? Probably not many. How many have passed without a demonstration of your love for Jesus?

1 John 4:19 "We love Him because He first loved us." NKJV

Life Lesson: Stay true to what you know is from God.

Dear Father,
Thank You for loving me. Thank You that You speak to me through Your Word. It is so amazing how the scriptures from long ago speak to my life today. Lord, You are so good, gracious and merciful. Thank You for Your forgiveness of my sins. Lord, help me to live a life of action. I know there are times when I put things or others before You. Lord, You are my True Love. Help me to put You first and give me the power to love others just as You love me. In Jesus' name, Amen.

FEBRUARY 15
DO YOU HEAR ME?

John 21:17-19

17 He said to him the third time, "Simon, son of Jonah, do you love Me?" Peter was grieved because He said to him the third time, "Do you love Me?" And he said to Him, "Lord, You know all things; You know that I love You." Jesus said to him, "Feed My sheep.18 Most assuredly, I say to you, when you were younger, you girded yourself and walked where you wished; but when you are old, you will stretch out your hands, and another will gird you and carry you where you do not wish."19 This He spoke, signifying by what death he would glorify God. And when He had spoken this, He said to him, "Follow Me."
NKJV

There is a concept in the church today that is unbiblical in understanding and application. We have somehow come to believe that only a select few in the church are called to serve. This was never the intention of Jesus. The plan for the church was that we would serve and love one another through acts of ministry. Someone saying, "I am not called to ministry," is almost like saying, "I am not called to love others." Through the scriptures, we are told to love one another as well as serve one another. We have been saved to be transformed or changed; transformed to serve. The calling may be different for each and every person, but the calling, itself, is there for all of us to hear. To he who has ears to hear, let him hear...and respond.

Life Lesson: We are all called into ministry.

Dear Father,
You have created me in Your image and I know that You are gracious, compassionate, slow to anger and abounding in love. I want to reflect Your attributes to everyone around me. I know I should be more concerned for others than for myself. Please help me to be. I pray this in Jesus' name, Amen.

FEBRUARY 16
BALANCED TEACHING

Acts 1:8
"But you shall receive power when the Holy Spirit has come upon you; and you shall be witnesses to Me in Jerusalem, and in all Judea and Samaria, and to the end of the earth."
NKJV

Luke 11:13
"If you then, being evil, know how to give good gifts to your children, how much more will your heavenly Father give the Holy Spirit to those who ask Him!"
NKJV

Most Christians know they should look to the Bible for their beliefs about salvation, heaven, and other important spiritual matters. In light of this, it amazes me how much of our beliefs and practices concerning the Holy Spirit are not Biblical. Both the denying of the power of the Holy Spirit and the unhealthy focus on the gifts of the Spirit are not biblically balanced. At The Bridge, I have been teaching verse by verse from the very beginning. As we explore God's Word together, we see what the Book has to say about this sometimes controversial subject. I am committed to teaching this in the clearest way possible from the Bible. We should allow the Bible to speak and the Holy Spirit to teach so that we can live in the fullness that God has designed for us. I am sure it will be an incredible adventure as we continue to live out the Bible at The Bridge.

PS – You can join us on this verse by verse adventure no matter where you are, through our live stream. Just go to aboutthebridge.com and click on "Live Streaming" and you will be able to join us live as I teach on Sunday mornings and Thursday evenings.

Life Lesson: We should base our beliefs about the Holy Spirit on the Bible alone.

Dear Father,
How many times have I turned to worldly counsel when I should have gone to Your Bible. Please forgive me for that. Please make me wise and give me discernment for life as I commit myself to daily time in Your Word. I pray this in Jesus' name, Amen.

FEBRUARY 17
ONE SURRENDERED LIFE

Acts 1:15-16

"And in those days Peter stood up in the midst of the disciples (altogether the number of names was about a hundred and twenty), and said, 'Men and brethren, this Scripture had to be fulfilled, which the Holy Spirit spoke before by the mouth of David concerning Judas, who became a guide to those who arrested Jesus;'"

NKJV

Luke 22:32

"But I have prayed for you, that your faith should not fail; and when you have returned to Me, strengthen your brethren."

NKJV

Peter is now doing what Jesus told him to do. In this passage of Luke, Jesus gave not only Peter, but all of us one of the keys to being restored; strengthen your brethren. Peter listened to what Jesus said in Luke 22 and Peter did what Jesus said in the first chapter of Acts.

The disciples are no longer asking about who would be the greatest. They aren't talking about who had the greatest sin or how Peter had fallen. They are standing together in unity and in prayer, doing the work of the kingdom. This is the way a body of believers will have maximum impact. By standing together, we discover that healing is found in pouring ourselves out for Jesus. Pour yourself out and discover the blessing of what God will do with one surrendered life. Together we can change the world.

Life Lesson: We mature spiritually, and often heal spiritually, as we serve others.

Dear Father,
Help me to focus on the important things and not be distracted by selfish want or foolish gossip. I want to commit myself to standing beside the body of believers in my church to serve You by serving others. I want to surrender my life to Your kingdom. Please give me a mind for it. I pray this in Jesus' name, Amen.

FEBRUARY 18
KNOW THE BIBLE

Acts 1:20
"For it is written in the Book of Psalms:
'Let his dwelling place be desolate,
And let no one live in it';
and,
'Let another take his office.'
NKJV

Here, Peter was quoting from the book of Psalms. Peter knew the Bible. At that time, the Bible was the Hebrew Scriptures, or the Old Testament. The people who followed Jesus quoted from it often. They knew the book. A hundred years ago, in the United States, most kids had read the Bible all the way through before they were 12. Now, there are Christians who are late in life and have yet to read the whole book. Join us here or online to study this incredible book of God's love, forgiveness and the redemption of mankind. The Bible shows us how salvation and joy can be ours and it gives us a way and a reason to live. We should read and study the Bible in our private time. Get to know the Word of God and you will get to know the God of the Word. Take the time to read because He took the time to bleed.

Life Lesson: We should know our Bibles.

Dear Father,
Thank you for the gift of Your Bible. I know I should read it and study it. Help me to commit time each and every day to do this. I want to seek Your face and so I want to read and study Your love letter to me. Help me to dedicate time every day to this. I pray this in Jesus' name, Amen.

FEBRUARY 19
LORD OF THE HARVEST

Acts 2:1
"When the Day of Pentecost had fully come, they were all with one accord in one place."
NKJV

Proverbs 10:5
"He who gathers in summer is a wise son;
He who sleeps in harvest is a son who causes shame."
NKJV

The Feast of Pentecost involved the wheat harvest. Jesus often referred to the harvest in scripture. The sheer volume of passages dealing with the harvest reveals just how important a subject it is. As a matter of fact, the Lord tells us He will not come back until the spiritual harvest is finished. (2 Peter 3:8-9). This point brings us to the question... how important is the harvest to you? Does it bother you that many people in other countries have not heard the Gospel at all? Does it bother you that many in this country know about God, but they have not heard an effective presentation of the Gospel? Does it matter that most Americans spend more on pet food than reaching other people with the Good News? Well, it bothers me and so The Bridge and Cross the Bridge Ministries makes it our goal to take the Gospel to every corner of this lost and dying world.

Won't you join with me in this? Your financial gifts and your faithful prayers carry the Gospel to people who might not otherwise ever hear. I want to encourage you to pray that the Lord of the Harvest would continue to use us to announce the Good News to this lost and dying world. Pray that God would use us to support other ministries that are doing the same.

May the harvest be important to you because it is important to the One we follow. Until the whole world hears...

Life Lesson: The Lord is interested in the harvest.

Dear Father,
Increase in me the desire to see the salvation of the lost of this world. Please give me opportunities to bring light to dark places. In the area of finances, Lord, I desire to show You my heart for others. In the area of prayer, Lord, I want to faithfully lift up The Bridge and Cross the Bridge Ministries. In my work, I ask that You give me opportunity to tell others about Jesus and in my own family. Lord, I want the harvest, Your harvest, to be important in my life. I pray this in Jesus' name. Amen.

FEBRUARY 20
GRACE FOR LIFE

Acts 2:14
"But Peter, standing up with the eleven, raised his voice and said to them, "Men of Judea and all who dwell in Jerusalem, let this be known to you, and heed my words." NKJV

One of the keys to studying the Bible is not skimming or reading too quickly. Every word is important. In this verse, I want you to notice the phrase "standing up with the eleven." Peter had denied the Lord not once, but three times. The disciples knew what Peter had done and yet accepted him back into the group.

It has been accurately spoken that the Christian army is the only one in the world that shoots its wounded. Think, for a moment, of those who have hurt you and wounded you. Perhaps someone wounded you at an important time in your life. Jesus, who has given you so much grace, now asks you to show others that same grace.

How many times should we give grace? Jesus told us 70 x 7. That totals 490 times, but Jesus meant even more than that. He meant an infinite number, or that we should keep showing people grace. By now, you may have thought about sending an email or a card or picking up the phone to speak to someone that needs grace from you. Freely give grace because you have been freely given grace.

Life Lesson: You have received grace in your relationship with God. Give grace in your relationships with others.

Dear Father,
Thank You for Your grace. You show it so abundantly to me and Lord, I should in turn show it abundantly to others. Please bring to my remembrance anyone that I need to forgive and show grace to and help others to show me grace as well. I pray this in Jesus' name, Amen.

FEBRUARY 21
TO BE NEEDED

Acts 2:44-46

"And all the believers met together constantly and shared everything they had. They sold their possessions and shared the proceeds with those in need. They worshiped together at the Temple each day, met in homes for the Lord's Supper, and shared their meals with great joy and generosity—" NLT

On many occasions, I have felt a little bruised and beat up from intervening in hairy and even scary situations. I have walked away from some of these dragging and feeling the effects of the battle I was just in. But then, someone comes up and encourages me in the faith or shares a God story from their life. Sometimes, perhaps, they just say, 'Hey Pastor David, thanks, I appreciate you.' I learned long ago that while you cannot live for those moments, God has a way of sending the right person with the right words at the right time. I am grateful for the many varying gifts in the people that I see represented in The Bridge. I am willing to admit humbly, that I need them as much as they need me.

Life Lesson: We need each other.

Dear Father,
Thank You for the people you have placed around me. Thank You that You bring encouragement when I need it, compassion when I need it and an arm around my shoulders when I need it. I want to be available to minister to those around me as well. Please open my eyes to the needs of others. I pray this in Jesus' name, Amen.

FEBRUARY 22
FIRST LOVE

Acts 3:6-7

"Then Peter said, 'Silver and gold I do not have, but what I do have I give you: In the name of Jesus Christ of Nazareth, rise up and walk.' And he took him by the right hand and lifted him up, and immediately his feet and ankle bones received strength."
NKJV

If you have been walking with the Lord for some time, let me ask you to take a moment and remember. Remember the ache you had to share the 'love of God' with others when you first got saved? That love looked for ways to express itself. It seemed like every day held an adventure of talking to people, praying with people, and sharing with people. Along the way, you may have noticed a few did not respond the way you thought they should, yet still several seemed to get it. You may have also noticed that as the years rolled on, in your spiritual wisdom and maturity you began to get a little too laid back. You overlooked showing the very love to others that has been shown to you. If you have found this happening in your own life, don't just sit and feel guilty, longing for the days of your 'first' love. Go back there.

Life Lesson: Expect God to use you in awesome ways to reach others.

Dear Father,
Please use me this day to reach out to someone. Open my eyes to see and open my ears to listen for those who need someone to stretch out a hand to them. Give me the strength and the words. I will look for these opportunities, and I will wait on You to show them to me. Lead me clearly and strongly to be a blessing to the others I come into contact with. In Jesus' name, Amen.

Now expect God to answer this prayer.

FEBRUARY 23
LOVE THE UNLOVABLE

Acts 3:17-19

"Friends, I realize that what you did to Jesus was done in ignorance; and the same can be said of your leaders. But God was fulfilling what all the prophets had declared about the Messiah beforehand—that he must suffer all these things. Now turn from your sins and turn to God, so you can be cleansed of your sins."
NLT

It really is amazing when you stop to consider the scene. Less than two months before, Peter had seen his leader and friend, Jesus, killed in a conspiracy involving these people. Peter could have tried to call down fire from heaven. He could have proclaimed that they were going to hell and he was glad. He did none of these things. With grace, mercy and love Peter reached out to these people. He called them friends or brothers. He offered them hope and salvation. He cared enough to tell them the truth and then present the Good News to them. Jesus told us to love our enemies, to do good and we will be rewarded (Luke 6:35). Truly Peter was listening when Jesus said to love your enemies. Are you listening now?

Life Lesson: Be motivated by love.

Dear Father,
Teach me to love. Teach me to love those who have hurt me. Teach me to love those who I have decided are unlovable. Change me. Now, please present me with opportunity to express love to my enemies. I pray this in Jesus' name, Amen.

FEBRUARY 24
REDEEMED

Matthew 12:20-21
"He will not crush those who are weak, or quench the smallest hope, until he brings full justice with his final victory. And his name will be the hope of all the world."
NLT

I do not want people to feel beat up about sharing their faith. I want to encourage people to share their faith. Why? Look at Peter! In his life we see certain things that are important for us to recognize. Peter had failed miserably not only by not sharing his faith, but also by denying his faith. Then, in the book of Acts we see a changed Peter. Here Peter is boldly declaring to Jewish leaders *"let it be known to you all, and to all the people of Israel, that by the name of Jesus Christ of Nazareth, whom you crucified, whom God raised from the dead, by Him this man stands here before you whole."* (Acts 4:10 NKJV). Despite Peter's failure, God still worked through him. Perhaps you have had some failures in sharing your faith. Maybe you have even denied Jesus in your words or your actions. However small or frail your desire to tell others about Jesus may be, God will take that desire and fan the flames of it until it is a roaring blaze. God wants us to share our faith and He works with us right where we are. All He asks for is a willing heart and mouth to speak on His behalf.

Life Lesson: God can give us a boldness to share our faith.

Dear Father,
Thank you for this gift of salvation. Help me to be bold in sharing it with others. I haven't been so bold in the past and have closed my mouth when I should have spoken. Please forgive me for that and renew my desire to share this message of forgiveness of sins to the world. I pray this in Jesus' name, Amen.

FEBRUARY 25
COZY

Acts 4:34-37

"Nor was there anyone among them who lacked; for all who were possessors of lands or houses sold them, and brought the proceeds of the things that were sold, and laid them at the apostles' feet; and they distributed to each as anyone had need. And Joses, who was also named Barnabas by the apostles (which is translated Son of Encouragement), a Levite of the country of Cyprus, having land, sold it, and brought the money and laid it at the apostles' feet"
NKJV

"The church is uncaring." It's a mantra heard more and more as Bible teaching and gospel minded churches become rarer. As a church body, we should be caring for one another more ... outside of the body and inside of the body. The Bridge has come to be known as a warm and caring place. Together, we can keep it that way or possibly make it even more warm and caring. One of the easiest ways to care for each other is to encourage one another. Encouraging each other must be something that we intentionally do. We should deliberately determine to encourage those around us. Encouragement is something we all need from time to time, and all of us are able to give it. Think for a moment. Could your life have been different if someone had encouraged you to do the right thing? I know my life was forever changed because someone else took the time to encourage me in my relationship with the Lord. Make a difference in someone's life today and encourage them. You might find that you are the one who ends up being encouraged. Love one another. Grace and peace to you.

Life Lesson: The people of the church and the church are to care for one another.

Dear Father,
Thank You for loving me. Lord, thank You for the encouragement I receive from others and give me opportunity to return that gift. Open my eyes to the needs of others and establish in my heart a desire to make someone's day better. I pray this in Jesus' name, Amen.

FEBRUARY 26
THE ENEMY WITHIN

Acts 5:1-4

"But a certain man named Ananias, with Sapphira his wife, sold a possession. And he kept back part of the proceeds, his wife also being aware of it, and brought a certain part and laid it at the apostles' feet. But Peter said, 'Ananias, why has Satan filled your heart to lie to the Holy Spirit and keep back part of the price of the land for yourself? While it remained, was it not your own? And after it was sold, was it not in your own control? Why have you conceived this thing in your heart? You have not lied to men but to God.'"
NKJV

It is worth noting that the most damaging attacks that happen to the church occur from within. One of the most divisive is gossip. The verbal airing of complaints and speaking of division should be seen for what they are, attacks.

In the military, one of the first things that happens after an attack is a damage assessment. Most of us have witnessed these spiritual attacks, and it wasn't until later that we realized the damage that occurred. We should not wait for a damage assessment. In fact, as a body of believers, we should be ready to act during an attack.

In Acts 5, we see that God felt strongly enough about this attack to take strong action. Should we not then speak to people who are divisive and attack the body from within? James speaks about how damaging the tongue can be. I have filed many 'damage reports' in ministry, and let me be the first to encourage you not be used by the enemy in this way. Confront those who try to attack the church from within (as the Bible tells us to). By taking action against these attacks, our focus will not be diverted from the real battle. The real battle is for the lives and souls of men and women all around us.

Life Lesson: Our enemy usually attacks the church from within it.

Dear Father,
The eternal destiny of people hangs in the balance. Please do not let me be a distraction, entertain distractions or cause a distraction from the battle. I know that I can be drawn into complaining and gossip. Give me wisdom to recognize the enemy trying to distract us from within and give me the courage to address it when I see it. I pray this in Jesus' name, Amen.

FEBRUARY 27
GOD KNOWS

Acts 5:12

And through the hands of the apostles many signs and wonders were done among the people. And they were all with one accord in Solomon's Porch.

NKJV

Unexpected events are a part of life. I have learned as a pastor that unexpected events, both good and bad, are also a part of church life. I am so glad that God works through and often in these events. Naturally, we are creatures of habit. When change comes along, our first reaction is to freak out. But loved one, does this response show we trust God? Does it show that we really understand He is still at work in us even in unforeseen events? What is unforeseen to us is not unforeseen with Him. God is still working in us and in this church. Have you ever sat and watched the tide roll in wave after wave? The waves are a work of God. Man can attempt to explain them, but man cannot change their pace, alter their coil or make them stop. Think of the powerful and relentless waves, their height, depth and length. In your life and in this church, you can be confident that God will be faithful to complete that which He started 'til the day of Jesus Christ.

Life Lesson: The work of God continues.

Dear Father,

There have been ups and downs in my life and I know there will be more. I am thankful that no matter how low the valley You are there with me and in control of the situation. There is no reason for the unforeseen to frighten me because You are my strength and my strong tower in the face of trouble. Thank You for that. I pray this in Jesus' name, Amen.

FEBRUARY 28
OPENINGS

Acts 6:3-4
"Now look around among yourselves, brothers, and select seven men who are well respected and are full of the Holy Spirit and wisdom. We will put them in charge of this business. Then we can spend our time in prayer and preaching and teaching the word."
NLT

In Acts 6, we see how important it became for these twelve men to raise up other Godly disciples to help in the work of the ministry. God had called these disciples to teach the Bible. In the midst of the grumbling among the believers, a decision had to be made. They could have either raised up other Godly disciples to help in the work, or they could have neglected their study of the Word of God. In order to teach the people, these men made a great decision. Instead of trying to delegate the order of business among themselves, they presented others with the opportunity.

It is important in ministry and in this body of believers to delegate and 'give away' ministry. God has given each and every one of us gifts in order to serve Him and the body of Christ. The gifts that each of us encompass are a necessary ingredient to the body of believers. Eph 4:11-12, "And He Himself gave some to be apostles, some prophets, some evangelists, and some pastors and teachers, for the equipping of the saints for the work of ministry, for the edifying of the body of Christ," NKJV

Loved one, step out and begin serving the Lord in the small things, and watch as larger doors open for you. He is so worthy to be served. Together, we will see God change lives, starting with our own.

Life Lesson: We should be willing to serve the Lord in any and all ways.

Dear Father,
Thank you for equipping me to serve within Your church. I crave opportunities to use these gifts You've given me to serve others. Help me to use these gifts faithfully so that leaders in the church will present me with more opportunities to glorify You in ministry. I pray this in Jesus' name, Amen.

MARCH 1
SURRENDER

Acts 7:9
"And the patriarchs, becoming envious, sold Joseph into Egypt. But God was with him
NKJV

Genesis 50:20 (Joseph speaking to his brothers)
But as for you, you meant evil against me; but God meant it for good, in order to bring it about as it is this day, to save many people alive.
NKJV

In the seventh chapter of Acts, we see Stephen reminding the Jewish leaders of their spiritual heritage. He recounts the life of Joseph. The most incredible and amazing thing about Joseph's story was that in many hard and difficult circumstances, God was with Joseph to bring him to just the right place at just the right time. God worked this way in the life of Joseph, Moses, and in the life of David. As a matter of fact, almost everyone in the Bible went through difficult times, and yet we see God use these trials to bless them and others. If God, Who has interacted with people for so long, can craft a plan for Joseph, He can certainly craft a plan for your life. Even as God was able to figure out how to give Abraham a son and land, place Joseph in prominence and power in Egypt, and turn Moses into the deliverer of Israel, God can and will lead you in your life. Trust Him through those hard times. Let me encourage you to learn about Him and follow Him. See the amazing things He will do to a life surrendered to Him and His will.

Life Lesson: God is leading us in our lives.

Dear Father,
My life is Yours. Use me for Your good things; to glorify You and bless others. I've had trials and You have seen me through them. I know there will be more and I know that You will deliver me through them into better things. Thank You. I pray this in Jesus' name. Amen.

MARCH 2
FORGIVE

Acts 7:59-60
"And they stoned Stephen as he was calling on God and saying, "Lord Jesus, receive my spirit." Then he knelt down and cried out with a loud voice, "Lord, do not charge them with this sin." And when he had said this, he fell asleep."
NKJV

Jesus gives so many wonderful things to those who follow Him. Some of them are obvious and some are not so obvious. Forgiveness is an obvious and incredible benefit to a relationship with Jesus. Our ability to forgive others is a benefit that might not be so obvious. Matthew, before following Jesus, was a tax collector. In his book, Matthew recorded a pertinent parable from Jesus. In this story, a certain man owed a king a great deal of money. The king was moved by compassion for this man and forgave him of all his debts. Ironically, this forgiven man was also owed money by another. Instead of offering compassion as the King had toward him, he had the man thrown into prison. When the king found out... well here is what happened.

Matthew 18:32-34 "Then the king called in the man he had forgiven and said, 'You evil servant! I forgave you that tremendous debt because you pleaded with me. Shouldn't you have mercy on your fellow servant, just as I had mercy on you?" NLT

You have the power to forgive just as you have been forgiven. Each of us has sinned many more times against God than others have against us. Since we have been forgiven of so much, we should in turn forgive. Forgiving or not forgiving others is an act of your own will. It's your choice. But to forgive others is imitating Christ. Jesus did it, Stephen did it, and you can do it.

Life Lesson: Do not carry baggage from people who have wronged you.

Dear Father,
Thank You for forgiving me of so much. I ask You now to help me forgive others. When bad and painful memories come to me, I ask that I would again be reminded to forgive those who have wronged me. I need Your help to do this because sometimes I don't feel like forgiving. Thank You for setting me free from carrying this baggage and guilt around. Thank You. In the name of Jesus, Amen.

MARCH 3
DONE WITH COMFORTABLE

Acts 8:5-6
"Then Philip went down to the city of Samaria and preached Christ to them. And the multitudes with one accord heeded the things spoken by Philip, hearing and seeing the miracles which he did." NKJV

The love of God is compelling. His love can overcome all differences between believers. It can drive us to brave and heroic deeds; to reach those who do not yet know God. We spend our lives building up walls through fear and insecurity. In the safety of God's love, He now asks us to tear those walls down; often with people who make us uncomfortable.

The Jews and the Samaritans did not get along; in fact they hated each other. The Lord led the early church at Jerusalem to minister and love on the Samaritans. They were willing to lay down their lives and reach out to others; God did incredible things in Samaria and beyond. What will the Lord do through us if we are willing to reach outside of our social groups? Stretch outside of your comfort zone and see what the Lord does on the outside and be amazed at what He does on the inside. The Bible says this...

Romans 8:38-39 "For I am persuaded that neither death nor life, nor angels nor principalities nor powers, nor things present nor things to come, nor height nor depth, nor any other created thing, shall be able to separate us from the love of God which is in Christ Jesus our Lord." NKJV

Life Lesson: We should love one another including other people groups.

Dear Father,
You alone see the fears inside me. I ask You to help me love others. Help me reach out to others who are just as scared as I am. Because You love me, I know I can love others. You tell us to do this so... Lord I need your help. Strengthen me to love others in the midst of a cold, dark and bitter world. May that light shine like a beacon of hope to all who see it and stand as a witness of Your love for the world. In Jesus' name, Amen.

MARCH 4
EXHIBIT U

Acts 8:18-19
"And when Simon saw that through the laying on of the apostles' hands the Holy Spirit was given, he offered them money, saying, 'Give me this power also, that anyone on whom I lay hands may receive the Holy Spirit.'"
NKJV

In this passage, Simon thought he could buy the power of the Holy Spirit. Simon wanted this power so that he could impress others. That is not what the power of God is for. The power of God is given that we may live for Him. We have the power of God that our lives might demonstrate God's work changing us. We should be good stewards, using our power and resources to reach people. We should want to encourage people in their faith. Throughout the Bible, we see Jesus using His power to touch lives, and He did so without weird displays. I believe this gives us our model of what using that power looks like. Why do you desire supernatural power? Hopefully it is to bless others. How do you use your God given resources? Is it to bless and reach others? I hope that it is. With what we have been given, we can make a difference in the hereafter, by making a difference in the here and now.

Life Lesson: God has given us power and resources to reach others.

Dear Father,
All the good things in my life have come from You. My life, my strength, my wisdom, and all that I am or hope to be is a gift from You. I want to use my power, strength, and resources to reach a lost and dying world. We know from Your life, Jesus, that You cared about people. As I follow You, help me to care for others. Help me to use what You have given me wisely as a good steward to reach others. In the name of Yeshua, Jesus, Amen.

MARCH 5
JUST TELL

Acts 8:35

"So Philip began with this same Scripture and then used many others to tell him the Good News about Jesus."

NLT

Jesus tells us to tell others about Him. He has asked us to impart truth to others; their sins can be forgiven if they come to Him. This news is transcendent and transformational. It is the best news that the world has ever heard. Why then is it so hard? First, there is a very real spiritual battle going on around us. In addition, we often think ourselves responsible for convincing someone to believe what we tell them about Jesus. The Bible tells us that God is the One who gives the increase. The Holy Spirit is the One Who convicts and convinces people of both their sin and their need for a Savior. What is our part? Our part is to simply deliver the message. When we realize that it is God's job to convert, suddenly we are free to tell others about Jesus. It makes something that could have been terrifying, a sheer joy. May you find the joy of telling others the great news about Jesus while placing the results in His capable hands. There are no better hands.

Life Lesson: We tell other people about Jesus because Jesus told us to.

Dear Father,

I know that I have thought converting others was my responsibility when it's in Your hands. My job is to simply tell them. I admit that at times I have been discouraged. I thank You for the honor of telling others about You, and I accept that You will strengthen me to do so. Help me to simply tell others of the joy that I have found in You, and direct them on how to find You. I know that You will be faithful to draw them to Yourself. Thank You for making me part of Your plan in telling others. Help me to serve You. In Jesus' name, Amen.

MARCH 6
LIFE INTERRUPTED

Acts 9:15-16
But the Lord said to him, "Go, for he is a chosen vessel of Mine to bear My name before Gentiles, kings, and the children of Israel. For I will show him how many things he must suffer for My name's sake."
NKJV

In Chapter nine of the book of Acts, we see Jesus interrupting the life of Saul of Tarsus. Saul was living out his life doing his 'own thing' with zeal. Unfortunately, Saul's 'thing' was harassing and persecuting Christians. Have you ever found your life interrupted by God? You were going about your life doing your own thing and all of sudden God interrupts, saves you and gives you a passion for lost souls. If you have met Jesus, you should have a passion for lost souls. Sometimes I hear people tell their life stories and wonder if they are grateful for this divine interruption. You have heard the stories. 'My life was great until I met Jesus, now I am barely getting by.' What a disservice that does to the treasure that we have found. We have now been graciously given a heavenly perspective in an otherwise earthly world. We have been given the high, holy and heavenly calling of offering hope to a doomed place. We have a calling to offer love to a world that long ago lost it, and light to a darkness that swallows the human soul. The only thing worse than having this kind of life changing interruption...is not having one. I am thankful for mine. How about you? Let's change the world, one life at a time, starting with yours.

Life Lesson: We are supposed to be a part of God's plan to reach the world.

Dear Father,
Thank you for coming into my life. I now give my life to You. If You can use my life to encourage one person, serve one person, or to see one person brought to You, please do so. There is no greater joy than to give our lives away. You not only told us that, but You showed us that. Lord, help me to look for ways to give my life away. Until the whole world hears. In Jesus' name, Amen.

MARCH 7
INSPIRED

Acts 9:27
"But Barnabas took him and brought him to the apostles. And he declared to them how he had seen the Lord on the road, and that He had spoken to him, and how he had preached boldly at Damascus in the name of Jesus."
NKJV

Acts 4:36
"And Joses, who was also named Barnabas by the apostles (which is translated Son of Encouragement), a Levite of the country of Cyprus,"
NKJV

Barnabas was used by God to encourage Saul. He could have turned away from Saul in disbelief, but instead he encouraged him. Encouraging another person is one of the easiest and most effective ways to influence someone's walk with the Lord. We pray for one another, but often the person may not know we are praying for them. It is only when we give them encouragement that they know. Do you like being encouraged? Of course you do. We all like to be encouraged. In fact, we all need encouragement. It only takes a few moments of time to inspire someone. A small amount of effort can make all the difference in the world. The next time you need encouragement, look for the opportunity to give encouragement to someone else.

Life Lesson: We should encourage one another in our faith.

Dear Father,
Please use me to encourage someone today. Help me to look for someone that is down or hurting. Give me the strength to encourage them in the things of the Lord. For some people, this may be pointing to the fact their sins _could_ be forgiven. For others it may point to the fact that their sins _have been_ forgiven. Give me the strength to encourage others in the same way that I would want to be encouraged. Thank You. In the name of Jesus. Amen.

MARCH 8
TWO WRONGS DON'T...

Acts 10:4
Cornelius stared at him in terror. "What is it, sir?" he asked the angel. And the angel replied, "Your prayers and gifts to the poor have not gone unnoticed by God!
NLT

This is one area that is a very sensitive issue. Certainly there are ministries who have hammered people into giving and that is wrong. Another problem is that many times there are people attending a church who never sow into that ministry. That also is wrong. I have made a commitment to teach the Bible verse by verse and chapter by chapter so I cannot avoid the hard topics; there are times that teaching on a subject is easier than others. I am encouraged by the fact that so many people in this church are 'givers.' However, I also realize that many Christians in this church and in other churches do not give and it is stunting their personal Christian growth. You see, tithing is not God's way of raising money, but God's way of raising children. If you attend here, I encourage you to make a commitment to sow into and pray for this church. If you attend another church, make a commitment to sow into and pray for it. By doing so, you can participate in changing the world.

Life Lesson: A serious follower of Jesus should be praying and giving.

Dear Father,
I now know I should be giving and praying for my church. Lord, you have blessed me through my church. Help me in return be a blessing. I ask for you to forgive me for not giving or praying for the ministry in the past. Please give me the strength to follow through with this. Thank you for the opportunity to give and pray. In Jesus' name. Amen.

MARCH 9
HOT POTATO

Acts 10:22-23

"And they said, "Cornelius the centurion, a just man, one who fears God and has a good reputation among all the nation of the Jews, was divinely instructed by a holy angel to summon you to his house, and to hear words from you." Then he invited them in and lodged them. On the next day Peter went away with them, and some brethren from Joppa accompanied him."
NKJV

In Acts chapter ten, we see the doors opening wide for all of humanity to hear the Gospel. Until this time, only a select few knew of the Good News about Jesus. That was about to change, drastically. The Good News to be presented and accepted by this group of gentiles would impact all of mankind. The world would never be the same.

Now that we have heard the Good News, we have the privilege to help others hear it. It is my desire to reach people with the Good News through any means possible, short of sin. In Genesis chapter four, Cain posed the question, "am I my brother's keeper?" The answer is a resounding 'yes'. We are responsible for reaching this generation with the good news that God loves them and died for their sins. Let's change the world one life at a time... starting with yours.

Life Lesson: We should work together to reach the world.

Dear Father,
I want to thank You that because I asked You to forgive me, You have indeed forgiven me. There are still many people who have not accepted You as Lord and Savior. Lord, please give me a burden to reach people. Lord I want to join together with my brothers and sisters to reach the world. Help me to care about whether they come to You or not. In Jesus' name, Amen.

MARCH 10
WHY R U HERE?

Acts 10:29
"Therefore I came without objection as soon as I was sent for. I ask, then, for what reason have you sent for me?"
NKJV

Peter asks a thought-provoking question in this passage. Why am I here? I think this is a great question to ask ourselves. We may _say_ we are here to serve and love God and to serve and love others, but if we never take the time to really _do_ these things... how important are they to us? I believe it is important to ask ourselves this question often and make decisions according to these priorities. I know I am guilty of getting caught up in things that don't really matter and disregarding the things that really do matter. I find myself 'majoring on the minors and minoring on the majors.' Jesus broke it down for us when He said, "love God and love others." It really can't be explained any simpler than that. We should remember that Jesus did something extraordinary. He loved us by giving His life away. In doing that, He has shown us how to love others.

Life Lesson: We should be asking ourselves the question, why am I here?

The answers should be:

1)...to love and serve God

2)...to love and serve others

3)...to show and tell others about Jesus

Dear Father,
Help me to remember what is important. I get confused about my priorities sometimes. Please remind me through Bible teaching, Bible reading and the love and care of others, why I am here. Help me to take the time to remember these things. Because when all is said and done, only what I have done for you will last. In Jesus' name, Amen.

MARCH 11
BICKERING BELIEVERS

Acts 11:1-4

"Now the apostles and brethren who were in Judea heard that the Gentiles had also received the word of God. And when Peter came up to Jerusalem, those of the circumcision contended with him, saying, "You went in to uncircumcised men and ate with them!" But Peter explained it to them in order from the beginning, saying:"
NKJV

Christians love to discuss their differences. While I do think some differences need to be discussed, I think we spend way too much time and energy on these discussions. There is so much to do for the Kingdom that we can't afford to waste this time. At the end of this brief season we call life; God will not ask how many arguments we have won but rather how many souls we have won. Believers accomplish little when arguing with one another. In discord, believers are not winning souls but instead are distracted by other issues and possibly giving a bad witness. Let's not over emphasize our differences but join together and serve side by side. Let's be careful not to argue differences. Instead, let's serve God alongside one another. John 13:35 reads, "By this all will know that you are My disciples, if you have love for one another."

Life Lesson: Be careful what you argue about with another believer.

Dear Father,
Help me to love the people You have placed around me in life. Help me not to argue and enter into strife with brothers and sisters. Lord while there are some things worthy of argument, there are many things that are not. Lord, please give me the wisdom to know the difference. In Jesus' name, Amen.

MARCH 12
LOUD SPEAKER

Acts 11:18
"When the others heard this, all their objections were answered and they began praising God. They said, "God has also given the Gentiles the privilege of turning from sin and receiving eternal life." NLT

In this verse, we see that the objections and accusations of the people were silenced through the actions of Peter. We should not be so quick to totally disregard critical comments about the church. For example, a comment you often hear is, "the church is all about getting your money." In an effort to remove the obstacle of finances from people hearing the Good News, here at The Bridge, we do not pass an offering plate. We discuss finances when we come across it in scripture. In allowing our actions to speak, we remove that obstacle and create disciples.

We often hear, "church is a fashion show." At The Bridge people are encouraged to come dressed as they are. We are just glad they are here. We do not impose dress codes or discourage one another with down-the-nose-over-the-glasses looks of disdain. Our actions prepare the way for us to use words and remove the obstacle. Follow Jesus and I guarantee people will notice. Live for Him, and the world will listen to the words you don't speak. Then may you have the opportunity to speak words the world longs and needs to hear.

Life Lesson: Do what's right, serve the Lord and let your actions speak louder than the words of others.

Dear Father,
Thank you that you know what it is like to have people say bad things about you. Help me to not let those things distract me from following you. Help me to examine my life and see if there is any truth in what they say. Help me to follow you and love and serve others. I may be the only Bible that someone ever reads so may I be careful what is written upon the pages of my life. In Jesus' name, Amen.

MARCH 13
NEXT STEPS

Acts 11:25-26
"Then Barnabas departed for Tarsus to seek Saul. And when he had found him, he brought him to Antioch. So it was that for a whole year they assembled with the church and taught a great many people. And the disciples were first called Christians in Antioch."
NKJV

At this point in the book of Acts, we believe Saul may have been in Tarsus for as long as 10 years. Saul had ten years to think about his calling and wait for his opportunity. Moses wandered around the desert for 40 years before going back to Egypt to see his people set free. Right in front of each and every one of us, there is an opportunity to step out and begin serving the Lord right where we are. There is a real God-given desire in each of us to make a difference. We all have a desire to belong to a group that is called to do something bigger than ourselves. To deny this God-given desire is to deny how and why we were created. To deny this desire is to live a life of frustration without meaning and purpose. Where are you in the great adventure we call life? Are you walking with Jesus step by step and excited about the possibilities? Are you still caught up in the dog eat dog world just thinking about yourself and looking out for number one? I want to encourage you to take the next step in your Christian faith and keep moving. Keep following Jesus who is so worthy to be followed.

Life Lesson: God uses and leads people for His purposes.

Dear Father,
Thank You for creating me with a desire to follow You. You have put in my heart a desire to serve and love others. When I do that, I will act more and more like You. Lord, please help me to rise out of the cycle of just thinking about me. May I begin to love others and serve others in my life. As I do this, I know that I will become more and more like You... a true follower of Jesus. I want to know You and make You known. Show me what the next steps are and help me to take them. In Jesus' name, Amen.

MARCH 14
DO YOU PRAY

Acts 12:5
"Peter was therefore kept in prison, but constant prayer was offered to God for him by the church."
NKJV

I encourage you to begin 'walking in prayer'. Paul tells us in 1 Thessalonians 5:17 to "pray without ceasing." At first glance, this seems impossible. In considering this further, we see that Paul is telling us to walk in prayer. A portion of my own prayer life is made up of simple short prayers as I commute to work, wait in line at a local store or on a walk alone. This makes me much more aware of the presence of God in my life. Often when someone asks me to pray for them, I pray for them right then and there. I want the person to know I have prayed for them. Let me encourage you to begin walking in prayer today. You will discover what an amazing difference it will make in your life.

Life Lesson: We should pray (which is simply talking and listening to God).

Dear Father,
Thank You for the gift of prayer. Thank You for the gift of being able to talk to You and listen to You wherever I am, whoever I am with and whatever I am doing. I ask, Lord, that I would develop a life style of talking and listening to You. Help me to pray throughout my day and enjoy the time I get to spend with You. Also, God, help me to remember to pray for others. Thanks God for listening to me. In Jesus' name, Amen.

MARCH 15
SOMEONE CARED

Acts 13:3-5

"Then, having fasted and prayed, and laid hands on them, they sent them away. So, being sent out by the Holy Spirit, they went down to Seleucia, and from there they sailed to Cyprus. And when they arrived in Salamis, they preached the word of God in the synagogues of the Jews. They also had John as their assistant."
NKJV

In the book of Acts, the progression of the life of Paul is revealed. Initially, we see Paul fighting against God. Paul is living out his life doing his 'own thing' when he meets God in a very real way. Paul's experience on the road to Damascus began this progression where we see him begin to give his life over to God. The book of Acts allows us to watch first hand as we see this man give his life away. One danger is to look at Paul's life and think, "Wow, that was great for Paul, but can my life really make a difference?" I used to ask myself the same question, but not anymore. You see, one of the beautiful truths of God's Word is that God will work through anybody who is willing. He is not looking for ability, but for availability. Throughout the Bible we see men and women accomplishing great and incredible things. These men and women had some of the same weaknesses and wanderings as us, yet the Lord used them to touch many lives. The most difficult part of this journey is the first step. I encourage you to take the first step. Step out in faith and begin to walk the incredible journey God has planned for you. You will look back in amazement at what the Lord will do. I know I do every day.

Life Lesson: We all should be ministers and make a difference in this world.

Dear Father,

You tell us to pray for workers in the harvest. Lord, I want to pray that You make me a worker in the harvest. Whatever my gifts and abilities are, Jesus, I lay them before You now and ask You to work through me to help change this world. I know I am not saved through these acts of service, but because I am grateful for Your forgiveness, I desire to serve so others may come to know You. I am a Christian because someone cared. Now it is my turn. In Jesus name', Amen.

MARCH 16
TUG OF WAR

Acts 13:7-8

"He had attached himself to the governor, Sergius Paulus, a man of considerable insight and understanding. The governor invited Barnabas and Saul to visit him, for he wanted to hear the word of God. But Elymas, the sorcerer (as his name means in Greek), interfered and urged the governor to pay no attention to what Saul and Barnabas said. He was trying to turn the governor away from the Christian faith."
NLT

In this story, we see the governor torn between Saul and Barnabas, who meant him well, and Elymas who tried to keep the governor from hearing about God. I believe we can relate to this in the many struggles in our own lives. We want to hear the Word of God, like during a teaching, but sometimes we allow ourselves to be talked out of it. One of the things that can make a huge difference in our lives is coming to church to hear the Bible studies. It encourages us, challenges us, and allows worship and fellowship with one another. It is obvious why the enemy of our souls would not want us in that kind of environment. He will try and use friends, family and loved ones to keep us from church, serving, giving, praying and reading the Bible. Above all the noise; however, the voice of Jesus rings true. Come to Him and He will give you rest. The world says 'get', Jesus says 'give'. The world says focus on 'you'. Jesus says focus on 'others' and upon Him. Be careful what voice you listen to my friend. It is very important.

Life Lesson: Every one of us is involved in a spiritual tug of war.

Dear Father,
Help me to hear Your voice over the noise of life. Lord it seems that others try to pull me down or keep me from being spiritual. Help me during those weak moments to know what You would say to me. Help me to hear and respond to Your voice and be forgiven. Help me to fellowship with and love others around me. Thank You for continuing to call me. In Jesus' name, Amen.

MARCH 17
ARE YOU MOVING?

Acts 13:14
"But when they departed from Perga, they came to Antioch in Pisidia, and went into the synagogue on the Sabbath day and sat down."
NKJV

In this verse, we see Paul active in his faith. Remember, this is the book of Acts. The church should be the most creative and most powerful force outside of God Himself. It is the vehicle through which God is moving. I do not believe that God is interested in maintaining the status quo while so many slip off to an eternity without Him. What about you? Are you moving? Are you moving in the right direction of loving, serving and worshipping God? I have personally never seen as much spiritual activity and spiritual fruit as I see in this place. I thank the Lord for that fruit. I ask Him to never let us be content with 'church as usual'.

Life Lesson: The church should always be on the move.

Dear Father,
It is an exciting thing to see You moving in people throughout the book of Acts. It is more exciting to realize that the God moving in the book of Acts is the same God who is moving in my church. Lord, it is You. Help me to be on the move with the church. Help us to move with You. Help the leaders to make wise decisions. Thank you Lord that I can play a part. Help me to find my part. In Jesus' name, Amen.

MARCH 18
YOUR GREATEST NEED

Acts 13:29-30
"Now when they had fulfilled all that was written concerning Him, they took Him down from the tree and laid Him in a tomb. But God raised Him from the dead."
NKJV

When we stop to consider the creation of the world, it is staggering. It is immense and huge and yet intricately beautiful to the smallest detail. Yet for all its wonder and beauty, it was not God's greatest work. His greatest work was the cross. If you were just a bystander on the day Jesus died, you would not have thought it a thing of beauty, yet strangely enough, it was the most beautiful thing ever created. This was a massive display of strength and power yet, at the same time, an overwhelming statement of grace, humility and love. In short, it was the most incredible picture of love this world has ever seen or ever will see. God, who was perfect, reached out to imperfect man so that He could have a relationship with him. Sin was in the way, and it had to be dealt with. God made the way and that way was the cross. This is our greatest need. Food is not the greatest need because there will come a day when we need food no more. Shelter is not the greatest need because we will not live eternally where we are now. The greatest need is to be forgiven and in a right relationship with God. If you are right with God, if you have been forgiven, then you have your greatest need already met. Now may your eyes be opened to those around you who have not had their greatest need met.

Life Lesson: God's greatest deed met man's greatest need.

Dear Father,
I thank You that because I asked You to forgive me and I believe in You, You have forgiven me. So often Lord, I think only of my needs. Lord, help me to be thankful that my greatest need has been met. Please help me to consider others in the world out there that have not had the joy of having their sins forgiven. Thank You for the cross and for making the forgiveness possible. Thanks God. In Jesus' name, Amen.

MARCH 19
CHOICES

Matthew 5:16

"Let your light so shine before men, that they may see your good works and glorify your Father in heaven."

NKJV

Many Christians, if asked "what are you called to do," have a difficult time answering the question. They feel like they need to respond with some grand scheme or plan that the Lord has lain on their hearts. Some feel that by answering the Lord has called me to clean hallways, serve in media or children's ministry, their calling pales in comparison to a Billy Graham or Greg Laurie. They could not be any more wrong in their assumption. You see, it is not one man's efforts that receive reward when a soul is won for Christ, but it is everyone who played a part. If there is a traffic jam in the parking lot, someone may see it and decide not to come to church. If they are not welcomed like a special guest when they come in the door, they may leave without hearing the Gospel. If nobody cleans the hallways and they are left dirty, that's another distraction that has to be overcome. If the lights and sound in the sanctuary are not functioning, there is another distraction. You see, it is all these things and all the people serving and ministering their gifts around the church that make the difference as to whether someone hears the Gospel presentation or not.

Sadly, some Christians will never be engaged. They will never step up to serve, and I have to wonder who their Lord is. Jesus said, "Anyone who isn't helping Me opposes Me, and anyone who isn't working with Me is actually working against Me." Luke 11:23 NLT

We have an immeasurable obligation to serve God. The blessings belong to everyone who participates, but do not do it for the reward... do it because God has called you, Christian.

Life Lesson: Answer the calling or miss the blessings, your choice.

Dear Father,

Thank you, that You provide the gifts and the opportunities to serve You. Help me to be open and available. Please forgive me for the times that I have not heeded Your call. Lord, I love You and I want to be faithful. Please place people in my life who will hold me accountable to serving. In Jesus' name, Amen.

MARCH 20
ENCOURAGE OTHERS

Hebrews 10:24
"Think of ways to encourage one another to outbursts of love and good deeds."
NLT

What is encouragement? Let's take a closer look at how God's Word reveals it to us. 1 Corinthians 12 tells us that spiritual gifts have been given to each believer by the Holy Spirit for the purpose of building up Christ's Body – the church. Every Christian has the gift of encouragement. Encouragement is in action every day here at The Bridge as we see brothers and sisters coming alongside one another in fellowship and prayer. This is a church full of people serving God and encouraging *one another to outbursts of love and good deeds."*

Do you need encouragement? Then be an encourager!

1 Peter 4:10 "As each one has received a gift, minister it to one another, as good stewards of the manifold grace of God." NKJV

If you are not already, start serving and watch what happens.

Life Lesson: Encouragement is a Spiritual Gift.

Dear Father,
Thank You for giving me the gift of encouragement. Forgive me for the times I have neglected to encourage my family, friends, co-workers, and people I don't even know. Help me to remember to use my gift and thank You for the encouragement that You give me every day. I pray this in Jesus' name, Amen.

MARCH 21
WHERE IS YOUR HEART?

Acts 14:11
"Now when the people saw what Paul had done, they raised their voices, saying in the Lycaonian language, "The gods have come down to us in the likeness of men! And Barnabas they called Zeus, and Paul, Hermes, because he was the chief speaker. Then, the priest of Zeus, whose temple was in front of their city, brought oxen and garlands to the gates, intending to sacrifice with the multitudes."
NKJV

We should be careful of worshiping others. "Pastor David, what do you mean 'be careful of worshiping others'? We live in an enlightened age; we are way beyond idol worship." Oh, Really? What about... NASCAR, MTV and Hollywood celebrities? Some people idolize Oprah or Dr. Phil; others worship movie stars, rock stars and athletes... All of which are people just like you and me. How easy it is to get sidetracked and take our eyes off the Lord! Some folks worship their children. They allow their children to decide what they do and when they do it.

Do not worship Mary, saints or angels. Angels are very sensitive to people worshipping them. Why? Because they saw many other angels get kicked out of heaven for rebelling. (Rev. 19:10; 22:9)

Be careful of worshipping people. Jesus said, "For where your treasure is, there your heart will be also." (Matthew 6:21, NKJV) So, where is your treasure? In Hollywood? In Wall Street? Then, I have to ask, where is your heart?

Life Lesson: Worship God and God alone.

Dear Father,
Thank You for loving me. Please forgive me for placing other people and things ahead of You in my life. Please show me where I have idols and help me to get rid of them. Thank you for loving me. In Jesus' name. Amen.

MARCH 22
SAINT YOU

Acts 14:18
"But even so, Paul and Barnabas could scarcely restrain the people from sacrificing to them."
NLT

How often we take our focus off God and place it on men. Paul is not Saint Paul in the religious sense; rather he is a Saint because he is new in Christ Jesus who forgave him of his sins. God did great things through Paul and Barnabas who were just people like you and me - people who had the mind of Christ. When we think of people as super heroes, we deceive ourselves in thinking they did things that we could never do, but you know what? God does great things through people today.

Jesus said that He did not come to be served, but to serve (Matthew 20:28). If we are to "arm ourselves also with the same mind" (1 Peter 4:1 NKJV) then we must serve others. Paul exhorts us saying, "You must have the same attitude that Christ Jesus had" (Philippians 2:5 NLT). What is your attitude toward serving others?

God wants to use you to do awesome things. People who forsake their own needs and wants by serving others demonstrate their focus is on Jesus. The kind of humility that it takes to deny yourself in order to serve others is unnatural to man, but through the incredible work of God it is made possible. There are more opportunities to serve others than there are of being served. What does that say about individuals willing to let others serve them, but never serve others? It speaks volumes about their focus. Have you positioned yourself to serve or to be served?

Life Lesson: Get your eyes off of people and put them on Jesus.

Dear Father,
Please forgive me for the times when I've taken my focus off of You and placed it on people. Please give me a heart to serve You by serving others. I want to be Your humble and obedient servant. Thank You. In Jesus' name, Amen.

MARCH 23
IT'S SIMPLE

Acts 15:5
"But some of the sect of the Pharisees who believed rose up, saying, "It is necessary to circumcise them, and to command them to keep the law of Moses."
NKJV

In the book of Galatians, Paul had to deal with legalists who were trying to add their own rules to the plan of salvation. Paul said, "I marvel that you are turning away so soon from Him who called you in the grace of Christ, to a different gospel, which is not another; but there are some who trouble you and want to pervert the gospel of Christ. But even if we, or an angel from heaven, preach any other gospel to you than what we have preached to you, let him be accursed. As we have said before, so now I say again, if anyone preaches any other gospel to you than what you have received, let him be accursed." Galatians 1:6-9 NKJV.

Be careful of those who try to add more to the plan of salvation or make it complicated. If it is not simple and clear, then it is not Biblical. God created the plan; the plan is perfect. Should we try to persuade God to add to His plan? Certainly not! Should we add to the gospel in order to please people? Never! Paul said, "For if I still pleased men, I would not be a bondservant of Christ." Galatians 1:10 NKJV

Romans 10:9-10 is very clear. "That if you confess with your mouth the Lord Jesus and believe in your heart that God has raised Him from the dead you will be saved." In addition, verse 13 states, "everyone who calls on the name of the Lord will be saved."

Have you asked Jesus to be your Lord and Savior?

It's real simple.

Life Lesson: Being forgiven is very simple and clear.

Dear Father,
I believe in You. I believe that You died on the cross for my sins. I am a sinner. Please forgive me for my sins. Thank You for forgiving me. Please give me the power to turn from sin and to live for You all the days of my life. I pray this in Jesus' name, Amen.

MARCH 24
GRACE GIFTS

Acts 15:10
"Now therefore, why do you test God by putting a yoke on the neck of the disciples which neither our fathers nor we were able to bear?"
NKJV

It is a sad reality that few Christians are willing to extend grace to one another as Jesus showed grace to us. On the day that we asked Jesus to forgive us of all our sins, He extended His grace toward us. God extends this same grace to each of us every day. What about your friends and family? Do they need grace? What about co-workers or the person sitting next to you in church?

How quick we can be to call out the sin in others while we ignore the sin in our own lives. This shows just how poor our understanding is of what Jesus did for us. If we truly understand just how far down God had to extend His merciful hand to reach us, certainly we should be willing to reach out with the same grace to others.

Think about this. When we accept God's grace for ourselves, but are unwilling to show grace to others, are we not claiming the gospel of grace for ourselves while charging the law to others? What pride! Colossians 3:12-13 reads, "Since God chose you to be the holy people whom he loves, you must clothe yourselves with tenderhearted mercy, kindness, humility, gentleness, and patience. You must make allowance for each other's faults and forgive the person who offends you. Remember, the Lord forgave you, so you must forgive others."

Be quick to show grace, Christian. Be ready to show mercy, child of God. After all, if when you look at someone else you see their sin, what do you think they see when they look at you? God's grace is not only sufficient for us, it's sufficient for us to show others.

Life Lesson: Grace is not just something we receive, it is also something we give.

Dear Father,
Thank You for Your grace. Please forgive me for the times when I have not shown that same grace to others. Help me to show grace from now on so that others will see You in me. I pray this in Jesus' name, Amen.

MARCH 25
USE THE COMPASS

Acts 15:19-21

"Therefore I judge that we should not trouble those from among the Gentiles who are turning to God, but that we write to them to abstain from things polluted by idols, from sexual immorality, from things strangled, and from blood. For Moses has had throughout many generations those who preach him in every city, being read in the synagogues every Sabbath."
NKJV

A compass is used to find the right direction to where you want to go. The compass has four main directions; north, south, east, and west. If you want to go north, then you go in the direction the needle is pointing. If you want to go south, then you go in the opposite direction. A compass does not force you to use it nor does it force you to go in the right direction. You get to choose whether to consult the compass or not. You also get to choose whether to follow its direction.

Romans 12:1-2 reads, "And so, dear brothers and sisters, I plead with you to give your bodies to God. Let them be a living and holy sacrifice—the kind he will accept. When you think of what he has done for you, is this too much to ask? Don't copy the behavior and customs of this world, but let God transform you into a new person by changing the way you think. Then you will know what God wants you to do, and you will know how good and pleasing and perfect his will really is." NLT

God has given us a spiritual compass through His Word. Some will choose to use it and some will choose not to use it. Some will read it, but others will choose to ignore it. Friend, don't let popularity or feelings be your compass. These things change. Jesus said, "I am the way, the truth, and the life. No one comes to the Father except through Me." John 14:6

God's Word does not move. God's Word will always point you in the right direction. It will always point to Jesus.

Life Lesson: Let God and His Word be your spiritual compass

Dear Father,
Thank You for giving us Your Word, the Bible as a lamp to our feet and a light to our path. Thank You that we do not have to depend on our own feelings, the feelings of others, popularity, or the world for guidance. Please forgive me for the times that I have looked to those things to guide me. I pray this in Jesus' name. Amen.

MARCH 26
MORE TO DO

Acts 15:35
"Paul and Barnabas also remained in Antioch, teaching and preaching the word of the Lord, with many others also."
NKJV

A lot of effort is put forth so that people can know God. I agree wholeheartedly that we should introduce people to God. Everyone has a need to have a relationship with Him. When someone makes a decision to accept Jesus, they have made the greatest decision they will ever make. The work of salvation is then complete, but there is still much to do. You see, once someone gets to know the God of the Word, they need to get to know the Word of God. We place great importance and emphasis on the teaching of the Word of God here at The Bridge. It is my joy and honor to walk you through the Word to help equip you to deal with life. I look forward to our walk together, and I am sure we will both learn many things. Take the time to read because he took the time to bleed. Get to know your Bible.

Life Lesson: We should intimately know the Word of God.

Dear Father,
Thank You for the Bible. I realize many men and women have died that I might have a copy of it in my life. It truly is a treasure and a light to my path. Please help me to read it, dig into it, and spend my days going through the incredible riches of this supernatural book. Thank You God for writing Your love letter straight to me called the Bible. In Jesus' name, Amen.

MARCH 27
I'LL TAKE DOOR NUMBER ONE

Acts 16:6-7

"Now when they had gone through Phrygia and the region of Galatia, they were forbidden by the Holy Spirit to preach the word in Asia. After they had come to Mysia, they tried to go into Bithynia, but the Spirit did not permit them."
NKJV

Have you ever had God close a door that you thought was open? What was your reaction? Did you moan and complain or did you thank God for the closed door while praying about what to do? Prayer is a good thing. Paul exhorts us to "pray without ceasing" (1 Thessalonians 5:17), but this doesn't mean to stop looking for other open doors. You can pray while taking action. What did Paul and his crew do when the Lord closed a door? Did they sit around and moan to one another about how difficult it was to be a Christian and how they wanted to minister in Bithynia but the Lord would not let them? No, they didn't! They kept moving forward as God revealed to Paul the door that He had opened.

Acts 16:10 "Now after he had seen the vision, immediately we sought to go to Macedonia, concluding that the Lord had called us to preach the gospel to them." NKJV

Although God closed some doors for Paul and his crew, God opened the doors to Macedonia in order that Lydia would be saved, and the door to Europe would be opened to the Gospel. You see, sometimes the door that God closes opens the door to something awesome that He has in store. What should we do when God closes the door? Don't try to kick in the door! Don't peep through the doorknob and don't look under the door. Instead, prayerfully try another door. That one's closed? Look behind you...there's another door. Try that one. It's open! Now what? Take a step of faith. The rest is up to God. Press forward.

Philippians 3:13-14 "Brethren, I do not count myself to have apprehended; but one thing I do, forgetting those things which are behind and reaching forward to those things which are ahead, I press toward the goal for the prize of the upward call of God in Christ Jesus." NKJV

Life Lesson: Closed doors are a blessing.

Dear Father,

Thank You for saving me. Thank You for allowing me to serve You in whatever way You have planned for me. Please forgive me for the times that I have tried to force open doors that You closed. Give me eyes to see the doors that You want me to go through and the courage to go through them. I pray this in Jesus' name.

MARCH 28
POKE!

Acts 16:14-15

"Now a certain woman named Lydia heard us. She was a seller of purple from the city of Thyatira, who worshiped God. The Lord opened her heart to heed the things spoken by Paul. And when she and her household were baptized, she begged us, saying, "If you have judged me to be faithful to the Lord, come to my house and stay." So she persuaded us."
NKJV

Lydia was not saved by good works, but saved in order to do good works.

Once saved, Lydia began to fellowship with other Christians. You see, it is the responsibility of every Christian to be in fellowship with other Christians. Fellowship helps you in your faith, and it will help other believers in their faith.

The Author of Hebrews says, "And let us consider one another in order to stir up love and good works, not forsaking the assembling of ourselves together, as is the manner of some, but exhorting one another, and so much the more as you see the Day approaching" Hebrews 10:24-25 NKJV.

The word used for 'stir up' also means to 'provoke'. It is like going to the dentist...stay with me here. When you go for a check-up, the dentist uses a sharp tool to poke around at your teeth, right? It is not until he pokes the one tooth that makes you jump that you discover you've got a cavity. Once you know that you have a problem with your tooth, you can take steps to fix it. It's not pleasant, but it's necessary as it keeps a small problem from turning into a big problem.

Interaction with other believers may not always be comfortable. Someone may see our sore spots - areas where we are weak or where we fail to glorify God. We may even get 'poked' in those spots. Sometimes we are not aware of the sore spot and the 'poking' brings to our attention the need to repent and change. Other times we are covering up the sore spot, and it takes encouragement from a brother or sister for us to make a change. Now, I'm not saying that you should nitpick all your friends until you find something wrong that you can point out to them - not at all! Rather, it's a natural part of fellowship with other believers. Solomon put it this way:

Proverbs 27:17 "As iron sharpens iron, a friend sharpens a friend." NLT

When you grind two pieces of iron together, you may get sparks, but it's not just one piece of iron that is sharpened; both pieces benefit from the process. Don't ignore this vital part of your Christian walk! I'm probably poking someone in a sore spot right now (poke!).

Life Lesson: We should fellowship or hang out with people in the church.

Dear Father,

Thank You for loving me. Thank You that I am not alone in this Christian walk. Please forgive me for the times when I have neglected fellowship. Please give me a desire to fellowship with my family in Christ. I pray this in Jesus' name, Amen

MARCH 29
THERE IS HOPE IN GOD

Acts 16:27-30
"And the keeper of the prison, awaking from sleep and seeing the prison doors open, supposing the prisoners had fled, drew his sword and was about to kill himself. But Paul called with a loud voice, saying, "Do yourself no harm, for we are all here." Then he called for a light, ran in, and fell down trembling before Paul and Silas. And he brought them out and said, "Sirs, what must I do to be saved?"
NKJV

All of us at some point in our lives are held captive by something. It could be that you are captive by a bad decision you made. Praise the Lord. Maybe you are held captive by habits or even by outside circumstances that you have little control over. Praise the Lord. Maybe it's your health. Praise the Lord. Is your hope in an escape? Then your hope is in the wrong place. Is your hope in healing? Then your hope is in the wrong place. Is your hope in the Lord? You got it, that's where it should be.

Jeremiah 29:11 "For I know the plans I have for you," says the LORD. They are plans for good and not for disaster, to give you a future and a hope." NLT

That's a promise that God has made to you, and He has an established track record of always keeping His promises. So, what are you doing while you are in the midst of your trials? Are you staying in His Word? Are you praising Him? Look around...who's watching? It could be that there are others...like you, or even jailors who are watching. What an incredible witness you can be by giving thanks to God despite your circumstances.

1 Peter 3:15 "Instead, you must worship Christ as Lord of your life. And if you are asked about your Christian hope, always be ready to explain it." NLT

You see, whether you have been beaten up like Paul and Silas or beaten down like the jailer, the Lord knows what is going on and wants you to turn to Him. His promises have not and will not change. So don't give up, friend. Stay focused on Jesus. Remember His words:

John 16:33 "In the world you will have tribulation; but be of good cheer, I have overcome the world." NKJV

Life Lesson: No matter how bad your circumstances are, there is hope in God.

Dear Father,

Thank You for sending Your Son, Jesus, to die on the cross for my sins. Thank You that He rose from death victorious so that I may have victory in life over darkness through Him. Please give me the ability to glorify and praise You in good times and bad. I pray this in Jesus' name, Amen.

MARCH 30
DECIDE

Acts 17:5-6
"But the Jews who were not persuaded, becoming envious, took some of the evil men from the marketplace, and gathering a mob, set all the city in an uproar and attacked the house of Jason, and sought to bring them out to the people."
NKJV

How often do you watch television shows about plush living or celebrity lifestyles? Many years ago, a very popular show was the "Lifestyles of the Rich and Famous." Today, it's "MTV Cribs" or a myriad of other shows with similar themes. What do you feel like after watching one of these shows? Do you covet what someone else has? Do you accuse the people in these shows of making too much money or owning too much house? "Oh, but that's television, Pastor David...if I'm envious of someone on TV it doesn't count because I don't know them." Well, that's not true. Let's bring it into the realm of daily life. Envy is spite and resentment at seeing the success of another. Are you envious of someone?

Envy not only affects you, it can affect those around you. It can wreak havoc in the workplace. It can hinder ministry. It can bring division in the home. I've heard a story about an old fisherman who was carrying a bucket of crabs with no lid on it. When approached by a young child to find out why he kept no lid on the bucket, the fisherman replied, "I don't have to keep a lid on the bucket. You see, whenever one starts to climb out, the others reach up and pull him down." Do you see how this applies to your own life? What is your reaction when someone has success in ministry or success in life? Do you say to yourself, "that's not fair" or "that should have happened to me." If so, then you are experiencing envy. Do you say, "He should have done it this way" or "I can't believe he did it that way?" What you really mean to say is, "I should have his job or ministry so that I can do it the way I want to." You can decide not to feel this way. You can thank God for blessing that person and ask Him to continue blessing them. What if you don't like them or if they are your enemy? Bless them all the more. The evil thing about being envious is that you cannot feel blessed and envious at the same time. You choose. Either you are blessed or you are envious. The opposite of envy is being grateful or feeling contentment. The Apostle Paul suffered greatly for the Gospel. He knew what it was to have nothing. He knew what it was to be persecuted, scoffed at, and imprisoned. He was beaten, stoned, and even shipwrecked. His life was always in peril from others. Yet in all this he wrote:

Phil 4:11 "Not that I speak in regard to need, for I have learned in whatever state I am, to be content" NKJV

Life Lesson: When you feel envy decide not to feel that way.

Dear Father,
Thank You for the blessings that You have given me; they are so much more than what I deserve. Help me to be content and not to be envious of anyone else. I thank You for the way You have blessed others, and I pray that You would continue to bless them. Please forgive me for the times that I have been envious of others. I pray this in Jesus' name, Amen.

MARCH 31
BE AN ENCOURAGER

Acts 17:13-14
"But when the Jews from Thessalonica learned that the word of God was preached by Paul at Berea, they came there also and stirred up the crowds." NKJV

Whenever you see someone trying to stir up others, ask yourself the simple question; why? What is their motivation? Is the motivation love because you know this person has so obviously cared about others in the past? Or, does the motivation seem unnatural because this person, who has shown little care in the past, all of a sudden is now saying something 'because they care.' Be careful.

Jeremiah 17:9 "The heart is deceitful above all things, And desperately wicked; Who can know it?" NKJV

The motivation of the crowd in Acts17:13 was envy. It is no great gift to stir others up in a bad way. It takes no talent nor discretion, and very little wisdom to stir up others in strife, envy or confusion. In the book of Hebrews, Paul exhorts us to stir one another up:

Heb 10:24-25 "And let us consider one another in order to stir up love and good works, not forsaking the assembling of ourselves together, as is the manner of some, but exhorting one another, and so much the more as you see the Day approaching." NKJV

Notice what Paul says 'stirring up' produces. Instead of strife, envy, confusion and discontentment, stirring up others should produce love and good works based in fellowship. This is important. Will the end result be encouragement or discouragement? It should be encouragement. Our faith, in action, should provoke others to love and good works. Sadly, there are Christians who do nothing. They don't stir even themselves up much less provoke anyone else to do good things. How self-centered. Fellowship with God should never be selfish, but should include others and serve others. We should love one another enough to be encouragers. It's not about what we get from fellowship, but it's what we give or contribute to fellowship.

- Can you stir people up in a good way?
- Can you help people continue on when they doubt?
- Can you help people hang in there when they are weak?

Yes, you can, and friend, that is an incredible gift.

Life Lesson: We should stir one another up to good works not to strife, envy, confusion and discontentment.

Dear Father,

Thank You for my church family and for the opportunity to fellowship with them and to serve them. I pray that I would be an encourager and please forgive me for the times when I have not. Please give me opportunities to encourage my friends and family to love and do good works, and give me the discernment to know when my motivation is wrong. I pray this in Jesus' name, Amen.

APRIL 1
BUILD BRIDGES

Acts 17:22-23
22 Then Paul stood in the midst of the Areopagus and said, "Men of Athens, I perceive that in all things you are very religious;23 for as I was passing through and considering the objects of your worship, I even found an altar with this inscription: TO THE UNKNOWN GOD. Therefore, the one whom you worship without knowing, Him I proclaim to you."
NKJV

It is easy to throw stones. It takes more effort to build something and costs much more to restore it. What then, is the price to redeem? Well, that price is far greater than we could ever pay. Only Jesus could pay that fine. Jesus died on the cross. He bore the penalty for our sins. It is by grace that we are saved and not by works (Ephesians 2:8, 9).

As Christians, we possess this knowledge. What should we be doing with it? Should we be using it as a crowbar to pry people apart? Should we use it as a wrecking ball to tear people down? Should we strike hard with this tool, pinning nail to wood with one mighty blow? Certainly not! What a horrible misuse of God's grace toward us that would be!

How we love to nest ourselves in the grace we have been given, and then, thinking ourselves to be on a higher branch, we drop stones on everyone else. We didn't have to earn our grace, but everyone else had better get to work! How hypocritical! When we are unwilling to show grace to others, we are misrepresenting God.

Jesus humbled Himself and dwelt with sinners.

Luke 5:31-32 Jesus answered them, "Healthy people don't need a doctor—sick people do. I have come to call sinners to turn from their sins, not to spend my time with those who think they are already good enough." NLT

In Acts 17:22-23, it would have been easy for Paul to start throwing verbal stones. Instead, he demonstrated God's grace by seeking to build a bridge of understanding so that the great news of the Gospel could be communicated. Instead of pointing out differences, he used a bridge to present the Gospel message to the people. Are you a bridge builder?

Life Lesson: We should build bridges with people who don't understand the good news about Jesus, not just stand back and throw stones at them.

Dear Father,

Thank You that it's not by any works of my own, but by Your grace that I'm saved. Please forgive me for times when I have torn down bridges instead of building bridges to tell people about Your Son, Jesus Christ. Please give me the fortitude to speak out of love instead of boasting. I pray this in Jesus' name, Amen.

APRIL 2
GOD WORKS IT OUT

Acts 18:2
"And he found a certain Jew named Aquila, born in Pontus, who had recently come from Italy with his wife Priscilla (because Claudius had commanded all the Jews to depart from Rome); and he came to them."
NKJV

Corinth was a very wicked city. It could be said that Corinth was the Las Vegas of the day. The population of the city was over 400,000, and it was a popular tourist destination due to the location as well as the loose morals of the city. In fact, the reputation of the city was such that calling someone a "Corinthian" was considered an insult and to 'corinthianize' was to engage in sin.

Around AD 49, a wave of anti-Semitism rolled through Rome and the Emperor, Claudius, expelled the Jews from the city. As a result of this edict, Aquila and Priscilla departed to Corinth. After being mocked in Athens, Paul also was in Corinth where he met Aquila and Priscilla. What seemed to be bad circumstances for Aquila, Priscilla and Paul, became a huge blessing. Aquila and Priscilla became a valuable part of Paul's ministry team, and Paul was able to minister the Gospel more effectively due to their help. God used a bad thing to produce a good result.

Romans 8:28, "And we know that all things work together for good to those who love God, to those who are the called according to His purpose." NKJV

Notice that it does not say 'most things' or 'some things,' but it says, 'all things'. This does not mean you will understand how God will work it out to your good. There will be many times where you will not know for days, weeks or even years, how He will do it. Throughout the Bible, we see God redeem events in the lives of people for His purposes. It is a theme of grace Christians can count on. Jesus said, "In the world you will have tribulation; but be of good cheer, I have overcome the world" John 16:33b NKJV. No mistake or circumstance can be too great to be used by God. The choice is yours. In difficult times, you can be freaked out or you can rest in the promises of God.

Life Lesson: When you follow God, He works things out for our good.

Dear Father,
Thank You that I do not have to worry. Thank You that because of Your mercy, faithfulness, and great love for me, I can be at peace in all circumstances. Please help me to remember this. I pray this in Jesus' name. Amen.

APRIL 3
COMMITMENT IS NOT BONDAGE

Acts 18:18

"So Paul still remained a good while. Then he took leave of the brethren and sailed for Syria, and Priscilla and Aquila were with him. He had his hair cut off at Cenchrea, for he had taken a vow." NKJV

Paul had taken a Nazarite vow that he would not touch a dead body; he would drink no wine, eat no grapes, eat no raisins, and allow his hair to grow before cutting it off as a sign of purification (see Numbers 6). But wait, you say, isn't Paul the one who told us that those under grace should not be under bondage? In Galatians 5:1, he wrote, "Stand fast therefore in the liberty by which Christ has made us free, and do not be entangled again with a yoke of bondage." This was not bondage for Paul because it kept the message of the Gospel of Jesus Christ relatable to the Jews. It was also profitable in that it gave Paul the opportunity to model service and sacrifice as an example for other Christians. Friends, I am going to let you in on something that may surprise you, commitment is not bondage. It is by God's grace that we have been given the opportunity to serve Him. How do we serve God? We serve Him by serving others and His church. Is commitment service or sacrifice? It is both. Every Christian should be ready to serve and be ready for sacrifice. What was the model set forth for us by Jesus? It was one of service and sacrifice. If we are to be "Christ-like" then we must be ready and willing to commit ourselves to live by the example He set for us. We hold ourselves to commitments everyday. Commitments we make at our jobs, with our family and friends. What about our commitment to Jesus and to His church?

Proverbs 16:3 reads, "Commit your work to the LORD, and then your plans will succeed." NLT

Service or sacrifice, whichever it may be, I'm ready. That is the mindset of a true servant of God. Maybe it is this church or maybe it is another church, but friend, find that place and be committed.

Life Lesson: We should be committed to God and to the church.

Dear Father,
Thank You for Your grace and Your mercy. Help me look for ways I can commit to serving others. Help me to be willing and ready when asked to serve. Lord, when my serving requires sacrifice, please help me not to grumble or complain. Help me to be glad that I can sacrifice my time and effort in serving others, and in turn recognize that I am serving You. Thank you Lord for Your serving and sacrifice for us. I pray this in Jesus' name, Amen.

APRIL 4
OPEN OR CLOSED

Acts 18:19
"And he came to Ephesus, and left them there; but he himself entered the synagogue and reasoned with the Jews."
NKJV

Earlier in Acts 18, Paul tried to minister the Gospel to the Jews in the synagogue in Corinth. It was not received. Paul decided that from then on he would go to the Gentiles. Later on in the chapter, we see Paul ministering again to the Jews in the synagogue in Ephesus. Paul realized that the door was not open for him to minister to the Jews in Corinth, but was open for ministry to the Gentiles. Now in Ephesus, he finds the door open to preach to the Jewish people for a short time prior to leaving for Jerusalem.

Sometimes you may have on your heart to do something and well...the time is just not right to do it. What do you do at those times? Do you force the door open or do you stand there and wait? Do you notice doors the Lord has opened, or do you wait only for the Lord to open that one door? Often, we get so distracted by the fact that one door is closed, that we overlook all of the open doors.

"Wait just a minute...this can't be right. How can this door be closed," we might say. "It was open five minutes ago. I've seen others go through it. There must be something wrong with the hinges! Certainly, God would want me to go through this door. *After all, I've seen others go through it,* and I have way more experience going through doors. Maybe if I stand here long enough, it will open back up."

Meanwhile, the doors of ministry that God has opened are closing. So, we see that Paul did not force the issue. He waited for the Lord to open the closed door, but did not ignore the door that was open. When the Lord opened the door for Paul in the synagogue in Ephesus, Paul used it. Paul was both willing to do it, and he was willing not to do it. This is important in following and serving the Lord. You need to be willing when the door opens. You also need to be willing when the door shuts. It will end up that Ephesus will be one of the healthiest growing churches that Paul starts. What if he had tried to kick the door down on God? It would not have gone well.

One of my frequent prayers is Lord, open the doors you want open so that no man can close them and close the doors you want closed so that no man can open them. That includes me. Keep serving and following the Lord. Charles Spurgeon said, "By perseverance the snail reached the ark."

Life Lesson: Wait on the timing of the Lord to open doors.

Dear Father:

Thank You for both the open doors and the closed doors in my life. Please forgive me for the times that I have tried to force open a door that You have closed. Please give me a willingness to serve You no matter where the door You open for me leads. I pray this in Jesus' name. Amen.

APRIL 5
REACH AND TEACH

Acts 19:10
"And this continued for two years, so that all who dwelt in Asia heard the word of the Lord Jesus, both Jews and Greeks."
NKJV

"Reach and Teach." This is the vision the Lord has given me for The Bridge. Notice the vision is not "sit and wait", "grow then maintain" but "Reach and Teach." The Lord has given me a heart to reach and teach people the Gospel message. The element to reach people is extremely important because without it, there would be fewer avenues to teach. I do not reach on my own. It is a team-effort.

The Lord has raised up faithful servants here who clean the building, park the cars, prepare the coffee, operate the soundboard, and many more things that I do not have room to list. These are the arm, hand, fingers and opposable thumb that work together so that I am able to teach more people verse-by-verse and chapter by chapter through the Word of God. Even if I were alone in this, I would still want to reach people with the good news of Jesus Christ, and so should you. I understand that life can get very busy. Between our jobs, school, families, and other activities that fill our schedule, days and weeks fly by. Looking back, do you remember where it all went? Do you remember all the activities, or do they flow together with only certain activities that come to mind? We often look back and wonder where all the time went. We wonder just how important those activities were, and what difference they really made. How many times did you share the Gospel with someone? How many times did you invite someone to church? How much time did you spend serving in church? Was most of your time focused on serving yourself or was it focused on serving others? How much did God occupy your time? You may say, "I shared the Gospel once and they laughed at me." You may even say, "I invited a few friends to church but they never came back." You may also say, "I served in church for a while, but nobody showed their appreciation for my hard work." Friend, do not serve God looking for the affirmation of people. If the work is unto the Lord, the results belong to the Lord. Let us share the vision and reach the world to teach it about the Gospel of Jesus Christ.

Life Lesson: We should reach out to the community with the Word of God.

Dear Father,
Thank You for saving me. Thank You for the opportunities that You provide for me to share with others about Jesus Christ. Please give me opportunities for faithful service and please forgive me for the times when I have not done so. Help me to do these things as unto You and not out of a desire for results. I pray this in Jesus' name. Amen.

APRIL 6
GOD STILL HEALS

Acts 19:11-12

"Now God worked unusual miracles by the hands of Paul, so that even handkerchiefs or aprons were brought from his body to the sick, and the diseases left them and the evil spirits went out of them."
NKJV

In this verse, we see that it is God who works the miracles out among people, not Paul. This is an interesting section of scripture that some have twisted for their own monetary gain in the selling of such items as prayer cloths and other "miracle producing items." The miracles were not from the handkerchiefs nor from Paul, but from God. These were merely the instruments God used. We should desire to be God's instrument. God used unexpected means to restore health to those who were ill.

The Bible is a supernatural book. Our leader is Jesus who died, and didn't stay dead, and offers us eternal life. While this passage is not a model for ministry, it does demonstrate that God can work through various unconventional means to draw people to Him. God used Paul to heal people, and God uses people today. Did God use Paul to heal everyone that he came across? No. Some were healed and some were not. Remember, Paul prayed for God to heal him and apparently Paul was not healed. We should pray for God to heal others and even expect God to heal them while trusting in His will.

2 Corinthians 12:8-9 "Concerning this thing I pleaded with the Lord three times that it might depart from me. And He said to me, "My grace is sufficient for you, for My strength is made perfect in weakness." Therefore most gladly I will rather boast in my infirmities, that the power of Christ may rest upon me." NKJV

God said to Paul, 'I am not going to heal you but give you the grace to get through it.' Sometimes God doesn't heal us and take us out of our situation or condition, but gives us the strength to go through it. When He heals, we can give Him the glory. When He doesn't, we are made stronger in our walk with Him.

Life Lesson: God can and does heal people.

Dear Father:

Thank You for loving me. Thank You for giving me the strength to endure the difficulties of this world. Please help me to keep my focus on You and not on those difficulties. I pray this in Jesus' name. Amen.

APRIL 7
STIR THINGS UP

Acts 19:23
"And about that time there arose a great commotion about the Way."
NKJV

The people of Ephesus either loved Paul or hated Paul. Why? Paul had a holy restlessness, a stirring in his heart that drove him to great lengths to share the Gospel message. It is important we understand that Christianity is not just about getting along with everybody. All of us are individually gifted and crafted for a unique purpose, but it doesn't end there. If we do not use our gifts, it profits no one. In the same way, if our relationship with one another does not transform us, it's not much of a relationship. Ministry changes people. It puts people together in situations that are often uncomfortable and stretches us in ways that we never thought possible. It causes us to drop our masks and be honest with one another.

Hebrews 10:24 "And let us consider one another in order to stir up love and good works."

We are to think about one another, and how we can love and encourage one another. We are to stir up (incite or provoke) love and good works in one another. This is not always going to be comfortable, and it is not always going to be received in the way that we intended. Maybe that's why the very next verse in Hebrews reads,

Hebrews 10:25 "not forsaking the assembling of ourselves together, as is the manner of some, but exhorting one another, and so much the more as you see the Day approaching."

I find it interesting that the verse telling us to stir up love and good works in one another is followed by a verse telling us to stay in fellowship. Why? Well, sometimes we can be offended by another's encouragement. We've been chugging along thinking we're doing great and then someone offers a word of encouragement that stirs us up. In a huff, we leave the fellowship. One of the resources God has provided for meeting our needs is other believers. When we sacrifice fellowship for comfort, we're like an antelope separated from the herd. Suddenly, it's not a question of 'if' we will be attacked, but 'when' we will be attacked.

Life Lesson: Ministry stirs things up.

Dear Father,

Thank You so much for the family that You have placed around me. Please give me a burden for the lost. Give me a burden to minister and encourage my brothers and sisters in Christ. Please take away any fear I have of doing this, and forgive me for the times when I have neglected to do this. I pray this in Jesus' name. Amen.

APRIL 8
CHANGE THE WORLD

Acts 20:15
"We sailed from there, and the next day came opposite Chios. The following day we arrived at Samos and stayed at Trogyllium. The next day we came to Miletus."
NKJV

Are you changing the world or is the world changing you? You see, the world can change you into something you don't like or want to be. It takes deliberate effort not to allow the world to change you. With God, you can go somewhere different with your life. If you partner with God, you will see yourself and the world changed. Because of those serving God and serving others, the world is not the same today as it was yesterday. Are you participating? If you are, then you are making a difference. If not, then you need to make some changes.

Matthew 25:21 "Well done, thou good and faithful servant: thou hast been faithful over a few things, I will make thee ruler over many things: enter thou into the joy of thy lord." KJV

Notice what Jesus said. He didn't say, "Well done thou good and faithful spectator", and He didn't say, "Well done thou good and faithful church critic". Start the changes today. God gives you the choice. You can live the way He created you to live, or you can live selfishly and miss out on a lot of awesome things the Lord wants to lead you in. It is your choice. No one can make the choice except you. If Gods' way is the best way, let's live like that. God has shown us how we should live. So, what's it going to be? The choices we make today will shape who we are forever. Let's follow God and play a part in restoring and redeeming a fallen, broken, hurting world. Let's live to be all that God intended us to be. Let's live to see the changes that we want to see in the world. Go for it. Live for God and God will take care of the details. Trust Him to do what He said He would do. May we live to be what He created us to be...Messengers of His mercy, His grace, His truth and His love. The book of Acts doesn't really end, it's still going on. We are the next chapter in Acts. We are Acts 29.

Life Lesson: We should change the world.

Dear Father,
Thank You for Your grace, Your mercy, Your truth, Your love and the provisions You have given me. Help me to live as a good and faithful steward of those things and to share them with my family, friends, neighbors, and the world. Please forgive me for the times when I've lived my way and not for You. I pray this in Jesus' name. Amen.

APRIL 9
PEACE

Acts 12:6
"And when Herod was about to bring him out, that night Peter was sleeping, bound with two chains between two soldiers; and the guards before the door were keeping the prison." NKJV

How often do you allow the troubles of life to steal your peace? Do you replay events over and over in your mind wishing you had done something differently, and sometimes even allow bad events to set the tone for the rest of your day? I am reminded of a story about a man who while on his way to work had a flat tire. When he finally got to work, his secretary asked him how he was doing. Through clenched teeth he said, "Terrible! I had a flat tire." He walked into his office, slammed the door, threw the chair back from his desk, and picked up a phone to speak harshly to an employee. At lunch, the waiter at the restaurant asked him how he was doing and he responded, "Terrible! I had a flat tire this morning!" Later that evening when he got home his wife asked him how his day went and he said, "It was terrible! I had a flat tire this morning!" That one event shaped his entire day and not only that, his bad attitude affected everyone he came across. In Acts chapter 12, we see James had been killed by Herod and Peter was imprisoned. Although Peter was probably about to be executed, he was sleeping! Now as far as 'bad days' go, I'd rank his pretty high on the list, yet Peter is comfortable and peaceful enough to sleep. Peter was at peace in the Lord as we should be. No matter what the circumstance.

Jesus said, "These things I have spoken to you, that in Me you may have peace. In the world you will have tribulation; but be of good cheer, I have overcome the world." John 16:33 NKJV

No matter what trial or tribulation you are facing, know that there will be a day when you will be free from it. It may not be until you are with the Lord in Heaven, but you will be free from it. Be at peace, Christian! You have an awesome promise to look forward to...

Revelation 21:3-4 "And I heard a loud voice from heaven saying, "Behold, the tabernacle of God is with men, and He will dwell with them, and they shall be His people. God Himself will be with them and be their God. And God will wipe away every tear from their eyes; there shall be no more death, nor sorrow, nor crying. There shall be no more pain, for the former things have passed away." NKJV

Life Lesson: Through Jesus, you may have peace.

Dear Father,

Thank You for sending Your only Son, Jesus to die on the cross for my sins. Thank You for the promise that one day, You will wipe the tears from my eyes and there will be no more death, sorrow or crying. Thank You that I can have peace through Jesus, no matter what trial or difficulties I am experiencing. Please forgive me for the times when I have surrendered my peace to a situation or problem and help me to live for You everyday. In Jesus' name, Amen.

APRIL 10
MAKE A DIFFERENCE

Acts 20:18-21

"And when they had come to him, he said to them: "You know, from the first day that I came to Asia, in what manner I always lived among you, serving the Lord with all humility, with many tears and trials which happened to me by the plotting of the Jews; how I kept back nothing that was helpful, but proclaimed it to you, and taught you publicly and from house to house, testifying to Jews, and also to Greeks, repentance toward God and faith toward our Lord Jesus Christ." NKJV

If you are living the same way you did before you met Jesus, then something is wrong. "Do you mean the bad things I used to do... like lying, drinking, and profanity?" Yes, but only in part because this kind of thinking is what's wrong with the modern day church. We tend to focus on the 'things' we have turned from and not on the 'One' we've turned to. You see, we should be following Jesus. Jesus said "Follow Me" and "DO the things I do". What did Jesus do? He reached out to the hurting, loved the unlovable, and He challenged the religious people of the day. We have made Christianity all about what we 'don't do' so that when we don't smoke dope or drink ourselves into a coma, we think we are living the Christian life. Certainly that is part of it, but it is when we love and serve one another that we are really living the Christian life. Look at the difference Paul made through his ministry. The world would never be the same because of the life of Paul.

Paul wrote, "Bear one another's burdens, and so fulfill the law of Christ." Galatians 6:1 NKJV

What is your commitment to God? You can judge that by your commitment to ministry, to the Church, and to serving others. Think about it. The fruit of our faith should be active. We should be 'Bible-doing' and not just 'Bible-reading'. It is my job to ask the hard questions and to help you with the answers. Here's a hard question... Are you making a difference? You probably already know the answer, but if you are not serving the Lord and others, then friend, you are probably not making a difference.

Life Lesson: We should make a difference in this work for God.

Dear Father,
Thank You for the gifts and abilities You have given me. Please forgive me for the times that I have failed to use them to glorify You by serving others. Please give me a burden for the hurting, the unlovable, the unsaved, and for my family in Christ. Give me opportunities to exercise that burden. Lord, I thank You for saving me from the bonds of sin. Please help me to serve You with all of my heart. In Jesus' name, Amen.

APRIL 11
FEEDING THE FLOCK

Acts 20:27
"For I have not shunned to declare to you the whole counsel of God."
NKJV

This is so important; in fact, it should be front and center of everything the church does. Here, in Acts, and in his letters, we see the heart of a pastor and a teacher in Paul. And what did he do? Paul taught the Word of God, and that is what the church should be doing. What about evangelism? If you are teaching the Word of God, evangelism will happen. Healthy sheep reproduce. If you are not teaching and evangelism happens then according to the Parable of the Sower (Luke 8:4-8) it will not happen for long.

I am willing to be your guide. I will dig into the Bible and show you what I know and what I have found. Together we will walk through the Word and it will help you to live, to love and to believe, but there is a decision you need to make . . . a stand you need to take. What is that? Get involved with a church that systematically studies the Word of God and faithfully attend. We would love to have you here at The Bridge. If you are unable to attend here, you can listen to the teachings online (www.aboutthebridge.com), on television, or on the radio, but be careful that you do not forsake fellowshipping with other believers. The folks who faithfully fill the services here have put a high priority on knowing and doing God's Word. They could be somewhere else doing something else but they are here and they are learning together, worshipping together, praying together, ministering together and serving together.

I believe that the way to spiritual balance is by scriptural balance, verse by verse and that is why I teach that way here, but verse by verse is not coast to coast, and I believe we can see some of the repercussions of this in the "Name it and Claim it" prosperity movements as well as other heretical movements that are out there today. How do you avoid these pitfalls? If you study the Bible verse by verse, you will be equipped for every circumstance.

2 Timothy 3:16-17 says, *"All Scripture is given by inspiration of God, and is profitable for doctrine, for reproof, for correction, for instruction in righteousness, that the man of God may be complete, thoroughly equipped for every good work."* NKJV

Are you equipped? If not, then take steps to be equipped.

Life Lesson: The church should feed the flock of God the Word of God.

Dear Father,

Thank You for giving us Your Word to equip me, encourage me, correct me, instruct me, and lead me as I become more like Your Son, Jesus Christ. Thank You for Pastors and Teachers who are committed to teaching verse by verse and chapter by chapter through the whole Bible. Help me to put what I learn from Your Word into action in my life. I pray this in Jesus' name. Amen.

APRIL 12
REAP WHAT YOU SOW

Acts 20:35
"I have shown you in every way, by laboring like this, that you must support the weak. And remember the words of the Lord Jesus, that He said, 'It is more blessed to give than to receive.'" NKJV

Do you give?

The Lord has placed in your stewardship blessings of finances, giftings, resources, and time. Just because blessings are placed under your stewardship, this does not mean that they are yours. Do not want what is not yours. There's always a lot of talk about pastors who speak too much about money, but if every Christian tithed, then every church would be out of debt, church buildings would be paid for, missionaries would be funded, and every starving man, woman and child would be fed. Not occasionally, not often, but in every instance what you do with material things is evidence of how you value spiritual things.

2 Corinthians 9:6-7 "But this I say: He who sows sparingly will also reap sparingly, and he who sows bountifully will also reap bountifully. So let each one give as he purposes in his heart, not grudgingly or of necessity; for God loves a cheerful giver." NKJV

'Sow much and reap much'; it's not the goal, but it's the benefit. How are you using the things God has entrusted you with? Are you investing them in the things of the world or are you hoarding them for yourself? You should give financially to the church you attend and serve there. If you 'reap what you sow', it seems to me that you ought to be careful of what you sow and where you sow it. It's not just about money... it's giving of yourself, talents, giftings, resources, time, and your finances in order to help people, serve people, support the weak, and reach people with the Gospel of Jesus Christ. There are 852 million hungry people in the world and around 3 billion people have never heard the Gospel. Those statistics are staggering, but as I stated previously, if every Christian tithed, then within two years every church would be out of debt, church buildings would be paid for, missionaries would be funded and every starving man, woman, and child would be fed.

Life Lesson: We should tithe or give a tenth of our income to the work of the ministry.

Dear Father,

Thank You for the blessings, talent, giftings and resources You have given to me. Please forgive me for the times that I have failed to use them to glorify You. Help me Lord to surrender the things of this world. Give me opportunities to give and serve others and my church. Thank You Lord for all that you have entrusted to me. In Jesus' name, Amen.

APRIL 13
BUT GOD

Romans 5:8
"But God demonstrates His own love toward us, in that while we were still sinners, Christ died for us."
NKJV

Ephesians 2:4-5
"But God, who is rich in mercy, because of His great love with which He loved us, even when we were dead in trespasses, made us alive together with Christ (by grace you have been saved),"
NKJV

Two of the most important words in the entire Bible are "But God." You and I were dead in our sins and trespasses, but God... Johnny was an alcoholic and Jane was a heroin addict, but God... The world needs to hear these words... they need to know "but God!". When I see the news, both local and world, it becomes more and more evident that this world is a mess... but God.

1 Timothy 2:3-4 "For this is good and acceptable in the sight of God our Savior, who desires all men to be saved and to come to the knowledge of the truth." NKJV

We have to step out of our comfort zones and tell people one on one about Jesus. We have to get Bibles into the hands of those who don't have them or who have never even seen one. We have to show the love of Jesus by bringing the Good News to those who have lost hope, to those who are living in the mess that has been made of this world. What mess have you made? God is in the business of fixing messes. God will break through the situation if you'll allow Him. Maybe you know this. Too often we keep this to ourselves when we should be telling others.

Life Lesson: But God...

Dear Father,
Thank you for sending Your only Son to die for my sins. Please forgive me for times when I have selfishly kept the light of the Gospel to myself and please give me the courage and desire to tell others about the reason for my hope which is Jesus. I pray this in Jesus' name. Amen.

APRIL 14
GIVE YOUR LIFE AWAY

Acts 21:12-13

"Now when we heard these things, both we and those from that place pleaded with him not to go up to Jerusalem. Then Paul answered, "What do you mean by weeping and breaking my heart? For I am ready not only to be bound, but also to die at Jerusalem for the name of the Lord Jesus." NKJV

Sometimes we say, "I would be willing to die for the Lord." If you say that and really mean it, then that's awesome. But are you willing to live for the Lord?

Paul wrote,

"I have been crucified with Christ; it is no longer I who live, but Christ lives in me; and the life which I now live in the flesh I live by faith in the Son of God, who loved me and gave Himself for me." Galatians 2:20 NKJV

If anyone lived for Christ, it was the Apostle Paul. He endured many trials and suffered greatly in order to further the Gospel. Paul did end up dying for the Lord, but by his living for the Lord, his life was "poured out as a drink offering" (2 Timothy 4:6). If you are living for the Lord, then you will be giving your life away and living sacrificially for others and not for yourself.

Jesus said,

"If you cling to your life, you will lose it; but if you give it up for me, you will find it." Matthew 10:39 NLT

Are you giving your life away?

Life Lesson: We should give our lives away as we follow Jesus.

Dear Father,
Thank You for giving me new life in Christ. Please help me to live for You and help me to serve others sacrificially. Please forgive me for times when I have lived selfishly. In Jesus' name, Amen.

APRIL 15
FREE GIFT

Acts 21:21
"but they have been informed about you that you teach all the Jews who are among the Gentiles to forsake Moses, saying that they ought not to circumcise their children nor to walk according to the customs."
NKJV

What are some of the traditions you hold that keep others from Jesus? In the verse above, you see the Jewish and Gentile conflict within the church and the traditions that the Jews wanted the Gentile church to follow. Although they rejoiced that God was at work among the Gentiles, they slipped in the word "but" revealing their "religiosity". They were concerned for the traditions set within the church.

It is important as you walk in relationship with others to speak leaving out the "buts". Often, you'll hear that word come up as you talk to others. We all are in danger of saying it. Have you ever said.

"I like the way you did this 'but'."

"It's a great church 'but'."

"I would show love to that other person 'but'."

Many times you can find yourself saying something and then filling in reasons why you don't approve of something. Tragically, it's the same thing that has put walls between the unbelieving world and personal relationships with Jesus Christ. On one occasion, I remember a guy who stopped by the parking lot of our church asking if it was okay for him to enter the church dressed as he was. The church down the road told him that he couldn't come in unless he dressed more respectfully. This man was simply wearing a t-shirt and pair of jeans. It was okay to come to church "but" he wasn't dressed nicely enough to be welcomed in. When God forgives us, there are no "buts". It is a free gift. When you are called to extend forgiveness to others, the Lord wants you to forgive them in the same way.

Maybe you are carrying around a number of reasons why you don't want to show God's love to someone else. If this is you, turn to the Lord right where you are and ask Him to help you purely embrace and show the gift of forgiveness to others as He has shown you.

Life Lesson: We do not earn forgiveness, it is given to us as a gift.

Dear Father,

Thank You for the free gift of Your forgiveness that You've shown to me by dying for my sins. Please give me the strength to extend the same gift of love and forgiveness to others. Keep me from putting up walls that hinder others in having a real relationship with You. In Jesus' name, Amen.

APRIL 16
BLOOM WHERE YOU ARE PLANTED

Acts 21:30
"And all the city was disturbed; and the people ran together, seized Paul, and dragged him out of the temple; and immediately the doors were shut."
NKJV

Although the door never really opened to the Jewish people, Paul continuously ministered to them. There was, however, an open door for Paul to minister to the Gentiles. Sometimes in ministry, you may want to do one thing but God wants you to do something else. Maybe you have a heart for a particular country, region, or a specific people group, but God wants you to 'bloom right where you are planted'. It could be that God has given you a heart to pray for missions in that area and not do it yourself. Paul supported the church at Jerusalem but was never really part of the church there. Look for open doors where you are. If there is an opportunity to join a ministry team in church, go for it! Maybe your heart is in Children's Ministry or Youth Ministry, but the open door is in another area of ministry.

"His lord said to him, 'Well done, good and faithful servant; you were faithful over a few things, I will make you ruler over many things. Enter into the joy of your lord.'" Matthew 25:21 NKJV

Friend, go for the open door. Perhaps later, God will open the other door. It's quite possible you are being tested whether you will be faithful in the small things.

Life Lesson: Bloom wherever God plants you.

Dear Father,
Thank You for giving me gifts that I can use to serve You and others. Please forgive me for times when I have not used them to serve. I ask you to show me the open door, even if it is not what I want, and give me the faith to go through it. I pray this in Jesus' name. Amen.

APRIL 17
THIS CHANGES EVERYTHING

Acts 12:11
"And when Peter had come to himself, he said, "Now I know for certain that the Lord has sent His angel, and has delivered me from the hand of Herod and from all the expectation of the Jewish people."
NKJV

Today, we rejoice in the most incredible event in the history of mankind. We celebrate the death, burial and the resurrection of Jesus Christ. Yet, how many of us stop and consider the wonder of what really happened? Often, we find ourselves caught up in the planning and celebration of this extraordinary event, never giving thought to the significance this has for us. Let me encourage you to take a few minutes to reflect on the impact of Jesus' victory. Take some time with your spouse, family or friends and read the story in Matthew 27 and 28. Reflect on what this means to you. For me, it means that I can be forgiven, death has been conquered and the guilt of my sins can be washed away. This event not only changed human history, it changed my history. Jesus is alive. His tomb is empty... this changes everything.

Life Lesson: We should live our lives in amazement at what the Lord does.

Please pray something like this...

Dear Lord,
Thank You for conquering death, sin and the grave. Help me to stop and consider what You have done for me. Lord, I often go through my life without pausing to reflect on the most important things. Help me to take the time to consider what happened. Lord, please forgive me afresh for all of my sins. Help me to live for You and to love others. In Jesus' name, Amen.

APRIL 18
SHARE YOUR STORY

Acts 22:2-3

"Then he said: 'I am indeed a Jew, born in Tarsus of Cilicia, but brought up in this city at the feet of Gamaliel, taught according to the strictness of our fathers' law, and was zealous toward God as you all are today.'"
NKJV

In Acts 22, Paul shares his 'God story', his testimony. Why is he doing this? Is it so others will be amazed at his religious upbringing or at the depth of his biblical training? Is it to glorify his past? No, Paul is sharing his testimony to lead others to Christ by explaining who he was before Jesus, what Jesus did, and the joy that he now has because of Jesus. This is one of the most effective ways of sharing your faith. You see...people can argue about historical facts and they can disagree over cultural details, but people cannot argue with the fact that you found love, joy and forgiveness at the foot of the cross. Brother or sister, don't be shy about telling your 'God story'. Tell it to as many as will listen and you will be amazed at how God will use it to change the lives of those around you.

Life Lesson: Share your life story often with people.

Dear Father,

Thank You for loving me and saving me. Though I was a sinner, You sought me out and saved me from who I was so that I can live for You forever. Please give me courage and opportunity to share my testimony with others and forgive me for times when I had opportunities to share and did not. I pray this in Jesus' name. Amen.

APRIL 19
FOCUS ON JESUS

Acts 22:17-18
Now it happened, when I returned to Jerusalem and was praying in the temple, that I was in a trance and saw Him saying to me, 'Make haste and get out of Jerusalem quickly, for they will not receive your testimony concerning Me.'
NKJV

In Acts chapter 22 Paul is sharing his testimony with an enraged group of Jews who were seeking to kill him. Notice, however, what Paul does NOT share in his testimony to these groups of men. Paul isn't saying anything about how difficult his life has been since he became a Christian. Certainly, he could have. Paul endured incredible hardships during his ministry. He was beaten many times; he was stoned with rocks, shipwrecked and imprisoned. Paul could easily have said, "Well, life's been pretty hard since Jesus saved me. I've been beaten, shipwrecked and imprisoned and now, once again, people are trying to kill me." Instead, Paul puts the focus on Jesus...and so should we. Brothers and sisters, when sharing your testimony, don't talk about the difficulties in your life. Jesus told us that in this world we would have tribulation, but He didn't stop there.

Jesus said, "Be of good cheer, I have overcome the world." John 16:33b NKJV

To talk about trials will only push people away. Talk about Jesus and salvation through Him. Keep the main thing the main thing.

Life Lesson: When sharing, always keep Jesus the focus. Keep the main thing, the main thing.

Dear Father,
Thank You for the life you have given me. Lord, when you bring me the opportunity to speak to someone about my testimony help me to always keep Jesus the main thing. Please do not let my words get in the way but let the Holy Spirit speak through me so that Jesus will be seen. Thank You for giving us Your Word to learn and obey. I pray this in Jesus' name. Amen.

APRIL 20
TRUST

Acts 22:21
"Then He said to me, 'Depart, for I will send you far from here to the Gentiles.'" NKJV

I'm often shocked at how arrogant we can be. The Scientific community thinks it knows everything. Many great discoveries have been made, but instead of demonstrating man's knowledge, they demonstrate that we don't know as much as we think.

It's pretty arrogant to drive around with bumper stickers that say things like, "God is my co-pilot." I mean, so you're OK with God's opinion as long as He is not behind the wheel? That, my friend, is "stinkin' thinkin'." Before you try to think of who you know with that bumper sticker, consider the times when you have failed to let God direct your path. Whenever we think we know better than God, we are wrong. Whenever we think we see something that God does not see, we are wrong. Whenever we think we know something that God doesn't know, we are wrong. As part of his defense, Paul shares his testimony with an angry mob in Jerusalem. Paul shares that God told him to...

"Depart, for I will send you far from here [Jerusalem] to the Gentiles." Acts 22:21 NKJV

It was 17 years prior when God told Paul that. Paul had traveled for 17 years and here he is in Jerusalem again. I wonder if Paul thought for those 17 years that God was wrong about how effective he would be in ministering to the Jewish people. God was not wrong. God is never wrong. You can trust God.

I'm reminded of a story about a 19th century acrobat named Blondin. He performed spectacular feats of courage and balance, crossing Niagara Falls on a tight rope. During one performance, there was a royal party from Britain in attendance. They watched Blondin as he crossed the rope over Niagara on stilts while blindfolded. After that, he stopped halfway and cooked and ate an omelet. Next, he pushed a wheelbarrow full of potatoes across from one side to another. He asked the royal party, "Do you believe I could take a man across this tightrope in a wheelbarrow?" A Duke replied, "Yes I do." "Hop in, then," replied Blondin. The Duke declined. He believed Blondin could do it, but wasn't willing to trust him with his life. God is looking for those who will trust Him with their lives. God tells us...

Life Lesson: Our heavenly Father knows best. Trust Him.

"For I know the thoughts that I think toward you, says the LORD, thoughts of peace and not of evil, to give you a future and a hope." Jeremiah 29:11 NKJV

Friend, God's plans for you are good. Give God the wheel. Please pray something like this...

Dear Father,

Thank You that Your plans for my life are good. I know I have not always demonstrated that I believe this. Please forgive me for the times when I have stubbornly directed my own path. Please give me the faith to take the steps You direct me in. I pray this in Jesus' name, Amen.

APRIL 21
GOD'S BEST

Acts 22:30
"The next day, because he wanted to know for certain why he was accused by the Jews, he released him from his bonds, and commanded the chief priests and all their council to appear, and brought Paul down and set him before them."
NKJV

Acts 23:1
"Then Paul, looking earnestly at the council, said, "Men and brethren, I have lived in all good conscience before God until this day."
NKJV

We see in the next seven chapters, Acts 22 to 28, Paul is either on his way to court or prison or is in court or imprisoned. If anyone would have had the right to mope around and complain about his problems, it would have been Paul... but he didn't. He could have been an 'Eeyore' and said, "I guess I'll never get out of here." Instead, he used those times by praying to God, and interacting with and encouraging others. Did you know that Paul wrote his letter to the Philippians while in prison?

Paul wrote in chapter 4, "I have learned how to get along happily whether I have much or little. I know how to live on almost nothing or with everything. I have learned the secret of living in every situation, whether it is with a full stomach or empty, with plenty or little." Philippians 4:11-12 NLT

How could Paul write this in the face of such overwhelming difficulty? He continues by saying, "I can do all things through Christ who strengthens me." Philippians 4:13 NKJV

That, my friends, is the key. We often hear slogans such as "Do your best and let God do the rest". Our best isn't even close to God's best. The next time you find yourself in a difficult situation, stop and ask God to make the best. Don't settle for your 'little' best. Ask God for His 'biggest' best. Trust God with today, and He will lead you into tomorrow's blessings.

Life Lesson: Ask God to make the best out of whatever situation you are in.

Dear Father,

Thank You for loving me. Thank You that I don't have to lean on my own striving or the hope that my best is good enough. Lord, I don't want my best, I want Your best. Please help me to commit all my plans to You. I pray this in Jesus' name. Amen.

APRIL 22
GOD'S ECONOMY

Acts 23:11
But the following night the Lord stood by him and said, "Be of good cheer, Paul; for as you have testified for Me in Jerusalem, so you must also bear witness at Rome."
NKJV

Notice that God did not say, "Paul, you big loser; no one got saved! You are so useless." God was pleased with Paul not because of the results, but because he stepped out. God did not say, "Now Paul, I told you not to go to Jerusalem and look what happened!" Instead, God encouraged him. In this 'results oriented' world, success is defined by payoff, not by obedience. But God operates on a different economy. God is pleased by obedience. This is great news! You are not responsible for the results. Understand, this isn't an excuse for doing shoddy work.

Romans 12:11 reads, "Never be lazy in your work, but serve the Lord enthusiastically." NLT

You can wholeheartedly serve God without worrying that the results aren't meeting His expectations. God is responsible for the results. You are responsible for doing what the Lord has told you to do. Sometimes, God may allow you to see the results of your labors. If He does, thank and praise Him... but be careful not to take the credit. If you serve only to see results, friend, you are going to become discouraged. If you serve because God wants you to, you will be in that place of peace and joy that comes through obedience to God.

Life Lesson: Don't always look with your eyes to see the effect you are having by serving God.

Dear Father,
Thank You for loving me so much that You allow me to serve You. Please give me the ability and the opportunity to be obedient to You. Please forgive me for the times when I have not. I thank You that the results are in Your almighty hands. I pray this in Jesus' name. Amen.

APRIL 23
DON'T GET DISTRACTED

Acts 24:1
"Now after five days Ananias the high priest came down with the elders and a certain orator named Tertullus. These gave evidence to the governor against Paul."
NKJV

What was Ananias doing chasing Paul around? As the High Priest, he should have been serving God and ministering to the people of Israel. Ananias was around 80 years old, yet he was so caught up in resentment that he was willing to make the 60 mile journey from Jerusalem to Caesarea to bring accusation against Paul. It's been said, that 'a distraction is what you see when you take your eyes off of the goal.' When we spend our time chasing distractions, we accomplish nothing. We only have so much time and so many hours in a day. In Matthew 5:37-40, Jesus told us to love God and love others, yet often we take our eyes off of Jesus and place them on ourselves.

Psalm 90:12 "So teach us to number our days, that we may gain a heart of wisdom." NKJV

If you are over 35, you are probably more than half way through your lifetime. At the age of 50, you have likely used seventy percent of your time. Friends, as you get older the numbers don't get better. Take a moment and reflect. Are you distracted? If you are focused on Jesus, then you will love God and love others. Do you love others? How? If you are making a long journey and your course gets off by even one degree, you will miss your destination by hundreds of miles. This is why we have to constantly make course corrections in our lives. Are you focused on Jesus or distracted by other things? Distracted? Uh oh, time for a course correction. Do you love other people? No? Oops... time for another course correction.

Life Lesson: As we follow Jesus we should not get distracted.

Dear Father,
I love You. Please help me to love and serve others. Please forgive me for times when I have been distracted. If I am off course Lord, I ask that You would show me through Your Word, through a Bible teaching church, and through fellowship with other Christians, so that I make corrections. I pray this in Jesus' name, Amen.

APRIL 24
ARE YOU CONCERNED?

Acts 24:15
"I have hope in God, which they themselves also accept, that there will be a resurrection of the dead, both of the just and the unjust."
NKJV

In his defense before Felix, Paul shares his faith as much as he defends his faith. Re-read the verse above. Who is the source of his hope? Is it Governor Felix? Is it himself? No, it is God, and he's letting all those within earshot know it.

If we are following Jesus, we should be walking in His path. We should be concerned about those things that concern Him. We should care about what Jesus cared about and should do the things that reflect His ministry.

Jesus did not come to make sure that people are living comfortably or 'feel ok' with themselves. He did not come to build up our self esteem or restore our self image. He came to save us out of our sins.

Luke 19:10 "For the Son of Man has come to seek and to save that which was lost." NKJV

Romans 6:23 "For the wages of sin is death, but the gift of God is eternal life in Christ Jesus our Lord" NKJV

What did Jesus care about? He cared about people being saved. If you are following Jesus, you should care about people being saved. Are you following Jesus? If you are, do you care?

Life Lesson: When we follow Jesus we should be concerned with other people knowing about Jesus.

Dear Father,
Thank You for saving me. Please forgive me for times I have kept the message of salvation to myself. Please give me opportunities to share Jesus with others. I pray this in Jesus' name, Amen.

APRIL 25
FIRST PLACE

Acts 24:24-26

"And after some days, when Felix came with his wife Drusilla, who was Jewish, he sent for Paul and heard him concerning the faith in Christ. Now as he reasoned about righteousness, self-control, and the judgment to come, Felix was afraid and answered, "Go away for now; when I have a convenient time I will call for you." Meanwhile he also hoped that money would be given him by Paul, that he might release him. Therefore he sent for him more often and conversed with him." NKJV

Governor Felix sent for Paul for one reason, and it was not to continue the conversation about Jesus. Felix wanted Paul to bribe him. Felix was shaken by what Paul said, but money was more important to him. Friends, be careful of the priority that you give money in your life. Money, itself, is not evil. The Bible does not say that money is the root of evil. We read in 1 Timothy 6:10, "For the love of money is a root of all kinds of evil, for which some have strayed from the faith in their greediness, and pierced themselves through with many sorrows." The love of money is the problem. You will be motivated by what you love.

I understand that finances have to take some sort of priority because it takes money to feed and keep our families warm and safe. However, the prominence money plays in our lives is up to us. Will you make money or Jesus first place in your life?

"Stay away from the love of money; be satisfied with what you have. For God has said, "I will never fail you. I will never forsake you." Hebrews 13:5 NLT

"No one can serve two masters. For you will hate one and love the other, or be devoted to one and despise the other. You cannot serve both God and money." Matthew 6:24 NLT

If money is the top priority in your life, then you will love and serve money. If God is the top priority, then you will love and serve Jesus. So which do you love and serve? Is it money or is it Jesus?

Life Lesson: Allow finances to have the right priority in your life.

Dear Father,

Thank You for being my provider. Please forgive me for times when I have given money priority over You. Please forgive me for times when I have served money rather than serving You. Lord, please present me with opportunities to serve You, and show me areas of my life where I am not serving You. I pray this in Jesus' name. Amen.

APRIL 26
RIGHT WHERE YOU ARE

Acts 25:11
"For if I am an offender, or have committed anything deserving of death, I do not object to dying; but if there is nothing in these things of which these men accuse me, no one can deliver me to them. I appeal to Caesar."
NKJV

What does God see when he looks at you? He sees you clearly right where you are. God knows your potential. He created you. He knows the gifts and talents that He has given you. God knows how He wants to use you to love and serve Him and others. Sometimes God will use things in our lives that we least expect Him to use. In Acts 25, we see God using Paul's Roman citizenship to give him the opportunity to preach the Gospel before King Agrippa and a huge audience in the amphitheater at Caesarea. Like Paul, God is able to use you to do incredible things right where you are. No gift or talent is too big or too small. No circumstance too dire, God can use it.

Do you want to be used by God? You can start right where you are in your home, workplace and in your church. How are you serving God today? How will you be serving God a month from now or even a year from now? I want to encourage you to start serving God right where you are. God has got an awesome adventure planned for you; a miraculous mission lays waiting for you if you choose to accept your mission. God will use you in ways you never thought possible.

Life Lesson: God wants to work through you right where you are now with what you have now.

Dear Father,
Thank You for loving me. Thank You for the gifts, talents and circumstances You have given me. I commit to using my gifts to glorify You... starting today. I pray this in Jesus' name, Amen.

APRIL 27
HOPE

Acts 26:6
"And now I stand and am judged for the hope of the promise made by God to our fathers."
NKJV

What is hope? The word hope conveys different ideas depending on the context. It can be... "I hope the stock market goes up," or "I hope I get a raise in pay," but in the Bible, hope means looking forward to the fulfillment of a promise or "it's going to happen." The first two hold no promise of fulfillment, but we can be confident in the third. As Christians, we have a "living hope."

1 Peter 1:3-5 "Blessed be the God and Father of our Lord Jesus Christ, who according to His abundant mercy has begotten us again to a living hope through the resurrection of Jesus Christ from the dead, to an inheritance incorruptible and undefiled and that does not fade away, reserved in heaven for you, who are kept by the power of God through faith for salvation ready to be revealed in the last time." NKJV

Although we know Jesus died for our sins, rose from death, and will return, we don't know the exact time of His return. However, God's track record of keeping promises demonstrates that our hope is well placed. In his first letter to Timothy, the Apostle Paul tells us that the foundation of our hope is Jesus Christ, and friend... all other hope is a sinking ship.

Hebrews 10:23 "Let us hold fast the confession of our hope without wavering, for He who promised is faithful." NKJV

Christian, if you let go of that hope every time life gets stormy you will be tossed around like a ship without an anchor.

Hebrews 6:19 "This confidence is like a strong and trustworthy anchor for our souls. It leads us through the curtain of heaven into God's inner sanctuary." NLT

Do you have hope? Do you want hope? Do you have something to look forward to every day? What about at the end of this life? If you are without hope, I want you to know that you can have hope today. All it takes is a prayer asking Jesus to come into your heart and forgive you of your sins. Friend, don't continue placing your hope in foolish things. Ask Jesus to be your "living hope!"

Life Lesson: Hold on to your hope. Hold on to Jesus.

Dear Father,

Thank You for giving me the hope of You. Thank You for the precious gift of You and the assurance that I have of Your salvation. Lord, when I go through a trial and lose hope, please draw me closer to You, and help me know that You are here with me. In Jesus' name, Amen.

APRIL 28
REJOICE

1 Peter 1:6
"In this you greatly rejoice, though now for a little while, if need be, you have been grieved by various trials,"
NKJV

I'm sure you have noticed that the Apostle Paul gets into a lot of tight spots. What do we then see him doing? Many times we see him recalling the incredible things God has done in his life in the midst of trials. Do you enjoy tests? Not many people do, but tests serve some valuable purposes. They reveal strengths and they reveal weaknesses. They demonstrate what we know and what we do not know and they teach us how to apply knowledge. Testing highlights God's faithfulness in our lives and in the lives of others. We can then patiently endure the test knowing that no matter the outcome, God is in control. When you are going through a test, remember all the things that God has done for you and then praise Him.

Philippians 4:8 "Finally, brethren, whatever things are true, whatever things are noble, whatever things are just, whatever things are pure, whatever things are lovely, whatever things are of good report, if there is any virtue and if there is anything praiseworthy — meditate on these things" NKJV

Life Lesson: Remember all that the Lord has done for you when going through trials and difficulties.

Dear Father,
Thank You for Your strength and comfort during times of testing. Please help me to praise You even in difficult situations. Please help me to be an encourager to others when they are going through a test. I pray this in Jesus' name, Amen.

APRIL 29
YOUR GOD STORY

Acts 26:16
"But rise and stand on your feet; for I have appeared to you for this purpose, to make you a minister and a witness both of the things which you have seen and of the things which I will yet reveal to you."
NKJV

How else could you explain the Apostle Paul's dramatic change outside of the supernatural? You simply cannot. How could you explain your personal change outside of the supernatural? Likewise, you cannot. Your story is a powerful witness to the grace of God. Your 'God' story could be the very thing that leads someone to make a decision for Jesus. Have you thought about your story? Have you thought about how you would communicate it to someone else? If not, you should.

Take a few minutes and think. Who were you before you met Jesus? Who are you now? What have you seen God do with your life? Paul recognized the power of his 'God' story to lead others to Jesus. How are you using your story to be a witness for Jesus? No matter who you are, you can and should share your 'God' story.

Life Lesson: Tell people your 'God' story.

Dear Father,

I love You. Thank You for saving me from my sins. Thank You for my 'God' story. Please give me the courage to share it with others. Please forgive me for the times when I should have but did not. I pray this in Jesus' name. Amen.

APRIL 30
WHAT WE DO

Acts 26:20
"I preached first to those in Damascus, then in Jerusalem and throughout all Judea, and also to the Gentiles, that all must turn from their sins and turn to God—and prove they have changed by the good things they do."
NLT

We often describe our Christian walk by the things we 'don't' do. We don't drink. We don't smoke pot. We don't cuss. In fact, for some of us, not doing these things is an incredible testimony of God's supernatural work in our lives. But we should also consider the things that we 'do'.

In Matthew 22:37-40, Jesus told us that we should love God and love others. Friend, you are not an accident; you were created with a divine purpose to be a blessing to others. You were created to hear the call, respond and be fruitful. In short, you were created to help God change the world. We know the things we shouldn't do because we would be ashamed of them. But why are we not ashamed of the things we 'don't' do? Jesus called the man who did not use his talent wicked and lazy. If you fail to 'do' something, you choose to fail at God's plan for your life.

James 2:17-18 "Thus also faith by itself, if it does not have works, is dead. But someone will say, "You have faith, and I have works." Show me your faith without your works, and I will show you my faith by my works." NKJV

James 4:17 "Therefore, to him who knows to do good and does not do it, to him it is sin." NKJV

Take a moment and reflect. What are you doing?

Life Lesson: It is what we 'do' that shows we are followers of Jesus, as well as what we 'don't' do.

Dear Father,
I love You and want to serve You by serving others. Please give me eyes to see where and how I may be a blessing to others. Give me love for those around me. Please forgive me for times when I've done nothing. I pray this in Jesus' name, Amen.

MAY 1
SERVE AND BE BLESSED...

Acts 27:3
"And the next day we landed at Sidon. And Julius treated Paul kindly and gave him liberty to go to his friends and receive care."
NKJV

Notice in the verse above, that Paul did not retreat to a quiet corner somewhere by himself to rest or 'get away from it all.' Instead, he went to his friends and they cared for him. Often, when we are going through difficult problems, we retreat to our house or our own room 'just to be alone for a while.' Do not get me wrong guys; it's great to find a quiet place to talk to God. You should do that every day. Nevertheless, there are times when you need to have friends who will come alongside of you, lift you up, and pray for you. The reality is... if you do not place yourself in a position where you develop relationships with others, you will never have that same encouragement in times of trouble. Where do you find these friends? Chances are you see them every Sunday. They are soldiers of Christ at church serving God and others. You will find them on the Media Team, parking cars, or greeting newcomers. They are sweeping, mopping floors and cleaning toilets. They are teaching and caring for the children. However, if you are not in the trenches with them, you may never know them.

When you serve in church, you develop relationships with people that you never would have otherwise. Take a moment to look around at those who are serving. You will see them laughing and joking, but you will also see them encouraging and praying. It is under the common ground of serving God that these relationships are founded. In the midst of amity or conflict, the strongest relationships are forged.

Proverbs 27:17 "As iron sharpens iron, a friend sharpens a friend." NLT

If you are not serving in your church, I want to encourage you to do so. You will never regret it.

Life Lesson: There is an incredible bond you have with people you serve with that sadly, most Christians will never know.

Dear Father,
I love You and want to serve You by serving others. Please forgive me for times when I have focused on myself instead of You and others. I want to have friends who will pray for me and encourage me. I ask You to give me the courage I need to take a step of faith and start serving at church. I pray this in Jesus' name. Amen.

MAY 2
HE CHOSE THE NAILS

John 15:13
"Greater love has no one than this, than to lay down one's life for his friends."
NKJV

Jesus' death on the cross is a historical fact. The fact that He rose from the dead is verified from literature. More documents exist that verify Jesus lived, died and rose from the dead than that George Washington crossed the Delaware or that Julius Caesar ever lived. Every one of the disciples except John died a martyr's death, but even under severe torture they would not and could not deny the truth of Jesus. Josephus, an ancient Jewish historian said, "He appeared to them alive on the third day as the divine prophets foretold."

Jesus said He laid down His life for His friends. The cross was no accident or tragic surprise. It was part of an incredible plan. Jesus orchestrated His own sacrifice. He willingly grew the tree He would be nailed to. He willingly picked Judas as an apostle to betray Him. He willingly put Pontius Pilate in power to order him crucified. Jesus was not held there by any man-made nails, but was held there by our need for a Savior and His love for you. The simple fact is He could have escaped at any time. When He chose you... when He chose to have a relationship with you, He needed to make a payment for your sins. When He chose you, He chose the nails.

Did Jesus die on the cross for your sins? You, my friend, have to make that decision. He is the Savior of the world; the question is, is He your Savior? You can often tell what something is worth by the price that is paid for it. God paid a very high price for you.

Life Lesson: God paid a very high price for you.

Dear Father,
Thank You for loving me so much. Thank You for paying the price that I could not pay. You died on the cross, held there only by Your love for me. You rose from the grave that I may have eternal life. Please forgive me for my sins and give me the power to live for You. In Jesus' name I pray. Amen.

MAY 3
OVERBURDENED

Acts 27:19
"On the third day, we threw the ship's tackle overboard with our own hands."
NKJV

Did you know that ships have a line drawn along the hull to indicate their burden? If the line goes too far beneath the water, the sailors know there is too much cargo on board. This allows the sailor to take the necessary steps to avoid disaster. Wouldn't it be great if we had indicators on us? In Acts 27, Paul, now a prisoner was taken by ship to Rome where he and the ship's crew encounter a mighty storm. In danger of shipwreck, the ship's crew threw overboard the cargo they once had considered necessities. Timing and events can really change the way we look at things. We fill our lives with 'tackle' and 'rigging' that is not important to the eternal plan. Often, we get distracted by those things and cling to them rather than to God. We think... "Oh, I need this" or "I just can't live without that," but soon, overburdened, we hit a storm and sink.

Hebrews 12:1 "Therefore, since we are surrounded by such a huge crowd of witnesses to the life of faith, let us strip off every weight that slows us down, especially the sin that so easily hinders our progress. And let us run with endurance the race that God has set before us." NLT

What's in your cargo hold? Are you carrying bitterness? Is there someone you need to forgive? Is your ship laden with shame? Are you hauling around guilt or sin? In Matthew 11:28-30, Jesus said "Come to Me, all you who labor and are heavy laden, and I will give you rest. Take My yoke upon you and learn from Me, for I am gentle and lowly in heart, and you will find rest for your souls. For My yoke is easy and My burden is light." NKJV

Friend, why carry burdens around when you don't have to? Won't you lay your burdens at the foot of the cross?

Life Lesson: Lay your burdens down at the foot of the cross.

Dear Father,
Thank You for loving me. Please forgive me for my sins and show me the burdens I carry that You want to remove. There may be things I'm not aware of that are distracting me from the best that You have for me. Please show me these things so that I can give them over to You. I pray this in Jesus' name. Amen.

MAY 4
ROUGH WATERS

Acts 27:30-32

"And as the sailors were seeking to escape from the ship, when they had let down the skiff into the sea, under pretense of putting out anchors from the prow, Paul said to the centurion and the soldiers, "Unless these men stay in the ship, you cannot be saved." Then the soldiers cut away the ropes of the skiff and let it fall off."
NKJV

The worst time to 'jump ship' is when the water is rough. If you make a decision when the storms are raging, it is hard to make a clear decision. Yet, isn't that when we often make life changing decisions, only to look back later, and discover we made the wrong decision? We hear ourselves saying, "I am tired of this marriage," "I am tired of my parents," "I am tired of my job," or "I am tired of this church." Weather the storms. When the storms get tough, do not bail out and give up. There is a huge blessing in pressing in.

In the verses above, Paul points out that the men 'jumping ship' were taking a selfish approach that ultimately would hurt them and the others. Be careful when you want to run, my friend. Please, don't have 'lifeboats' for yourself as a way out. Do not keep the mind set that "If this doesn't happen" or "if that happens, I am out of here." "I will work where I am appreciated, and when I don't feel appreciated, I am gone." Often, we walk into situations already planning our escape route or our way out. Of course in thinking like that, we soon have a reason (more like an excuse) to 'jump ship.' Instead of looking for a way out, maybe we should look at these circumstances as a way in. We want to be more like Jesus... who obviously did not turn and run in the face of opportunity, offense or crisis. Friend, look for the 'growth opportunity' in the storm to grow as a person, a believer, and as a follower of Jesus. You will soon find it.

Life Lesson: Don't jump ship when the waters are rough.

Dear Father,
I know I have made bad decisions in the midst of the storms in life. Please forgive me. I know some of the consequences of my bad decisions are still here. In the future, please help me to make better decisions. Please send others to help me through these tough times. I ask for Your peace to comfort me. I ask, Father, for Your power to strengthen me. When I want to run because I am afraid or hurt, I ask that You help me to stand. I know that You will guide me to grow through these things. Lord, I know You will be there to help me through every storm of life and even in the final storm of death. You will be with me. Thanks God. In Jesus' name, Amen.

MAY 5
LOVING GOD AND LOVING OTHERS

Acts 28:2
"And the natives showed us unusual kindness; for they kindled a fire and made us all welcome, because of the rain that was falling and because of the cold."
NKJV

When someone is going through a tough time or tough place, they especially need love and mercy. It could be a waiter or waitress struggling with serving your meal or the cashier having a hard time at the grocery store. Sometimes, just asking someone how they are doing makes all the difference. Believers should be so much more loving and kind than people who do not believe in Jesus. In fact, the comparison shouldn't even be close. Isn't it often though that these folks are more loving, kind, and gracious than those of us who say we follow Jesus? Since we've been shown so much love and mercy, shouldn't we be quick to show that same love and mercy to others? Sometimes though, it all gets lost in the shuffle, doesn't it? I mean, you see someone who is obviously struggling, and you have every intention of walking up to them to comfort and encourage, but then this is going on over there and then that other thing and soon we've forgotten about the person who is struggling. Jesus, in the midst of all that was going on around him, always managed to love and encourage those who were hurting. So should we.

1 John 4:20 "If someone says, "I love God," but hates a Christian brother or sister, that person is a liar; for if we don't love people we can see, how can we love God, whom we have not seen?" NLT

Life Lesson: Love God, love people.

Dear Father,
Thank You for Your love. Please help me to show others the love that You show me. Please give me an attitude of Jesus in seeking to show love and mercy to others. Give me a heart of humility, and forgive me for those times when I have not shown love. I pray this in Jesus' name, Amen

MAY 6
BLOOM WHERE YOU ARE PLANTED

Acts 28:9
"So when this was done, the rest of those on the island who had diseases also came and were healed."
NKJV

God places us in situations where we can be a blessing to others. If you find yourself in the middle of a trial, work as unto the Lord and bless the people around you; whether you are in a tough job or circumstances that seem impossible, look for occasions to bless others. It is so easy to spend our time and energy complaining about situations and fail to notice the opportunities.

"What opportunities?" "Pastor David, how can there be opportunities where I am?" Friend, there are always opportunities to bless others and there are always those who need help more than we do... to think otherwise is quite prideful. Take your focus off your own person and your own plight and place it on Jesus. The greatest preparation to stand through the storms of life comes when we spend time at the feet of Jesus. Focus on Jesus and you will be devoted to blessing others and in turn you will be blessed.

2 Corinthians 1:4 "He comforts us in all our troubles so that we can comfort others. When others are troubled, we will be able to give them the same comfort God has given us." NLT

Galatians 6:2-3 "Share each other's troubles and problems, and in this way obey the law of Christ. If you think you are too important to help someone in need, you are only fooling yourself. You are really a 'nobody'." NLT

In the case of Paul and the gang in Acts 28, they could have sat around talking about how unfortunate it was that they were shipwrecked and almost died. They could have commiserated about how messed up their timetable now was. They did not. They recognized that God had given them a chance to help others in need, which they did and they were blessed.

Life Lesson: Allow the Lord to lead you through the storms to where He wants you.

Bloom where you are planted.

Dear Father,

So many times in the middle of trials, I've focused on myself and taken my focus off of You. Please forgive me. Please give me such love for others that I can take my eyes off of myself and see how I can be a blessing to those around me, even in the midst of difficulty. I pray this in Jesus' name. Amen.

MAY 7
THE ONLY WAY

Acts 28:23-24
"So when they had appointed him a day, many came to him at his lodging, to whom he explained and solemnly testified of the kingdom of God, persuading them concerning Jesus from both the Law of Moses and the Prophets, from morning till evening. And some were persuaded by the things which were spoken, and some disbelieved."
NKJV

Interesting... Paul used what part of the Bible? He used the Hebrew Scriptures. Paul used the Old Testament to show that Jesus was the Messiah; Yeshua HaMashiach in Hebrew. It's amazing to me how many churches, pastors, and Christians are willing to throw aside the Hebrew Scriptures, calling them outdated or not relevant for today. We see Jesus all through the Old Testament! He's in Genesis, Exodus, Leviticus, and all the way through the Psalms and into the prophets. Friend, you cannot throw out the Hebrew Scriptures without saying that Jesus is no longer relevant. Some would try to say that there are other paths to God. It is true that all paths do lead to God, but there's only one path that leads to heaven. Everyone will stand before God, but without Jesus, you will be eternally separated from heaven and God at that meeting.

John 14:6 "Jesus said to him, "I am the way, the truth, and the life. No one comes to the Father except through Me." NKJV

Jesus did not say, "I am one of many ways." Friend, God has provided THE way for forgiveness and restoration to Him and that way is through His Son, Jesus Christ who died on a cross and was resurrected from the grave for our sins.

Jesus is the way to God's forgiveness. He's the only way.

Acts 4:12 "Nor is there salvation in any other, for there is no other name under heaven given among men by which we must be saved." NKJV

Romans 10:9-10 "That if you confess with your mouth the Lord Jesus and believe in your heart that God has raised Him from the dead, you will be saved. For with the heart one believes unto righteousness, and with the mouth confession is made unto salvation." NKJV

Life Lesson: Jesus and the Bible teach us that Jesus is the only way to heaven.

Dear Father,

Thank You for providing the means for my salvation. Thank You, Jesus, for dying on the cross for my sins so that I can be saved. Thank You for forgiving me of my sins. Please give me the courage to be a witness for You here on earth. I pray this in Jesus' name. Amen.

MAY 8
UNSTOPPABLE

Acts 20:24
"But my life is worth nothing unless I use it for doing the work assigned me by the Lord Jesus—the work of telling others the Good News about God's wonderful kindness and love."
NLT

Life Lesson: When filled with God's purpose and power the church is an unstoppable force and nothing is impossible.

Are you willing? Are you willing to be used by God? Are you willing to play a part in saving lives? Are you willing to do things that you never thought were possible for you to do? You may say, "God has not called me to do anything." Yes, He has. Jesus showed us how to love and serve others. Jesus told us to love and serve others.

Jesus also said...

John 13:17 "If you know these things, blessed are you if you do them." NKJV

Perhaps you might say, "God can't use me. I'm disqualified by the things I've done." Friend, if that were the case, nobody would be qualified. No one is too small, too weak, or too messed up for God to use him or her. Join me in this battle. Church is not a playground; it is a battleground. You might say, "I've been called to teach, but they want me to clean toilets." Every ministry has a starting point. Start there. Get involved at church. Serve God by serving others. Take a moment and read the life lesson above again. You are the church. So let us look at that life lesson again...

Life Lesson: When filled with God's purpose and power <u>I am</u> an unstoppable force and nothing is impossible.

Brother or Sister, let us change the world. Let us reach the world. The book of Acts will not be finished until Jesus calls us home. God is still taking prideful religious people and the deepest darkest sinners and working through them to show His marvelous light. Won't you join me in this adventure of a lifetime?

Dear Father,

Please forgive me for the times I have not shown love toward others. Forgive me that when there were opportunities to serve others, I chose not to. Please Lord; empower me to do the work of Your will. Help me to reach others and change the world. In Jesus' name, Amen.

MAY 9
HONOR OR BURDEN?

Romans 1:1
"Paul, a bondservant of Jesus Christ, called to be an ápostle, separated to the gospel of God."
NKJV

Consider all that God has done for you and where you would be without His grace. When you truly realize what Jesus did for you, serving is not a chore or a burden. It is an honor and a privilege. How do you view serving? How do you express your love for God? One way you can tell God you love Him is by serving others.

1 Corinthians 6:20 "For you were bought at a price; therefore glorify God in your body and in your spirit, which are God's." NKJV

Matthew 22:37-39 "Jesus said to him, "'You shall love the LORD your God with all your heart, with all your soul, and with all your mind.' This is the first and great commandment. And the second is like it: 'You shall love your neighbor as yourself.'" NKJV

Do you express thanksgiving to God by serving others? Service out of an attitude of love for God will not express itself in a self seeking manner. Love for God is deeply expressed through love for others. When we serve others, we are demonstrating our thanks to God for all that He has done for us. By serving others, we demonstrate the love of God to those who may not know Him and we model His love to other Christians.

Life Lesson: We should serve God out of love. It shows we are truly thankful for all He has done for us.

Dear Father,
Thank You so much for all You have done for me. I want to show You how much I love You and thank You by serving. I ask that you give me opportunity after opportunity to serve others and to demonstrate my love and thanksgiving to You. I pray this in Jesus' name. Amen.

MAY 10
THE CALLED AND CHOSEN

Romans 1:5-6
"Through Him we have received grace and apostleship for obedience to the faith among all nations for His name, among whom you also are the called of Jesus Christ."
NKJV

Your mission, should you accept it, is to reach the world with the Gospel and to teach the world to follow Jesus. At The Bridge, 'Reach and Teach' is our vision and mission. As Pastor here, I want this church to reach every corner of this world with the message of the Gospel. Will you play a part in accomplishing that mission?

You are the called of Christ. You are chosen for this mission. Never mind your fears, weaknesses, or inadequacies. As "the called of Jesus Christ", you have been chosen for this mission. The Apostle Paul wrote...

1 Corinthians 1:26-29 "Remember, dear brothers and sisters, that few of you were wise in the world's eyes, or powerful, or wealthy when God called you. Instead, God deliberately chose things the world considers foolish in order to shame those who think they are wise. And he chose those who are powerless to shame those who are powerful. God chose things despised by the world; things counted as nothing at all, and used them to bring to nothing what the world considers important, so that no one can ever boast in the presence of God." NLT

Never be content to just sit and be a spectator to what is going on here. I encourage you to step out. Make that journey from 'the stands, to the bench, to the playing field'. In this game of life in following Jesus Christ, you win by playing and lose... by not playing. If you attend church here, get involved and join us in making a difference. If you listen to the teachings online, on the radio, or watch on television, play a part in reaching the world by contributing financially according to the blessing that you received through that ministry. If you attend another church, then find a way to get involved there. Whatever you do, wherever you are, please don't be content to be a spectator. Partner with us in reaching and teaching the world.

Life Lesson: We should all be a part of reaching and teaching the world.

Dear Father,

I want to be a part of reaching the world with the Gospel of Jesus Christ. Thank You for giving me the opportunity to do that. Please forgive me for times when I was content to be a spectator. Give me the courage to step out in ministry. I pray this in Jesus' name. Amen.

MAY 11
PRAYER

Romans 1:9-10

"For God is my witness, whom I serve with my spirit in the gospel of His Son, that without ceasing I make mention of you always in my prayers, making request if, by some means, now at last I may find a way in the will of God to come to you."
NKJV

God always hears and answers the prayers of His children. He may not answer them in the way we want Him to, but God does answer. His answer may sometimes be "no." But even so, praise Him... God knows our needs much better than we do. Too often when we pray, it is like we are writing up a contract that we ask God to sign.

"Alright God, just need your signature right there and we're done. I've got it mapped and planned out. No reason for You to get involved in the 'hows' or the 'whys'. Just sign and we're all done."

Sound familiar? Instead, we should pray for great things with a willing heart seeking to be obedient to God's will. We should give thanks in all circumstances and say...

"Lord, thank You for loving me. What is Your will in my situation? You know my needs and my desires, but I want Your will to be done in Your own way. Use me however You want to Lord."

Do you have a willing heart?

Life Lesson: God answers prayer in His own timing and in His own way.

Dear Father,
Thank You that Your will for me is good. Thank You for Your grace and mercy. Lord, You know my needs and wants. You know my troubles and fears. I want Your will to be done in my life in Your own way. Use me however you want to. I pray this in Jesus' name, Amen.

MAY 12
WHICH WAY DO YOU WANT TO STAND?

Romans 1:17
For in it the righteousness of God is revealed from faith to faith; as it is written, "The just shall live by faith."
NKJV

Habakkuk 2:4 "Behold the proud, His soul is not upright in him; But the just shall live by his faith."
NKJV

This is the verse that started the reformation. It is quoted in Romans, Galatians and Hebrews. We are not saved by works; we are saved by grace for works. In other words, the faith that does not change your life will not save your soul.

Ephesians 2:8-10 "For by grace you have been saved through faith, and that not of yourselves; it is the gift of God, not of works, lest anyone should boast. For we are His workmanship, created in Christ Jesus for good works, which God prepared beforehand that we should walk in them." NKJV

Paul is speaking of everyone who believes. Once you are forgiven, you begin to do things that honor God and in that He reveals His righteousness to those around us. Faith should be living and active. If you believe in what Jesus said it should affect your life. You should begin to want to go to church; you should want to hang out with other believers. You should begin loving God and loving people. These things are an overflowing of your faith. It starts with faith and overflows to good works. If you do not see good works as a result of your faith, you should be concerned. If we stand on our own righteousness then we stand ashamed. If we accept Jesus as our Savior and we stand in His righteousness, then we stand not ashamed. Which way do you want to stand?

Life Lesson: We are saved by faith alone.

Dear Father,
Thank You for loving me and saving me by grace through faith. Thank You that it is not something that I have to strive for, hoping my good outweighs my bad. Thank You that it is by faith. Lord, please show me opportunities to do good works in Your name. In Jesus' name, Amen.

MAY 13
ACKNOWLEDGE GOD

Romans 1:28
"And even as they did not like to retain God in their knowledge, God gave them over to a debased mind, to do those things which are not fitting;" NKJV

Go to church... don't go to church. Read your Bible... don't read your Bible. Serve at church... don't serve at church. There is a constant battle going in our minds and that battle can positively affect or negatively affect what we choose to do with our time. All you have to do is flip through the channels on TV, glance at the advertisements on websites, read billboards on the road, or open up the newspaper to discover that there is a war being waged for control of your thoughts. All it takes is one seed of 'stinkin thinkin' to kick-start a thought pattern leading to an ever-widening downward spiral of sinful behavior. You are bombarded on a daily basis by thousands of suggestions about how to spend time and what to spend it doing. What are you to do? How do you fight a battle that takes place all around you, even in your own mind?

Philippians 4:8 "Finally, brethren, whatsoever things are true, whatsoever things are honest, whatsoever things are just, whatsoever things are pure, whatsoever things are lovely, whatsoever things are of good report; if there be any virtue, and if there be any praise, think on these things." KJV

Friends, this rules out 99% of television, internet, email, newspapers and magazines, but is 100% inclusive of the Bible. You need to submit to the will of God... outwardly in creation, inwardly in conscience and biblically in scripture. Serve the Lord at church and outside of church; praise God, pray to God, memorize scripture, listen to teachings and do what you've learned. These things point to God.

Romans 12:2 "And be not conformed to this world: but be ye transformed by the renewing of your mind, that ye may prove what is that good, and acceptable, and perfect, will of God." KJV

You are either being changed by this world or by God. Your will, influenced by the Holy Spirit, is incredible power to change your life and the world in which you live.

1 Corinthians 10:31 "Therefore, whether you eat or drink, or whatever you do, do all to the glory of God." NKJV

Acknowledge God.

Life Lesson: There is a battle for your mind.

Dear Father,

Thank You for the faithful mercy You show so abundantly to me. Thank You for the weapons that you have given me so the battle in my mind can be won. Thank you for giving me truth, righteousness, readiness in the gospel of peace, faith, salvation and Your Word. Lord, these things I will clothe myself with in preparation. In Jesus' name, Amen.

MAY 14
OUR MISSION

Romans 2:1

"Therefore you are inexcusable, O man, whoever you are who judge, for in whatever you judge another you condemn yourself; for you who judge practice the same things."
NKJV

In Romans chapter one, we learn about the unrighteousness of man. In chapter two, Paul addresses our self-righteousness; our desire to consider ourselves better than everybody else. Nobody wants to be called self-righteous, yet we are so quick to judge others. Friend, be aware of your own weakness and sinfulness. If you think that once you became a Christian you stopped sinning, you should check out the passage below:

1 John 1:8-10 "If we say we have no sin, we are only fooling ourselves and refusing to accept the truth. But if we confess our sins to him, he is faithful and just to forgive us and to cleanse us from every wrong. If we claim we have not sinned, we are calling God a liar and showing that his word has no place in our hearts." NLT

Judge yourself. If you look long at the sins of others and not enough at your own sins, you will develop spiritual pride, which is a stench to God. Have you ever looked at someone and thought there is no hope for them? Well then, you are making the statement that the mercy of God is limited. You are pridefully saying that your sins are covered, but another's are not. Every person, whether we deem them good people or not, needs God's saving power and grace. Stop and think... How much have you been forgiven? Does this mean we cannot speak into other's lives? Absolutely we can and should, but not in condemnation. Just as God has heaped His grace so abundantly on you, in discernment you can speak into someone's life from your experiences with an attitude of love, peppered with grace. You cannot condemn someone and offer hope at the same time. The moment we start to condemn people is the moment we forget our mission. What is our mission? Our mission is to tell people about Jesus.

Life Lesson: Seeing the evil in others does not root out the evil in you.

Dear Father,
Thank You for forgiving me of my sins. I am so grateful for Your grace. Please forgive me for times when I, in my own pride, looked at someone else and condemned them in my mind. Please give me opportunities to tell people about Jesus. Thank You. In Jesus' name, Amen.

MAY 15
FRUIT

Romans 2:13

"for not the hearers of the law are just in the sight of God, but the doers of the law will be justified;" NKJV

Knowledge of Jesus as your savior always changes your actions. Always. People who have no fruit (tangible evidence of faith) in their life and then fall on the fact that they repeated some words in a prayer should be very concerned. It's interesting to note that people who wonder about their eternal security are usually the ones who do not need to, and those that don't wonder at all, should be the ones concerned. In Luke chapter 13, Jesus shares a parable about a tree that does not bear fruit. The owner of the vineyard instructs the keeper to cut down the tree, but the keeper asks for one more year in order to fertilize it; then if the tree does not bear fruit he will cut it down. As Christians, we should be bearing fruit with no excuses. We should be 'doing' the things that the Bible tells us to be doing.

James 1:22-25 "But don't just listen to God's word. You must do what it says. Otherwise, you are only fooling yourselves. For if you listen to the word and don't obey, it is like glancing at your face in a mirror. You see yourself, walk away, and forget what you look like. But if you look carefully into the perfect law that sets you free, and if you do what it says and don't forget what you heard, then God will bless you for doing it." NLT

What do you do with this? Do you set aside God's grace to earn your salvation by works? Absolutely not! Good works should be manifested in your life because you are saved! If you call yourself a brain surgeon, but you never perform brain surgery, are you really a brain surgeon? If you are a Christian and you don't do any of the things that Christians should do; you don't go to church, you don't serve, you don't give, you don't study the Bible, you don't tell others about Jesus, are you really a Christian?

Life Lesson: Bible study should lead to 'Bible doing'.

Dear Father,

Thank You that my salvation is not dependent on my being good enough to earn it. Thank You that because of Your love for me, Jesus bore the burden of my failures and sins. Thank You that salvation is by grace through faith... just calling out to Jesus to put my trust in Him. Please forgive me for not doing things that I should be doing as a follower of Jesus. Help me to be a 'doer' of your Word. I pray this in Jesus' name, Amen.

MAY 16
WHO OR WHAT?

Romans 2:28-29
"For he is not a Jew who is one outwardly, nor is circumcision that which is outward in the flesh; but he is a Jew who is one inwardly; and circumcision is that of the heart, in the Spirit, not in the letter; whose praise is not from men but from God."
NKJV

Who or what are you trusting in? Do you trust in rituals, or Jesus? Do you place your trust in baptism, catechism, confirmation or church membership? If your trust is in these things, then my friend, it is misplaced. Do you think you are a Christian because you go to church or because your parents were Christians? None of these things mean you are a Christian. The Apostle Paul says we should examine ourselves to make certain we are in the faith (2 Corinthians 13:5). Faith leads to works, not the other way around. If you are counting on works, you need to re-evaluate. God is concerned with the inward man, not with outward pomp or show.

Joel 2:13 "So rend your heart, and not your garments; Return to the LORD your God, For He is gracious and merciful, Slow to anger, and of great kindness; And He relents from doing harm."
NKJV

God is interested in the heart, the inward you. He is not interested in our outward traditions or rituals. So test yourself, what works are in your life? "Wait a second, Pastor David. I thought it wasn't about works." Friend, if you have repented and accepted Jesus as your Lord and Savior the 'outward works' should change according to the 'inward working' of the Spirit of God in you. Let your heart be softened, and let your actions be changed; not placing your confidence in your own works, but in the work that God is doing in you.

Life Lesson: Let your heart and your actions be changed.

Dear Father,
Help me to place my trust in you. Change my heart so that my actions reflect the work you are doing in me. Thank you for working in me so that I may be a blessing to others. In Jesus' name, Amen.

MAY 17
WHAT TIME IS IT?

Romans 3:1-2
"What advantage then has the Jew, or what is the profit of circumcision? Much in every way! Chiefly because to them were committed the oracles of God."
NKJV

A.W. Tozer once said, "If God gave you a watch, would you honor Him more by asking Him what time it is or by simply consulting the watch." God has provided us with the instruction book He authored and it is our responsibility to read it and heed it. Friend, there are places in this world where simply possessing a Bible brings a death sentence. Many Christians have been martyred and continue to be in astounding numbers across the globe for the very thing which many of us take for granted.

God has blessed you with a Bible and with the freedom to read it. What, my friend, do you do with it? Is it simply a 'coffee table' book, a drink coaster or a paperweight? Does it sit unused on a bookshelf? The Bible, which God has given you, will keep you and your family from boatloads of trouble, but only if you read, study and apply it. It is the very Word of God.

John 8:31-32 "Then Jesus said to those Jews who believed Him, "If you abide in My word, you are My disciples indeed. And you shall know the truth, and the truth shall make you free." NKJV

Friend, I want to encourage you to study your Bible. Make certain that you and your family faithfully attend a Bible teaching church. If you do not already attend a Bible teaching church, we would love to have you here! Get into the habit of praying and reading your Bible daily. Lead your family in prayer and devotions. Be diligent to do these things, and you will be amazed by the changes, miracles and blessings that are poured out on you and your family.

Life Lesson: There is a blessing and a responsibility in having a Bible.

Dear Father,
Thank You for giving me Your Bible. Please forgive me if I have been slack in reading and studying it. I ask You to give me a hunger for Your Word. Open my heart to receive Your counsel and do the things You tell me. I pray this in Jesus' name. Amen.

MAY 18
GLORIFY GOD

Romans 3:13-14
"Their throat is an open tomb; With their tongues they have practiced deceit";"The poison of asps is under their lips"; "Whose mouth is full of cursing and bitterness."
NKJV

A forest fire can start by very simple means. All it takes is one small spark landing on dry timber and quickly lives are displaced or even destroyed. James 3:5 reads,

"Even so the tongue is a little member and boasts great things. See how great a forest a little fire kindles!" NKJV

If you have ever witnessed a forest fire, then you have probably noticed that individual embers can soar to incredible heights and travel enormous distances - far greater distances than you would think. My friend, the words that come out of our mouths do the same. Words of gossip and cursing travel far and wide, causing destruction wherever they go, whether to the heart of a child or to the ears of an adult. Words of grace; however, build up, encourage and glorify God. Our words can hurt people; they can derail lives, ruin reputations and sidetrack the work of God. They can also glorify God and lead people to Him. The things that we say carry much farther than we may ever know and once we speak them, we cannot take them back. Speaking again of the tongue, James 3:9-10 reads,

"With it we bless our God and Father, and with it we curse men, who have been made in the similitude of God. Out of the same mouth proceed blessing and cursing. My brethren, these things ought not to be so." NKJV

Friend, do you speak words that build or words that destroy?

Life Lesson: We should seek to glorify God with what we say.

Dear Father,
Thank You for loving me. Please give me the power to speak grace into the lives of others. By my own strength, my words are polluted. By my own strength, my words can destroy. By Your strength, my words can build and encourage. I want to glorify You in my speech. I pray this in Jesus' name, Amen.

MAY 19
PRIDE

Romans 3:27

"Where is boasting then? It is excluded. By what law? Of works? No, but by the law of faith."
NKJV

Because salvation is not something we can earn or merit, we cannot brag about it. Salvation is a gift we do not deserve. It is not a reward for our 'innate goodness'.

Ephesians 2:8-9 "For by grace you have been saved through faith, and that not of yourselves; it is the gift of God, not of works, lest anyone should boast." NKJV

Friend, do not have spiritual pride about your salvation. Forgiveness does not give you the right to look down on anyone else. Jesus is the One who saved you, because you were the one that needed to be saved. A drowning man rescued from an ocean does not brag about how well he was drowning; rather he thanks his rescuer. Sometimes as Christians, we can get aloof and condescending because of our salvation. We act as if we have climbed on some ladder of importance. God loves everyone, and He wants everyone to be saved from the wages of their sins. Friend, thank Your Savior Jesus and tell others about Him.

Life Lesson: We should not have spiritual pride or brag about being forgiven.

Dear Father,
Thank You for loving me. Thank You for saving me from my sins even though I do not deserve it. Thank You that it is a gift and not something earned. Please forgive me if I have become prideful or boastful and give me opportunity to tell others about You. In Jesus' name, Amen.

MAY 20
WRONG THINGS

Romans 4:1-2
"What then shall we say that Abraham our father has found according to the flesh? For if Abraham was justified by works, he has something to boast about, but not before God."
NKJV

There is absolutely no work that we can do to earn our salvation. If there was, we would glorify the work and not God. Think about it. We all are quick to place our faith in the wrong things. We place our faith in jobs, money and family. Suddenly, those things become our priority instead of the very God who gave us those things.

James 2:14 "Dear brothers and sisters, what's the use of saying you have faith if you don't prove it by your actions? That kind of faith can't save anyone." NLT

Although salvation is not earned, works are a good indicator of what you believe. Friend, if you say you are a Christian, but there is no fruit demonstrating it, then you need to take a serious look at your priorities.

Life Lesson: Good works are not the basis for salvation but are the fruit of salvation.

Dear Father,
Thank You for loving me so much. Thank You that it's not what I do that affords me salvation but it is faith in Jesus that does. I pray that You will help me to honestly look at my life and see if my works demonstrate my faith. In Jesus' name, Amen.

MAY 21
LIVE IT

Romans 4:3-4

"For what does the Scripture say? "Abraham believed God, and it was accounted to him for righteousness." Now to him who works, the wages are not counted as grace but as debt."
NKJV

When was Abraham saved? He was saved when he believed God. It wasn't Abraham's actions that saved him. His actions, however, did demonstrate his belief.

So, when are you saved? You are saved when you believe. If you work for your salvation, it cannot be of grace because then it would be owed to you. You do good things because you have been given salvation, not because you needed to earn salvation. You should serve God not for what He might do for you, but for what He has already done. Praise God that we do not have to work for our salvation, because we already have a sin-debt that we can never pay.

Romans 6:23 "For the wages of sin is death, but the gift of God is eternal life in Christ Jesus our Lord." NKJV

The wages we've earned? That's death. God's grace? That's life. "God's Riches At Christ's Expense." Got grace? Then live it.

Life Lesson: We should serve God with a grateful heart for what He has already done for us.

Dear Father,
Thank You for loving me so much that You were willing to be the atoning sacrifice for my sin. Thank You that I do not have to earn salvation. Please give me the faith to continue in Your grace and to demonstrate it to others. I pray this in Jesus' name, Amen.

MAY 22
KEEP THE FAITH

Romans 4:12
"And the father of circumcision to those who not only are of the circumcision, but who also walk in the steps of the faith which our father Abraham had while still uncircumcised."
NKJV

In this verse, Paul is saying that these things are meaningless symbols without faith behind them. A light switch without electricity is useless. No matter how many times you flip the switch up and down, without electricity, nothing meaningful is going to happen. Works without faith are meaningless. Baptism without faith is meaningless. Communion without faith is meaningless. Saying a prayer without faith is meaningless. Even with the law, the Jewish people were not made heirs through their works but through their faith. When they gave sacrifices, they did so because of their faith. Their actions were the result of their faith and likewise, your actions should be a result of your faith. The outpouring of your faith should be love.

1 Corinthians 13:3 "If I gave everything I have to the poor and even sacrificed my body, I could boast about it; but if I didn't love others, I would be of no value whatsoever." NLT

Friend, do you love others? Do your friends know you love them? Does your family? What about your friends at church? You can do this whole 'Christian thing'... sacrifice, serve, and give, but if the outpouring of your faith is not love, all these things are nothing.

Life Lesson: Salvation is not keeping the law but keeping the faith.

Dear Father,
Thank You for Your love. Please forgive me if I have been unloving. Help me to show my faith in an outpouring of love. Please present me with opportunities to love people I never thought I could love. I pray this in Jesus' name. Amen.

MAY 23
TRUST

Romans 4:18-19
"...who, contrary to hope, in hope believed, so that he became the father of many nations, according to what was spoken, "So shall your descendants be." And not being weak in faith, he did not consider his own body, already dead (since he was about a hundred years old), and the deadness of Sarah's womb."
NKJV

Abram was 100 years old and Sarai was 90 years old. Think about that. What God was promising was not possible, yet it was possible because God promised it. As you may be aware, God called me to spend many years on the road with my family in a national music ministry. Our life on the road was fraught with unknowns. Many times, I was faced with situations where I could not see how it could possibly work out. Time and again, I saw God come through and it built my faith. What has God brought you through? Think for a moment of all the situations that God has brought you through. Let your faith fight your fear. Do not be controlled by fear because when you fear, you are not controlled by faith. You have to make the choice. Will you choose faith or will you choose fear?

Life Lesson: We should believe and trust in God even when it doesn't make sense.

Dear Father,
Thank You that You are a God who keeps His promises. You tell us in Your Bible that all things work together for good to those who love You. What an incredible promise! Lord, please help my faith and give me the occasion to help encourage another in their faith. I pray this in Jesus' name. Amen.

MAY 24
PEACE

Romans 5:1-3
"Therefore, having been justified by faith, we have peace with God through our Lord Jesus Christ, through whom also we have access by faith into this grace in which we stand, and rejoice in hope of the glory of God."
NKJV

Peace is mentioned over 400 times in the Bible. The Hebrew word for peace is Shalom, which means wholeness and health in every area of life. The Apostle Paul used an interesting salutation in most of his letters: "Grace to you and peace from God our Father and the Lord Jesus Christ." I have never met anyone who claimed they had enough peace in their life. All of us want more peace but sadly enough, most are not willing to go to the Source, which is God. Christian, if you are not at peace in your life, the fault lies squarely with you. No one has the power or authority to take away your peace. You have to give them that power; you have to give them that authority. Whether it is the difficult boss or the unexpected bill, giving your peace away is, quite frankly, your choice.

John 16:33 "I have told you all this so that you may have peace in me. Here on earth you will have many trials and sorrows. But take heart, because I have overcome the world." NLT

Matthew 11:28 "Come to Me, all you who labor and are heavy laden, and I will give you rest." NKJV

Ahhh... how wonderful is the peace of grace. You can lay your head down on your pillow at night because you have peace with God. How incredible is that? You cannot find that anywhere except at the cross. In Jesus, there is grace and peace. In the world, there is tribulation. Which do you choose?

Life Lesson: Jesus gives us peace. We can give our peace away or we can keep our peace.

Dear Father,
Thank You for giving me grace and peace. Forgive me for times when I have turned my peace over to frustration or anger. You love me and You have forgiven me. My peace is secure in You. In Jesus' name, Amen.

MAY 25
TO DO

Romans 5:6
"For when we were still without strength, in due time Christ died for the ungodly."
NKJV

What do you have to do in order to be righteous with God? Do you have to die a martyr's death before God will allow you into paradise? No. Do your good deeds need to outweigh your bad deeds for God to allow you into heaven? No. Do you have to be at peace with nature when you die, so that God will absorb you into heaven? No. What if you have done enough works, will God then allow you into heaven? No. Man pridefully wants to play a part in his salvation. We invent hurdles to jump, thinking we can earn God's approval. I don't want what I've earned because according to Romans 6:23 I've earned death. I need God's grace.

2 Corinthians 5:21 "For God made Christ, who never sinned, to be the offering for our sin, so that we could be made right with God through Christ." NLT

Every world religion is based on what you 'have to do' to convince God you deserve to go to heaven... that is, except one - Biblical Christianity. You see, the Bible tells us that God has already done everything for you. Your part is simply to accept Jesus' gift to you. He did the work, dying on the cross for your sins. Friend, you don't have to reach for God because He's already reaching out for you. Please don't reject Him.

Life Lesson: God has done everything needed for us to be at peace with Him.

Dear Father,
Thank You for giving Your Son, Jesus, to pay the penalty for my sins through His death on the cross. Thank You that He rose again and defeated death so that I may have eternal life. Thank You that in weakness, I am made strong through You. In Jesus' name, Amen.

MAY 26
GREAT JOY

Romans 5:11
"And not only so, but we also joy in God through our Lord Jesus Christ, by whom we have now received the atonement."
NKJV

The Hebrew word for atonement is kaphar which means "to cover." In the Greek, the word is katallage (kat-al-lag-ay') which means "to make one." The New King James Version of this verse uses the word reconciliation, and the New Living Translation reads, "making us friends of God." Christ's death can put away our sins and we can be one with Him. There are two states we can be in; friends with God or enemies of God. What makes the difference? Friend, the difference is made by whether we have accepted Jesus as our Lord and Savior or, in our hardheartedness we have rejected His offer of friendship.

Many Christians walk around all sour-faced, acting like they've been baptized in vinegar. Where's the joy? Christian, you should have great joy because you are forgiven. If you are having a bad day, think about God's great joy of forgiveness and your day will get better. If you are already having a good day, thinking of this joy will turn your good day into a great day. If you are having a great day, hold on to keep from flying!

Psalm 32:1 "Oh, what joy for those whose rebellion is forgiven, whose sin is put out of sight!" NLT

Life Lesson: We should have great joy because we are forgiven.

Dear Father,
Thank you for forgiving me. I have joy knowing that I am Your friend. What joy it is to know that what I 'cannot do' has been done by Jesus and that what I 'cannot pay' has been paid by Jesus. Lord, help my joy overflow to others in such a way that they cannot help but know who my Father is. I pray this in Jesus' name, Amen.

MAY 27
BUT GOD...

Romans 5:20
"Moreover the law entered that the offense might abound. But where sin abounded, grace abounded much more,"
NKJV

We allow 24,000 people to die from hunger or hunger related causes every day; that's one thousand an hour or one every 3.6 seconds. Not counting individual murders, but counting war and genocide in the last 100 years, we've killed 200 million... and it doesn't stop there; as time continues so does sin and death. We all own a part in this. This is the world God died for. But God...

Romans 5:8 "But God demonstrates His own love toward us, in that while we were still sinners, Christ died for us." NKJV

The Bible talks about God's grace abounding. There are a lot of people in this world and each one of us needs every last bit of God's grace. We should be very thankful that His grace does not have volume or measure; it's unlimited. He pours out grace, He pours out mercy, and He does not empty. His grace is available to everyone who is willing to accept it. God will never say, "Nope, that's it. You're all done. You had your share of grace and you squandered it." No friend, in contrast, He stands with arms outstretched, waiting.

Life Lesson: God has an infinite amount of grace and mercy available to each of us.

Have you accepted God's grace? Will you? If you would like to do this right now, please pray something like this...

Dear Father,
Thank You for loving me. Thank You for Your grace and mercy. I confess to You that I am a sinner. Lord Jesus, please forgive me for my sins. Thank You for forgiving me. Thank You for dying on the cross for my sins and defeating death. Please give me the power to live for You all the days of my life. In Jesus' name. Amen.

MAY 28
KNOW THE BIBLE

Romans 6:3
"Or do you not know that as many of us as were baptized into Christ Jesus were baptized into His death?"
NKJV

In Romans 6:3, Paul asks a very pertinent question, "Do you not know?" Multiple times in the New Testament Jesus is recorded asking the question, "have you not read?" Both Jesus and Paul seem to be hinting that we should know our Bibles. God does not ask us to be ignorant about His plan for our lives. In fact, He's given us a supernaturally detailed game plan through His Bible. We have the choice between knowledge and ignorance and it is a shame how many Christians choose the latter.

Proverbs 25:2 "It is the glory of God to conceal a matter, But the glory of kings is to search out a matter." NKJV

Personal study time in God's Word and devotions - these are very important to your spiritual growth and maturity. Everything you need is contained within the pages of our Bible. Do you realize that? There is not one single situation you will ever encounter that is not dealt with in the pages of scripture. Any Pastor should desire to teach his flock God's Word. Yet, we find ourselves in a time when there is a famine of good expositional Bible teaching going on in the world. How can we expect people to do the Word if they are not taught it? Knowing the Bible is one of the keys to doing the Bible. At The Bridge, you can rest assured that you are going to receive the full counsel of God, verse by verse and chapter by chapter whether you attend the services, listen to them at aboutthebridge.com, on the radio or via television. It is my desire to equip you to do the Bible. And if the Lord should ask you, "Have you read?" you can answer, "Yes, Lord. I have."

Life Lesson: Knowing the Bible is one of the keys to doing the Bible.

Dear Father,
Thank You for Your love, Your grace, and Your mercy. Thank You for giving me Your Bible to read, study, and learn so that I am equipped to live according to Your plan and purpose for my life. As I study Your Word, I ask that you would give me opportunities to live it. In Jesus' name, Amen.

MAY 29
DRAFTING GOD

Romans 6:9
"For the death that He died, He died to sin once for all; but the life that He lives, He lives to God."
NKJV

Jesus lived His life for God and the world will never be the same. He died, I died; He lives, I live. He went to heaven, I am going to heaven. He beat death, I will beat death. Jesus died once, for all. He changed all the rules. He broke death's back. He paid the penalty for sin and He crushed sins power over all who call on His name. Through Jesus, the warrant of death becomes a covenant of eternal life and pointless existence becomes a purposeful mission. Friend, you have been drafted into God's army.

Matthew 12:30 "He who is not with Me is against Me, and he who does not gather with Me scatters abroad." NKJV

Let's join together to reap a harvest. You may have accepted Jesus, but have you joined with Him in God's mission? Does it matter to you that there are people in our world that have not heard the Word of God? Do you care that there are multitudes that have never heard the Gospel message? If we live for God and not ourselves we can change the world we live in. A life sacrificed for God... your life or someone else's? People don't know because they have not been told and people die everyday without God. They may live down the street or on the other side of the globe, but one thing is sure, they need us to care enough to tell them about Jesus... and I do... and I will. Will you? Onwards, for our King!

Life Lesson: If we live for God and not ourselves we can change the world we live in.

Dear Father,
Thank You for loving this world. Thank You for Jesus. Please give me opportunities to share the Gospel with others and please forgive me for times when I may have selfishly remained silent. Please use me to change the world. In Jesus' name. Amen.

MAY 30
FREE

Romans 6:18
"And having been set free from sin, you became slaves of righteousness."
NKJV

If you are a Christian, the shackles of sin are shattered and you are free. Having been in bondage to sin, you are now free to live in Christ. Friend, remain fast in that freedom! Although free from the fetters of bondage, should you slip the shackles back on your wrists? Certainly not! Yet we do that, don't we? Why tarry in a dungeon with the door open? Let's leave the brig behind.

John 8:34-36 "Jesus answered them, "Most assuredly, I say to you, whoever commits sin is a slave of sin. And a slave does not abide in the house forever, but a son abides forever. Therefore if the Son makes you free, you shall be free indeed." NKJV

Friend, be victorious. Not in your own strength, but in yielding to the Holy Spirit. We cannot live the Christian life under our own capacity. We can live life through the power of God. Bread in a toaster will not become toast until you plug the toaster in. You cannot break the bondage of sin without Jesus. When plugged in, you are powerful. Are you plugged in?

Life Lesson: We are free to live for God.

Dear Father,
Thank You for saving me from my sins. Thank You for the gift of freedom through You. Please remind me of that freedom when I feel like a slave to the world. Help me live in liberty by the power of Your Spirit like You want and intend for me. I pray this in Jesus' name, Amen.

MAY 31
BEAR GOOD FRUIT

Romans 6:21-22
"What fruit did you have then in the things of which you are now ashamed? For the end of those things is death. But now having been set free from sin, and having become slaves of God, you have your fruit to holiness, and the end, everlasting life."
NKJV

The fruit we used to bear is common to this world. Its harvest is death. Now, as Christians our fruit should be spiritual - freaky fruit if you will - peculiar in this world. However you phrase it, the outpouring of a Christian's life is extraordinary compared to the works of the world.

I'm sure we've all heard the question, "If you were arrested for being a Christian, would there be enough evidence to convict you?" While that's a great question, let's take it a step further. Would the case be built on circumstantial evidence, "His family was seen entering church on Sunday morning" - "Her car has a fish on the bumper?" Maybe the case would be built on direct evidence, "He has shared his faith with me and with others."

Friend, it should be a mix of both. Good fruit is the visible effect of our Christian life - sharing your faith, serving the Lord. Good fruit is also the invisible affect of our Christian life on others - "I want the same joy that she has" - "her upbeat attitude is such a blessing at work." Jesus told us to be salt and light. Salt cultivates thirst. Does your life leave the people around you thirsty for Jesus?

Matthew 5:16 "Let your light so shine before men, that they may see your good works and glorify your Father in heaven." NKJV

Life Lesson: We should bear good fruit.

Dear Father,
Thank You for freeing me from my sins. Please remind me of that freedom when I feel like a slave to the world. Give me the power to live my life according to Your will. Thank You for the gifts that You place within me to serve others. Lord, help me to bear good fruit and give me a boldness to share my faith with others. I pray this in Jesus' name, Amen.

JUNE 1
PRUNING

Romans 7:5
"For when we were in the flesh, the sinful passions which were aroused by the law were at work in our members to bear fruit to death."
NKJV

The technological advancements made by mankind in the last century or even the last 20 years are astounding. Yet with all our technology, we still have to wait for lettuce to ripen and for olives to mature. Lettuce ripens a month and a half after planting, but for an olive the wait is at least four years. Some of us, like the lettuce, are maturing quickly while others, like olives, are improving more slowly. Something changed in you when you were saved, and still... God is making changes to you.

Romans 7:6 "But now we have been delivered from the law, having died to what we were held by, so that we should serve in the newness of the Spirit and not in the oldness of the letter." NKJV

We should all be bearing fruit. There may be times that you may need to endure pruning before you bear fruit. Pruning redirects energy to the right places. If you are not being fruitful, maybe you need to redirect energy toward the Lord. Don't just come to church, be the church. Be praying, giving, serving - joining hands with your church to achieve something far greater than any one of us could achieve alone.

Life Lesson: Christianity is not a do-it-yourself religion.

Dear Father,
Thank You for loving me. Give me the desire to grow in righteousness through the washing of Your Word; in serving You and prayer. Help me to love and serve others in the place where You want me to grow and bear good fruit. In Jesus' name. Amen.

JUNE 2
ACTION OR REACTION?

Romans 7:7
What shall we say then? Is the law sin? Certainly not! On the contrary, I would not have known sin except through the law. For I would not have known covetousness unless the law had said, "You shall not covet."
NKJV

Coveting is a sin without action. It is a disposition of the heart often expressed in motive. When you want something that you should not have, that is coveting. Unchecked coveting will manage your actions and your reactions when you receive truth. Tithing is a great example. Your tithe does not belong to you... even before you write the check. First fruits belong to God before you have even earned them... even during weak economic times. Spurgeon wrote, "It is the teaching of Scripture that the Lord enriches the liberal and leaves the miserly to find out that withholding tendeth to poverty." Stingy Christians do not see the overflowing bounty that God has for them, but God blesses those who place their trust in Him.

Psalm 18:30
As for God, His way is perfect;
The Word of the LORD is proven;
He is a shield to all who trust in Him.
NKJV

That is the truth. Are you geared toward action or reaction? You will not hear about tithing from me often except when there is scriptural application. God's Word not only tells us what is wrong, but how to make it right. When you take your car to the garage for repairs, the mechanic will tell you what is wrong and what is needed to fix it. That's not being closed-minded... that's recognizing the truth. The Bible does just that, but for people. Every time you study the Bible the Bible studies you.

Life Lesson: God's Word not only tells us what is wrong but how to make it right.

Dear Father,
Thank You for the truth of Your Word. Examine my heart. Show me Your truth and reveal in me Your ways. Please bless me with opportunities to bless others. In Jesus' name, Amen.

JUNE 3
IT'S GOD

Romans 7:15
"For what I am doing, I do not understand. For what I will to do, that I do not practice; but what I hate, that I do."
NKJV

If you think you cannot identify with this statement, then you need to look in a mirror. The Apostle Paul, who wrote Romans and much of the New Testament, is being open and honest with his struggles... and we can also. We all struggle with doing wrong things. In fact, if it was not for God working through us, every attempt of our hands would be blameworthy. We all want to do well, but many times we give in to our flesh and end up doing wrong. The only way we can transact righteousness is by consequence of God in us. It is not just the 'doing'. Your appetite to affect virtue is an indication that God is working.

Philippians 2:13 "For it is God who works in you both to will and to do for His good pleasure." NKJV

Your reading this devotion is affirmation. You are hungry for something more. Every time you do something good, you can know and believe that God is working in you. My Christian friend, take heart and be encouraged. The Creator of all the universe sees Jesus reflected in you.

Life Lesson: The fact that we want to do good is God.

Dear Father,
Thank You for Your love. Thank You for working through my insufficient efforts to produce something that is glorifying and profitable for Your kingdom. Please present me with greater opportunities to do right. I know that it is only through Your strength that I can do them. In Jesus' name, Amen.

JUNE 4
ACCORDING TO THE SPIRIT

Romans 8:3-4

"For what the law could not do in that it was weak through the flesh, God did by sending His own Son in the likeness of sinful flesh, on account of sin: He condemned sin in the flesh, that the righteous requirement of the law might be fulfilled in us who do not walk according to the flesh but according to the Spirit."
NKJV

No man has ever been a better example of righteous living than Jesus Christ. He lived a perfect, sinless life. He was giving, loving, benevolent, caring, serving and passionate about saving people. He was selfless in every action and relentless in pursuit of His goal. In John 15:13 Jesus said, "Greater love has no one than this, than to lay down one's life for his friends." When you place the wants and needs of others before your own wants and needs you lay down your life for them. Serving others is serving God. We should be following Jesus' example. Is that example too lofty for us? No, friend, it is not! Once you have accepted Jesus as your Lord and Savior, He starts His work in you. Through the power of the Spirit, you can rise above the flesh. You can be the example of Jesus in the lives of everyone around you.

Life Lesson: Jesus shows us how to live.

Dear Father,
Thank You for Your selfless gift of dying for my sins. Please give me Your love and passion for people. Help me to place the wants and needs of others before my own. Fill me with Your Holy Spirit so that I can show the love of Jesus to those around me. In Jesus' name, Amen.

JUNE 5
DO YOU MIND?

Romans 8:6
For to be carnally minded is death, but to be spiritually minded is life and peace.
NKJV

Who or what is controlling your life? To be carnally minded (self-centered) is death. To be spiritually minded (Christ-centered) is life and peace. According to Romans 8, when you are out of rest, you are not in the Spirit. Do you have peace? If you do not have peace, do not blame it on the world or others; the blame lies with you. When you surrender to God, you do not have to surrender to your flesh. Live the Spirit-led life and you will live according to God's will and in God's power.

John 13:8-9 Peter said to Him, "You shall never wash my feet!" Jesus answered him, "If I do not wash you, you have no part with Me." Simon Peter said to Him, "Lord, not my feet only, but also my hands and my head!" NKJV

Life, in its fullest, comes through being led by the Lord. Fellowship is broken with God when you sin. You are still His child, but sin is in the way. Confess your sin to Jesus and let Him wash you clean. Then, you will be able to enjoy His presence.

What are you living for? Your reason for living should be set apart from the rest of the world. If you live for the riches of the world, you may be alive in the body, but you are dead in your spirit. Live for God! As an heir to the riches in Christ, you will enjoy the fullness of joy that comes through walking in the calling of God.

Life Lesson: The way to walk in peace is to be spiritually and heavenly minded.

Dear Father,
Thank You for the awesome riches You have given me through Your son, Jesus Christ. Please give me wisdom and discernment as I seek to follow after You. I want to walk in the joy and peace You have given me. Set me apart to do Your will for my life and help me to live a surrendered, Spirit-filled life. In Jesus' name, Amen.

JUNE 6
LIVE THE CHANGE

Romans 8:11
"But if the Spirit of Him who raised Jesus from the dead dwells in you, He who raised Christ from the dead will also give life to your mortal bodies through His Spirit who dwells in you."
NKJV

The same power that raised Jesus from the dead is available to you. Do you realize that? The defining moment of the world and all the power that was behind His glorious resurrection is for you. That is what Romans 8:11 says. Are you living life defeated by sin? Friend, seize the moment! Now is the time! Never before have you been more able to live life to its fullest. The potential of your Creator is dwelling in you. The Holy Spirit, given to you by Jesus wants to perform a work in you so amazing you will never be the same. Victory has been declared ... are you taking part in it?

Philippians 4:13 "I can do all things through Christ who strengthens me." NKJV

You are being perfected. As you allow God to work in you, you are being conformed to the image of Christ. That's powerful! Friend, you can do all things through Jesus, including overcoming that sin that you keep going back to. Stop feeding it. Feed your spiritual nature. Going to church, personal time in the Bible, prayer and serving others is the way to grow in God and these things are products of the Holy Spirit working in you. You don't owe sin anything, but you owe Jesus for dying for you. You were purchased at a high price. Jesus changed your life. Live that change.

Life Lesson: You have resurrection power available to you to overcome sin in your life.

Dear Father,
Thank You that I do not have to be a slave to sin, but can be a bondservant of righteousness through You. Please forgive me for my sins and give me the power to live for You. Help me to grow in You through church, study, prayer and by loving and serving others. In Jesus' name, Amen.

JUNE 7
LOOK FORWARD

Romans 8:18-19
"For I consider that the sufferings of this present time are not worthy to be compared with the glory which shall be revealed in us. For the earnest expectation of the creation eagerly waits for the revealing of the sons of God."
NKJV

I read a story about twin boys who, though they looked alike, were different in almost every other way. Perhaps the most decided distinction was their outlook on life. One was a constant optimist while the other was a perennial cynic. One Christmas, their father decided to experiment. On the pessimist's side of the Christmas tree, the father piled up games and toys and on the optimist's side, he piled up horse manure. When morning came, the cynic sat amongst his gifts crying. When the father asked why, the child responded, "because now I'll have to share and I'm sure I'll constantly be changing out batteries in these toys and losing pieces to these games." In contrast, the optimist was singing and dancing around joyfully. When his father queried, he said, "with all this manure there's got to be a pony around here somewhere!"

Seems rather silly, doesn't it? Yet we can all be like the cynic. We focus on the world and all its trials and tribulations and forget that Jesus told us He has overcome the world. Buried in the short term and forgetting about the long term, we get so tied up in our pessimism that we lose sight of our inheritance.

Philippians 3:13-14 "Brethren, I do not count myself to have apprehended; but one thing I do, forgetting those things which are behind and reaching forward to those things which are ahead, I press toward the goal for the prize of the upward call of God in Christ Jesus." NKJV

Friend, don't be a pessimist. You have God's promise that even the worst this world will throw at you will work to bring about the best that God has for you. This world has enough cynics. Pessimists seldom solve problems. Optimists change the world. Friend, press toward the goal. Don't sit on the sidelines. Got trials? There's probably more to come. "But God", two words that turn the tables on trouble and strike fear in the heart of Satan. Don't allow yourself to be discouraged. Take heart and play a part. Now is the time, before it's too late.

Life Lesson: If you are following Jesus then you have much to look forward to.

Dear Father,

Thank You for adopting me into Your Kingdom. Thank You that no matter what the trials are and no matter how high the hill to climb, You are there to pull me through. Don't let me be a cynic. I want to make a difference in this world and in the lives of others and I can't do that if I am on the sidelines. Please give me opportunities to serve You and make a difference. In Jesus' name, Amen.

JUNE 8
WHERE'S YOUR FOCUS?

Romans 8:23
"Not only that, but we also who have the first fruits of the Spirit, even we ourselves groan within ourselves, eagerly waiting for the adoption, the redemption of our body."
NKJV

In this Christianity thing, what do you bring to the table? There are really only two possibilities - either you are bringing heaven to earth, or you are not. It's so easy to get caught up in today's trials that we forget our Lord is triumphant. When your focus is on the world, you will be entangled in adversity. Focus on Jesus and the tribulations of this earth are ephemeral.

Have you ever spoken with someone who is fixated on trouble? They bear a brand of defeat. Only the conquered should wear this badge of defeat. Christians are anything but conquered. Now, imagine some gentleman - not a believer - observing a Christian enamored with this world. Would he see hope? Would this fellow be inclined to follow?

Romans 8:24-25 "For we were saved in this hope, but hope that is seen is not hope; for why does one still hope for what he sees? But if we hope for what we do not see, we eagerly wait for it with perseverance." NKJV

So, what do you bring to the table? What do you set before others for them to see? Is it heaven or hell? Your faith is their evidence. If non-believers see you living out the substance of your faith they will know that your God is greater than this world's woes.

If you are sitting at the station of this world waiting for your go on the gravy train, you are sitting at the wrong station. That train, while tempting on the outside, has a disappointing destination. Christian, if the substance of your hope is worldly success and not Jesus, then you need to review your faith because others already are.

Life Lesson: Don't focus on today's groaning but on tomorrow's glory.

Dear Father,
Thank You for the hope You have freely given to me through Your Son Jesus. Lord, help my doubt when I cannot see. As I eagerly wait in expectation of Your coming, strengthen me to persevere in the calling You have laid before me. I know that all things work together for good to those who love You Lord. I commit my life to Your purposes today. In Jesus' name, Amen.

JUNE 9
BUMPS

Romans 8:36-37
"As it is written: 'For Your sake we are killed all day long; We are accounted as sheep for the slaughter.' Yet in all these things we are more than conquerors through Him who loved us."
NKJV

As the Pastor of a large congregation, I often speak with and pray for those who are in the midst of monumental life changing challenges. It might be unemployment, eviction, addiction, separation, divorce or even death. Whatever it is, for those going through it, it seems to be a Mount Everest of a challenge. One thing I've noticed is that those who dare to take on mountains often triumph while those who survey the towering heights and presume defeat... buckle. Colossal cliffs teach the deepest lessons - the kind you never forget.

Genesis 22:8 "And Abraham said, My son, God will provide himself a lamb for a burnt offering: so they went both of them together." KJV

From the stable to sacrifice, Jesus knew His mountain. Awaiting Him at the top were false accusation, humiliation, torture, pain, suffering and death on a cross. For us, our Savior set His jaw and pressed forward. Jesus made the greatest climb - to Calvary.

Willingly, Jesus took that hill. He knew what was waiting, and He went. It was His joy to do so. He did it to purchase you and change your destiny. Friend, because Jesus made His ascent, you can climb your mountains with victory in hand. The next time you see a mountain looming in the distance, remember, you're a conqueror. With Jesus, you will take that hill.

Life Lesson: Bumps are what you climb on.

Dear Father,
Thank You for loving me. It is through You that I do not have to fear the difficulties of this world and that I have everything I need for the challenges of life. Please forgive me for times when I've stalled in the face of trials instead of relying on You. In Jesus' name, Amen.

JUNE 10
HANG UP THE EXCUSES

Romans 9:1-3
"I tell the truth in Christ, I am not lying, my conscience also bearing me witness in the Holy Spirit, that I have great sorrow and continual grief in my heart. For I could wish that I myself were accursed from Christ for my brethren, my countrymen according to the flesh,"
NKJV

The Apostle Paul's legacy endures as a challenge for us to re-think our obligation toward others. He was willing to make a sacrifice of his own life so that others could know Jesus. Are you willing? Whether we want to admit it or not, Christians place conditions on compliance. We draw lines of feasibility. I will do this or that as long as it falls within certain parameters. What conditions did Jesus place on His love and His willingness to sacrifice?

Here's a common situation... the homeless man asking for a little cash... how do you react? "If I give that homeless man a few dollars, he will go and buy alcohol. I don't want to be an enabler." Yeah, maybe he will buy alcohol, but what if you share Jesus and pray for him? Jesus died for that man just as he died for you. God took the action for you to claim the opportunity. Friend, be an enabler... enable others with the choice - Jesus... yes or no?

What about sharing with that long time friend, family member or passing acquaintance? How will they react? If your friend or family member were drowning would you be considering their reaction before throwing a life line to them? Of course not! I say let's hang up the excuses and get beyond comfortable. There is no inappropriate time to share Jesus.

Life Lesson: Followers of Jesus should care and be willing to sacrifice for those that do not know Jesus as their Savior.

Dear Father,
Thank You for saving me. Please soften my heart towards others and give me a deep caring for them. Open up opportunities for me to share and help me to be faithful to do so. In Jesus' name, Amen.

JUNE 11
A GIFT TO BE SHARED

Romans 9:6-7
"But it is not that the word of God has taken no effect. For they are not all Israel who are of Israel, nor are they all children because they are the seed of Abraham; but, "In Isaac your seed shall be called."
NKJV

Never before has Christianity been so accessible within the United States. Just walk a few blocks down any city street and you will pass a church. Take a drive down any country lane and you will find chapels and churches satisfying the scenery. Christian radio and television are making waves while religious readers have easy access to the latest best-seller.

So why are so many starving for Jesus? Well friend, the mantra of the modern Church has become self-improvement, self-empowerment and self reliance. In effect, this leaves multitudes drowning in a sea of self-centeredness.

2 Thessalonians 1:8-9 "in flaming fire, bringing judgment on those who don't know God and on those who refuse to obey the Good News of our Lord Jesus. They will be punished with everlasting destruction, forever separated from the Lord and from his glorious power" NLT

This situation is serious. Many Christians have become so self-centered that they think about no one else. They do not comprehend the consequences of hoarding the Good News. The light we have received is desperately needed by others, yet so many "saved" will never know the joy of sharing it. If we really believe what we lay claim to, how can we be OK with letting someone perish? It goes beyond indifference or fear of rejection; it is either unbelief or hatred. How much do you have to hate someone to let them go to hell? I'm not OK with it and never will be. Won't you join with me in living to tell what Jesus died to say?

Life Lesson: The Gospel is not a treasure to be stored but a gift to be shared.

Dear Father:
Thank You for the Good News of Jesus Christ. Thank You for the freedoms of owning a Bible and being a part of a church home. Lord, forgive me for the times I have been self-centered and thought only of my own salvation. Please show me the opportunities to tell someone about You. I want to join in the joy of reaching others with the Gospel of Jesus Christ. In Jesus' name, Amen.

JUNE 12
CHOICES

Romans 9:17
"For the Scripture says to the Pharaoh, "For this very purpose I have raised you up, that I may show My power in you, and that My name may be declared in all the earth."
NKJV

Our decisions can lead to good things or they can lead to bad things. Now, you probably think that I'm about to make an appeal for any non-believer reading this message to accept Jesus. Well, in a way I am, but in a roundabout kind of way. You see, I'm writing specifically to you, Christian, because the choices you make may determine whether or not someone else chooses to accept Jesus. Do you speak to others about Jesus? That's an obvious way that your choices can influence decisions for Christ. We can never know how far our choices in the form of words or actions travel. If you have children, you may have already learned this. If you don't have children, ask someone who does.

The book of James tells us that the words we consider to be of little consequence have the power to destroy and that our actions are the showcase of our faith. Take a moment and think of the people in your life who don't know Jesus. What part are your words or your actions playing in the choice they are making?

Life Lesson: God wants to reveal Himself through us to the world.

Dear Father,
Thank You for Your grace and mercy. Lord, help my choices and my actions influence others to know Jesus. Please forgive me for times when I've been careless in my choices, words or actions. In Jesus' name, Amen.

JUNE 13
YOU ARE LOVED

Romans 9:25-26 (As He says also in Hosea)
"I will call them My people, who were not My people, And her beloved, who was not beloved."
"And it shall come to pass in the place where it was said to them, 'You are not My people,' There they shall be called sons of the living God."
NKJV

Paul is pulling verses from the book of Hosea, a "minor prophet", with a major league message. Hosea was guided by God to marry a prostitute named Gomer. She left the lifestyle; they grew in love and established a family. Soon, though, she returned to her former practice. Time and again, she would come back to Hosea only to abandon him for another. One day she chose not to return. Hosea searched high and low and when he found her, she was for sale in a slave market. In an outpouring of his undying love, Hosea paid the price and purchased her back. It is an incredible story of unfaltering love and loyalty and is an eloquent rendering of God's never-ending love even when His people turn to idols.

1 John 4:16 "And we have known and believed the love that God has for us. God is love, and he who abides in love abides in God and God in him." NKJV

God sees our faults and loves us. He finds us slaves of sin and frees us. When we go back to the chains, Jesus doesn't turn His back, but holds out His pierced hands. "I love you, and I miss you." Friend, have you wandered off? God's heart for you is restoration and love. What will you do?

Life Lesson: God is love. You are loved.

Dear Father:
Thank You for Your love. Lord, at times I will admit, I feel like a slave to my sins. Thank You for looking past my faults and freeing me of my sins. Remind me when I see the faults of others, to examine them with Your unfaltering love and loyalty toward them. In Jesus' name, Amen.

JUNE 14
POEM

Romans 10:1
"Brethren, my heart's desire and prayer to God for Israel is that they may be saved."
NKJV

The summer twilight breeze carried the scent of distant rain. The beach was pressed in the white noise of water cresting - spilling in against its surge. Sea foam soda-pop-fizzed then went missing leaving its briny deposit. A businessman, phone in hand to ear watched a young boy knock about on the beach tossing starfish back to their home. Like the night sky that was quickly appearing, hundreds of starfish spotted the sand and one by one the boy picked them up and threw them back into the water. Puzzled by his observation, the businessman ended his call and approached the boy. "Look," he said, "There must be hundreds of them. You'll never be able to save them all." The boy bent down and plucked another from the sand. Throwing it into the life preserving water he replied, "No, but I can save this one."

We should desire that others follow Jesus and find love and forgiveness. How can we be content when people are dying without the Savior? Is it your heart's desire to see people saved? Does it matter to you? It matters to God.

Who do you know that does not know Jesus? Write down their names and commit to pray for them and invite them to church.

Life Lesson: We should desire that others follow Jesus and find love and forgiveness.

Dear Father:
Thank You for saving me. Please give me Your desire for people to be saved. Bring to my mind those people I know who do not know You. Please give me the courage to invite them to church and open their hearts to be receptive to my invitation. In Jesus' name, Amen.

JUNE 15
SAY WHAT?

Romans 10:10
"For with the heart one believes unto righteousness, and with the mouth confession is made unto salvation."
NKJV

We are capable of doing incredible harm with our speech. With slash and burn efficiency, angry words sear into the lives of those around us. "I hate you!" "You're stupid!" "You'll never amount to anything!" What do little ears hear when you speak? What about your spouse? How many people carry around shrapnel from your tongue?

Philippians 2:11 "and that every tongue should confess that Jesus Christ is Lord, to the glory of God the Father." NKJV

Let us be God's representatives of grace and love in this world. With the same mouth that we asked Jesus to forgive us, let us forgive others. Let us lead the world in the kind of love that desires to forgive even to the point of sacrifice. Let us commit ourselves to speaking things glorifying to the Lord even when we want to let a cutting comment fly. Let us be forgiving of others because God has forgiven us.

Life Lesson: We can be forgiven.

Dear Father:
Thank You that Your mercy is new every morning. Thank You for the grace and love You have given to me freely. Lord, forgive me for the times I have hurt others. Likewise, remind me to have the same grace toward others who have hurt me. Help me use my words in the way that is glorifying to You. In Jesus' name, Amen.

JUNE 16
LIVE FOR REAL

Ezekiel 37:3
"And He said to me, 'Son of man, can these bones live?' So I answered, 'O Lord GOD, You know.'"
NKJV

My friend, where are you spiritually right now? Are you frustrated? Are you tired? Devastated? Do you feel like your world is caving in and you just can't handle it? Are you dry... weary from crying? Do you feel spiritually dead?

Lamentations 3:21-24 "This I recall to my mind, therefore I have hope. Through the LORD's mercies we are not consumed, because His compassions fail not. They are new every morning; great is Your faithfulness. "The LORD is my portion," says my soul, "therefore I hope in Him!" NKJV

To the stale soul, hope sounds impossible... I know it does. I once searched for hope in dry and desolate places. I remember what it's like.

In Matthew 7:7, 8 Jesus said, "Ask, and it will be given to you; seek, and you will find; knock, and it will be opened to you. For everyone who asks receives, and he who seeks finds, and to him who knocks it will be opened." NKJV

Stop and look around you. What you surround yourself with is a good indication of where you seek. What surrounds you? Is it television, music, gadgets, computers... or maybe it is drugs and alcohol? There is no hope in these things. Hope is in Jesus. God's promise lasts forever. You can live - I mean really live, but it's in Jesus and not in the world.

Life Lesson: You can live for real.

Dear Father,
Thank You for the hope You give to me in Jesus. Lord, help me to stay determined and not lose hope even when I find myself in a valley of dry bones. Remind me to feed upon Your Word. I give you all praise and glory for the promises you set before me. In Jesus' name, Amen.

JUNE 17
THE CHAIN

Romans 10:17
"So then faith comes by hearing, and hearing by the word of God."
NKJV

I receive many emails that turn out to be chain letters. Usually I disregard the chain letters, but for some reason, I decided to read this one. After reading the skillfully crafted yet doubtlessly erroneous story, it ended with a warning of dreadful things happening if I didn't forward the letter to ten other people. That's one of the reasons why I hate chain letters... they usually end with bad news. Now, the idea of the chain... that is a great concept; I share with you, you share with others and so on... until everyone hears.

Romans 10:17 "Yet faith comes from listening to <u>this message of good news</u>—the Good News about Christ." NLT (my emphasis)

We've got good news to share. Sometimes when sharing the Good News of Jesus Christ, people put more emphasis on the bad news than on the good news. The "you're going to hell and let me tell you why" approach often comes across as "I'm better than you and here's a list of the ways." After berating someone about their failings, how likely do you think they are to tune in while you share the Gospel? Build a bridge, don't burn one. Certainly, people have to understand why they need a Savior... I'm not saying anything different. That job has already been filled. The Holy Spirit convicts of sin. Our job is to go and tell... or maybe better put, "show and tell." I want to carry this message of good news to all the earth because someone shared it with me. I want to continue the chain. Will you?

Life Lesson: We should have a living and active faith not a dead faith.

Dear Father,
Thank You for Your love. For some reason, You looked down on me and loved me enough to die for me. You did that for everyone else too and I need to tell them. Please give me opportunities to share the Good News about Christ. Embolden me so that I do not let those opportunities slip away. In Jesus' name, Amen.

JUNE 18
IMITATE CHRIST

2 Kings 17:4
"And the king of Assyria uncovered a conspiracy by Hoshea; for he had sent messengers to So, king of Egypt, and brought no tribute to the king of Assyria, as he had done year by year. Therefore the king of Assyria shut him up, and bound him in prison."
NKJV

The old adage goes... is there anything in your house that you would not want Jesus to see if He were to visit? What about in your life... your decisions? You see, our tendency is to make idols. Sometimes we look up to entertainers, musicians or sports stars and begin to model our lives after them. Subtly, as we admire their work, read about them in magazines and study them online, the choices we make begin to reflect their ideals instead of God's ideals. Their lives look so good to us, and then the time comes where we realize just how miserable they are because it has become manifest in our own lives.

1 Corinthians 11:1 "Imitate me, just as I also imitate Christ." NKJV

The Apostle Paul was an imitator... he imitated Christ. Do you know what manifested in his life? Christ likeness. We should take note and do likewise.

Life Lesson: Sin will keep you longer than you want to stay and pay you more than you want to be paid.

Dear Father,
Thank You for loving me. Please forgive me for allowing idols in my life. Please help me to take my eyes off of people or things they should not be on. Help me to keep my eyes on You. In Jesus' name, Amen.

JUNE 19
LOOK TO THE BIBLE

Romans 11:1
"I say then, has God cast away His people? Certainly not! For I also am an Israelite, of the seed of Abraham, of the tribe of Benjamin."
NKJV

There are a lot of books out there about the Bible and a lot of books offering man's counsel for life's circumstances. Only one book, the Bible, is authored by God and offers God's counsel for life's circumstances. That being said, sometimes we come across a section of scripture that seems to raise more questions than it answers. When that happens, keep reading. It's been well said that the best commentary on the Bible is the Bible. If you come across a question in the Bible, keep looking and you will find the answer.

Friends, be very careful searching for answers about the Bible from sources outside of the Bible. Many false doctrines have started that way. Now, don't get me wrong, there are some very good commentaries out there, but commentaries are not "inspired scripture." Always make certain that what you read or hear balances with scripture.

Some churches pay homage to what's called "Replacement Theology." Basically saying that Israel messed up too many times (and the church hasn't?) and so God is through with Israel and the church has now inherited all of Israel's promises. If you have ever heard that or even believed that, look at this verse. Some finer points of theology can be debated looking into word tense, origin and original languages, but others are as plain as the nose on your face. This is as plain as the nose on your face. God is not finished with Israel.

Life Lesson: We look to the Bible in spiritual and theological matters to form our opinions and beliefs.

Dear Father,
Thank You for Your love, Your grace and Your mercy. Thank You that even though I make mistakes, You do not withdraw Your promises from me, just as You have not withdrawn them from Israel. Lord, Your Word is faithful and Your covenant is forever. In Jesus' name, Amen.

JUNE 20
WHAT'S YOUR COMPASS?

2 Kings 17:7-8
"For so it was that the children of Israel had sinned against the LORD their God, who had brought them up out of the land of Egypt, from under the hand of Pharaoh king of Egypt; and they had feared other gods, and had walked in the statutes of the nations whom the LORD had cast out from before the children of Israel, and of the kings of Israel, which they had made."
NKJV

What is your spiritual compass? What is your moral compass? I am not asking if you do everything right but I am asking where do you go to figure out what is right? Do you go to the news or the internet? Do you go to other people or look to the culture? Public opinion and world culture - these things are always shifting and stuff within culture (trends, styles, fashions and the world's opinion on what is right and what is wrong) will always be changing. If you depend on the world, then you will always be changing. Why does a compass work? A compass works because it points North. The compass does not decide to base its reading off East because that is what is comfortable or it is the new fad. If you use a compass correctly, you will always know the direction in which you are headed. Too many Christians allow the things of this world to be their spiritual compass and all they have to show for it are messed up worldly lives. Allow God, His Word, your love for Him and your love for people to be your spiritual compass in this ever-changing world. Then, you will never be lost.

Life Lesson: Allow God, His Word, your love for Him and your love for people be your spiritual compass in this ever-changing world.

Dear Father,
Thank You for loving me. Please forgive me for times when I have wandered off. Thank You for Your Word and help me remember to always keep it at the forefront of my mind. In Jesus' name, Amen.

JUNE 21
CURTAIN CALL

Revelation 16:15
"Behold, I am coming as a thief. Blessed is he who watches, and keeps his garments, lest he walk naked and they see his shame."
NKJV

As I sit looking out over the Valley of Megiddo in Israel (where the Bible says the final battle will take place), I thank the Lord for His patience; that many may be saved.

2 Peter 3:9 "The Lord is not slack concerning His promise, as some count slackness, but is longsuffering toward us, not willing that any should perish but that all should come to repentance." NKJV

In earlier times and at the completion of a public performance, the author of a play would walk on stage; this was how people knew who wrote, created and orchestrated the play. In the same way, Jesus will walk on the stage of the world and all will recognize Him as the Author. For some, that day will be glorious, but for others it will be disastrous.

Romans 10:9-10, 13 tells us all who believe and call on the name of Jesus will be saved. The Bible also tells us that we should take a close look at ourselves to be certain we are in the faith. You see, there are visible evidences in our lives of where we stand as Christians. A couple of those things are love for others, self sacrifice and good works. These things don't save you, but they are an indication of your faith. Perhaps you should take a moment to reflect. Are you prepared to meet Jesus?

Life Lesson: Prepare your heart.

Dear Father,
Thank You that You are not slack concerning Your promises. I desire to live a life surrendered to You. I desire that my life reflect Your promises, love and great mercy so that it encourages the lives of others around me. Thank You for Your longsuffering toward us. Your Word is faithful and Your covenant is forever. In Jesus' name, Amen.

JUNE 22
INDEPENDENCE DAY

Ezekiel 37:21
"Then say to them, 'Thus says the Lord GOD: "Surely I will take the children of Israel from among the nations, wherever they have gone, and will gather them from every side and bring them into their own land;"
NKJV

The fortress palace of Masada is located about 1500 feet above the surrounding land. With its sloping walls, most armies would have found it unreachable - but not the Roman army. In 66 AD, nearly 1000 Jewish men, women and children made a final stand against the forces of the Roman army. The standoff culminated in their mass suicide in order to avoid capture and slavery. Masada is significant in the hearts of Israelis who proclaim "Masada will never fall again."

In 1948, Israel became an independent nation once again. The people here love their land and their country. God gave them this land.

While excavating in the synagogue of Masada, archaeologists discovered a fragment of scroll. This scroll contained Ezekiel 37, a prophecy about the rebirth of Israel. Today, this scripture has been fulfilled. God has given the Israeli people this land, and no one can take it away.

Friends, Jesus is coming soon. The prophetic timepiece is in place... Israel is back in the land. Are you prepared? A student once asked his Rabbi, "When should someone repent?" The rabbi responded, "One day before you die." "I do not know when that will be", protested the student. "Then repent now", said the Rabbi. Friend, where are you with Jesus?

Life Lesson: The time is now.

Dear Father,
Thank You for the truth of Your promises. Just as You brought life again to Israel, You also bring the same hope of vitality to me through Your Son, Jesus Christ. Remind me to feed upon Your Word daily. I give You all praise and glory for the promises You set before me. In Jesus' name, Amen.

JUNE 23
TO DO OR NOT TO DO

Isaiah 56:5
"Even to them I will give in My house and within My walls a place and a name better than that of sons and daughters; I will give them an everlasting name that shall not be cut off."
NKJV

Today, we visited the Israeli Holocaust Museum "Yad Vashem". Yad Vashem means "hand and a name" in Hebrew. I would encourage everyone to make the trip to Israel at least once, and if you do, be certain not to miss Yad Vashem. It will change you forever.

One thing that should be striking to any Christian is the role the Christian Church played in the Holocaust. Six million Jews were slaughtered including one and a half million children. Where was the church? They were standing aside in silence.

Each day, we are faced with the decision to take an action or not; to speak out or say nothing; to help a need or disregard; to love or not to love. Sin is not only something done but also something not done.

James 4:17 "Therefore, to him who knows to do good and does not do it, to him it is sin." NKJV

Take a moment to pray and reflect. Allow the Holy Spirit to speak to your heart. What have you neglected to do? Now what do you need to do?

Life Lesson: Actions you do not take can be as bad as actions you do take. What you do not say may speak louder than what you do say.

Dear Father,
Thank You for loving me. Lord, speak to my heart the ways I have neglected to serve You in my actions toward others. I am sorry Father. I truly love You and desire to serve You faithfully. Please fill me with wisdom and discernment to make decisions that reflect the truth of Your Word. In Jesus' name, Amen.

JUNE 24
IN WHOM DO WE TRUST?

2 Kings 18:4-8

"He removed the high places and broke the sacred pillars, cut down the wooden image and broke in pieces the bronze serpent that Moses had made; for until those days the children of Israel burned incense to it, and called it Nehushtan. He trusted in the LORD God of Israel, so that after him was none like him among all the kings of Judah, nor who were before him. For he held fast to the LORD; he did not depart from following Him, but kept His commandments, which the LORD had commanded Moses. The LORD was with him; he prospered wherever he went. And he rebelled against the king of Assyria and did not serve him. He subdued the Philistines, as far as Gaza and its territory, from watchtower to fortified city."
NKJV

Having just returned from Israel, I am freshly reminded how man can turn anything into an idol ... even a gift from God. While I was there, I was able to visit some traditional and historical sites. Traditional is code for "it probably did not happen here" while historical means "it probably did happen here". At many of the traditional sites, you will find people "worshipping" the place rather than the God who performed the miracle there. This was the very thing happening here in 2 Kings. The people of Israel had turned the bronze serpent, which God had worked healing miracles through, (Numbers 21:6-8) into an idol.

It's so easy to turn your trust from God to things that God has given you as a blessing. In other words, you love the gift and not the Giver. Money is a big one these days. Is it in 'God we trust' or in 'money we trust'? These present-days are testing where you place your trust.

Psalm 121:1-2 "I will lift up my eyes to the hills — From whence comes my help? My help comes from the LORD, Who made heaven and earth." NKJV

Are you looking to the high places of money worship or are you placing your trust in the Lord God who made heaven and earth? God wants to bless you. He loves to bless His children. He wants you to place your trust in Him and not the world. When you trust Him to provide, He does.

Life Lesson: God is a blessing God and wants to bless His children.

Dear Father,

Thank You for Your love. Lord, I know it is easy for me to be distracted with the things of this world. Help me to keep my focus on Your will for my life. I surrender to You and place all my trust in You to provide. In Jesus' name, Amen.

JUNE 25
GRACE ALONE

Romans 11:6
"And if by grace, then it is no longer of works; otherwise grace is no longer grace. But if it is of works, it is no longer grace; otherwise work is no longer work."
NKJV

Salvation through works is at odds with salvation through faith. Counting on the former, as a matter of course means, we cannot count on the latter. The very nature of 'doing' to earn is in contrast to receiving without merit. So what of those seeking to earn their entrance to heaven based on their works?

Matthew 7:22-23 "Many will say to Me in that day, 'Lord, Lord, have we not prophesied in Your name, cast out demons in Your name, and done many wonders in Your name?' And then I will declare to them, 'I never knew you; depart from Me, you who practice lawlessness!'" NKJV

Why not salvation by a system of works? That, my friend, is an act of 'chesed' (Hebrew for loving-kindness) from our Lord. God knows that in our fallen state we can never do a truly righteous work.

Isaiah 64:6a "But we are all like an unclean thing, and all our righteousness are like filthy rags;" NKJV

There is no other way. It has to be by God's grace through the mechanism of faith, which in itself, is a gift of God (see Ephesians 2). If we could do it ourselves, we would receive glory instead of giving God the glory.

Jesus paid the price so that we wouldn't have to; all we have to do is believe. Two of the most beautiful words in the Bible are, "but God".

Romans 5:8 "But God demonstrates His own love toward us, in that while we were still sinners, Christ died for us." NKJV

Life Lesson: You can either be saved or forgiven through grace or works. You get to choose.
(this is a trick life lesson, salvation is by grace alone)

Dear Father,

Thank You for Your loving-kindness toward me. I am truly grateful that I do not have to earn entrance to heaven based on my works. Thank You that Jesus paid the price. Thank You, Lord, for your grace and mercy. In Jesus' name, Amen.

JUNE 26
TRUST IN THE LORD

2 Kings 18:19
"Then the Rabshakeh said to them, "Say now to Hezekiah, 'Thus says the great king, the king of Assyria:"What confidence is this in which you trust?"
NKJV

It is very easy to begin trusting in the 'things' of this world because of the subtle way they steal our attention away from God. It is because of this subtle infiltration of worldly things that every Christian should take the time to evaluate themselves. Is there something that you give a larger role in your life than God? Has your focus become a kaleidoscope of 'things' preventing you from clearly focusing on serving God? If so, you had better confess to God and turn your gaze toward Him before the subtle deception of accumulation leaves you trusting in the stuff instead of God. Otherwise, there will come a day when you will find yourself spiritually and possibly physically famished.

Life Lesson: We should know who or what we are trusting in. We should trust in the Lord alone.

Dear Father,
Thank You for Your love. Lord, forgive me for the times I have placed my focus on the 'things' in my life rather than You. Give me the discernment and wisdom to see the deception in the things of this world and keep my eyes fixed upon You. I surrender everything to You. In Jesus' name, Amen.

JUNE 27
JESUS SAVES

John 5:7
"The sick man answered Him, "Sir, I have no man to put me into the pool when the water is stirred up; but while I am coming, another steps down before me."
NKJV

During the Cross the Bridge Outreach in Miami we've seen an amazing work of the Lord as hundreds of people have made a decision for Christ. And that's just it - it's a decision. Only Jesus saves. No matter how much I teach and invite, if a person is not willing to call out to Jesus there is nothing I can do. Empty and broken we come before the cross of Jesus, each one of our own accord.

John 5:8-9 "Jesus said to him, "Rise, take up your bed and walk." And immediately the man was made well, took up his bed, and walked." NKJV

I can bring the message, but I cannot put someone into the "pool" of living water. No man can but one - the Son of Man, Jesus Christ. I will take advantage of every opportunity to "stir up the water" but only Jesus can heal the heart.

Life Lesson: Only Jesus can save.

Dear Father,
Thank You.
In Jesus' name. Amen.

JUNE 28
GO TO CHURCH

2 Kings 19:1
"And so it was, when King Hezekiah heard it, that he tore his clothes, covered himself with sackcloth, and went into the house of the LORD."
NKJV

Many people find themselves in difficult circumstances... whether in their family, their finances or some other facet of life. King Hezekiah faced a huge crisis situation with the Assyrian army besieging Judah. His actions give us a wonderful model of what we should do when times turn tough. Read the verse above. What did Hezekiah do? He went to church.

Far too often, when Christians encounter difficulties, instead of going to the church, they seek comfort and counsel in the world. That, my friend, will only compound the problem. Go to church. Worship God. Seek counsel from godly people. Pray. Don't listen to your enemy, the devil.

How big is your God? Now, how big is your problem? If you think your problem is too big for God to handle, you need to think again. God created the universe and He created you. He chooses kings and cuts down nations. I guarantee you that He will overcome your problems.

Psalm 121:7-8 "The LORD shall preserve you from all evil; He shall preserve your soul. The LORD shall preserve your going out and your coming in From this time forth, and even forevermore." NKJV

Life Lesson: We should make a commitment to go to church.

Dear Father,
Thank You for Your love. Thank You that I do not have to fear or worry because You will preserve me. Though this world would seek to destroy me, You have surrounded me in Your love and protection. I give to you every trouble in my life. In Jesus' name, Amen.

JUNE 29
LET'S GO

Romans 11:13-14

"For I speak to you Gentiles; inasmuch as I am an apostle to the Gentiles, I magnify my ministry, if by any means I may provoke to jealousy those who are my flesh and save some of them."
NKJV

Real Christianity has to be about reaching others or it is not real. Jesus reached out to others with the Good News of His coming. If you are to be like Christ, then you also have to be reaching out to others with the Good News. Jesus said go and reach the world. You are to take the church to the world, not just bring the world to church. This is the heart behind Cross the Bridge...to take the church to the world; to look outside the church instead of inside. I want to go where the unsaved are instead of waiting for them to come to us. I would love for you to partner with me in this. We just held a massive Cross the Bridge Outreach event in South Beach, Miami and saw over 165 people commit their lives to Jesus. That is 165 people that may never have stepped foot inside a church building, but were willing to come to listen to awesome music and hear a simple evangelistic message they needed to hear. Cross the Bridge Ministries not only reaches through outreach events but also through our television, radio, and social media...speaking to people right where they are and not waiting for them to come where we are. Your partnership counts. Every prayer, every dollar and every moment you are willing to dedicate to our shared endeavor will see a life changed... maybe even your own.

Life Lesson: God's plan for you includes you reaching other people.

Dear Father,
Thank You for Your love for each person on this earth. Lord, it's not Your will that any should be left out, but that everyone should have the choice to make; think about life, think about Jesus. I ask you to bless Cross the Bridge Ministries and show me how I can actively partner with them in reaching the world. I pray this in Jesus' name. Amen.

JUNE 30
DON'T WAIT FOR THE RAIN

Romans 11:25
"For I do not desire, brethren, that you should be ignorant of this mystery, lest you should be wise in your own opinion, that blindness in part has happened to Israel until the fullness of the Gentiles has come in."
NKJV

"The fullness of the Gentiles has come in." The New Living Translation puts it this way, "this will only last until the complete number of Gentiles comes to the Lord." So, there are a fixed number of Gentiles who will come to the Lord and then that is it...no more.

Genesis chapters 6-8 is the record of Noah building an ark as God commanded, which spared him and his family from God's judgment on the whole earth. The Bible says that once the ark was loaded with animals, Noah and his family were inside the ark for seven days before the flood waters came upon the earth. Now, think about this...Noah, over the course of a hundred years, built a giant covered barge on dry land in preparation for a world-wide flood. "Where's the flood, Noah?" "Looks like rain, Noah, you better hurry!" "You're crazy, Noah!" Can you imagine the ribbing he was taking? Those who mocked him were the same people banging on the door when the floods hit. Unfortunately, the door to the ark had been closed by God. They had made their decision, and God honored it. Things, as they are now, will not last forever. The door is open now. There will come a day when that door is shut. Don't wait until it rains friend, it may be too late.

Life Lesson: Things will not be as they are now forever.

Dear Father,
Thank You for the gift of salvation through Your Son Jesus Christ. Your love is clearly revealed to me by the prophetic truths of the scriptures. Thank You for Your infinite grace and mercy toward me. Lord, through Your Word, you have reminded me afresh of the importance of living ready. I am surrendered to Your will to do the work of the ministry. In Jesus' name, Amen.

JULY 1
PERSPECTIVES

2 Kings 21:8-9
8 "and I will not make the feet of Israel wander anymore from the land which I gave their fathers — only if they are careful to do according to all that I have commanded them, and according to all the law that My servant Moses commanded them."9 But they paid no attention, and Manasseh seduced them to do more evil than the nations whom the LORD had destroyed before the children of Israel. NKJV

In looking at this chapter about the reign of Hezekiah in Judah, we see some of the fruit of his pride. God had sent the prophet Isaiah to tell him that God's plan was for him to die. Hezekiah then appealed to the Lord to let him live. God heard his prayer and allowed his request. As a result, a series of events began that led Judah to destruction and its people to be carted away. Had Hezekiah accepted God's will, all this would have been averted.

From our perspective, God's will seems harsh at times. Sometimes, it may even seem absurd or impossible. Friends, that is from our limited perspective. God's perspective is not limited. He knows what the best is for us and it is His desire to give it to us; but He will not force it on us. When you pray to God, make your requests and then go with God's flow of what He is trying to do. Then, you will know the goodness of God's will in your life.

Jeremiah 29:11 "For I know the thoughts that I think toward you, says the LORD, thoughts of peace and not of evil, to give you a future and a hope" NKJV

Life Lesson: Desire God's best for your life and don't demand your own way.

Dear Father,
Thank You for loving me. In all things, Your desire toward me is good and perfect. Sometimes, I want my own way and I try to force it. Please forgive me and when I do it again, please send a reminder to me that Your way is better than my way. I pray this in Jesus' name. Amen.

JULY 2
SON-HAS-RISEN

Romans 11:30-32
"For as you were once disobedient to God, yet have now obtained mercy through their disobedience, even so these also have now been disobedient, that through the mercy shown you they also may obtain mercy. For God has committed them all to disobedience, that He might have mercy on all." NKJV

God offers all mankind His mercy. Who are we to put limits on His mercy? When we choose not to minister the Gospel to another, we do just that. The definition of mercy is that you do not receive what you deserve. As we remember the resurrection of Jesus Christ, let us remember that in no way did we deserve God's merciful action. By no means did we merit Jesus' suffering at the hands of the unrighteous...that He would bear the tremendous weight of our own sin on that cross. Through no power of our own, these events unfolded through the benevolent and merciful loving-kindness of a Father which many want to push away. Let us commit ourselves to making sure that everyone hears God's message of mercy to the broken. May all mankind hear the Gospel and make their choice. Let us brace ourselves as we begin each new day, embrace our God given duties and make sure that the whole world hears.

Life Lesson: God is a merciful God.

Dear Father,
Thank You for being my God of mercy. I believe that Jesus is alive and accept Him as Lord of my life. May I live only for You. Purify my heart with Your truth and guide me in the way of Your will for my life so that I may always do what is pleasing in Your sight. In Jesus' name, Amen.

JULY 3
MOMENTS

2 Kings 20:1
"In those days Hezekiah was sick and near death. And Isaiah the prophet, the son of Amoz, went to him and said to him, "Thus says the LORD: 'Set your house in order, for you shall die, and not live.'"
NKJV

What if God told you that you were going to die? People every day are informed by doctors and juries they have only years, months, days, or even moments left to live. Those could be moments of regret or moments of satisfaction...it all depends on what we 'make' of moments God allots to us. Make? Yes, God has given to each one of us creativity, time, a sense of right and wrong, and free will. What we do with these raw materials is up to us. Most of us dole out the moments on frivolous, self-centered activities. Sometimes, it takes moments of shock to make us change course.

Do something for the Lord or do something for the world? The first is a path leading to satisfaction and the latter is a highway leading to regret. It has been said, "Life is not measured by the number of breaths we take, but by the moments that take our breath away." Life is much more than just a measure of our days. It is what we do for the Lord and that, my friend, will last forever. What if God told you that you were going to die? Well...He has.

Hebrews 9:27 "And as it is appointed for men to die once, but after this the judgment," NKJV

What are you doing with your moments? Are they going to last?

Life Lesson: There are things worse than death.

Dear Father,
Thank You for Your love. Thank You for the moments You have given to me. Please forgive me for times when I have selfishly squandered those moments. Please give me the courage to make the most of the time and abilities You have given me. In Jesus' name. Amen.

JULY 4
FREE CHOICE

2 Kings 22:1-2
"Josiah was eight years old when he became king, and he reigned thirty-one years in Jerusalem. His mother's name was Jedidah the daughter of Adaiah of Bozkath. And he did what was right in the sight of the LORD, and walked in all the ways of his father David; he did not turn aside to the right hand or to the left."
NKJV

Josiah's grandfather, Manasseh, and his father, Amon, were two of the worst kings of Judah. They killed prophets, sacrificed their children, and rebuilt places of idol worship - even placing them in the house of the Lord. Josiah chose to do differently. He chose to walk in the ways of the Lord. That is just it, friend. We get to choose. People will say that you are doomed to follow in the sins of your father. Josiah proves that is not the case. You may be predisposed to those sins, but you get to make the choice. Maybe you watched your father get drunk every day of his life - that does not mean you have to. Even when you choose not to walk in the sins of your mother or father, you will still have to deal with it just as Josiah did. You will have to make the decision of whether you follow or choose something better.

1 Corinthians 10:13 "No temptation has overtaken you except such as is common to man; but God is faithful, who will not allow you to be tempted beyond what you are able, but with the temptation will also make the way of escape, that you may be able to bear it." NKJV

Maybe your father followed Jesus and lived his life for the Lord. If so, what an awesome privilege; those are great footsteps to follow. For others, their childhood was full of parental failures and disappointments. The trail blazed was bleak. Be encouraged. You may face the temptation my friend, but God has provided the means by which you can overcome and choose a better way. It would have been easier for Josiah to continue in the way that was paved by his father and grandfather; instead, he chose a better path. What path will you choose?

Life Lesson: Christianity offers you the power to make a free choice.

Dear Father,
Thank You for loving me even in my failures. Thank You for forgiving me. Help me to make wise decisions by looking to Your Word to receive Your counsel and instruction. In Jesus' name, Amen.

JULY 5
LIVE FOR HIM

Romans 12:1
"I beseech you therefore, brethren, by the mercies of God, that you present your bodies a living sacrifice, holy, acceptable to God, which is your reasonable service."
NKJV

In the verse above, the Apostle Paul pleads with us to be fully devoted to God in our lives because He gave Himself fully for us. Jesus died for us; therefore, we should live for Him. You know that... right? Are you doing it? Wisdom is knowledge put to work. To know the Bible should be to do the Bible. Worship, service and sacrifice are things all Christians should be engaged in. The word for reasonable, in this verse, is the Greek word logikos, which means logical. It is logical that since Jesus gave His life for us, we should be willing to devote our lives to Him. That word service? It is latreia in Greek or avodah in Hebrew, which means service in the temple. To sum it up, service is worship. Worship is not just the music before the teaching at church. Worship is a way of life. Worship is a pattern of living. It is serving and giving. It is being a steward of the things God has given you and leveraging them to produce good things for the kingdom of God. This is the work that Jesus wants to perform in you. He wants to change you from the inside out - if you will let Him. This is Paul's wish in the first couple of verses of Romans 12 and it is my prayer for you as well. Will you allow Jesus to transform you from the inside out?

Life Lesson: Jesus died for us so we should live for Him.

Dear Father,
Thank You for loving me so much that You would send Your Son, Jesus to die for my sins. I give You my life. Please transform me from the inside out that I may have the mind of Christ to worship You with all that You have made me a steward of. In Jesus' name, Amen.

JULY 6
BE A DOER

2 Kings 23:3-4
"Then the king stood by a pillar and made a covenant before the LORD, to follow the LORD and to keep His commandments and His testimonies and His statutes, with all his heart and all his soul, to perform the words of this covenant that were written in this book. And all the people took a stand for the covenant. And the king commanded Hilkiah the high priest, the priests of the second order, and the doorkeepers, to bring out of the temple of the LORD all the articles that were made for Baal, for Asherah, and for all the host of heaven; and he burned them outside Jerusalem in the fields of Kidron, and carried their ashes to Bethel."
NKJV

I've met many Christians who know the Bible inside and out. They can quote scripture after scripture, word for word with verse references and even comment on the meaning. I've met fewer who actually do the Bible. This astounds me. What if a 16 year old kid memorizes the driver's exam study book and aces the exam, but then goes out and runs every stop light he comes across? He's going to get hurt and will probably hurt someone else in the process. The same is true with the Word of God. Think of the Christians on street corners with sandwich boards and megaphones hardening the hearts of everyone around them. They have the "head knowledge" but they have not made the "heart application". To the other extreme are Christians who use church as a social club. They nod their heads and "amen" the pastor, but their day to day life speaks nothing of following Jesus. Solid biblical teaching assigns the hearer the responsibility to act on what they learn. Someone who goes to Med School but begs on the street is not really a doctor. They may carry the title, but they don't do the work. So, where do you fall in this? Are you a Bible doer or just a Bible hearer?

Life Lesson: We need to be acting on the Word of God.

Dear Father,
Thank You for loving me. Please forgive me for times when I have failed to live by Your Word. I thank You for giving me Your Bible. Help me to make doing what You tell me the priority in my life. Help me to love You and to love others. In Jesus' name, Amen.

JULY 7
HEALTHY BODY

Romans 12:4-6a
"For as we have many members in one body, but all the members do not have the same function, so we, being many, are one body in Christ, and individually members of one another. Having then gifts differing according to the grace that is given to us, let us use them:"
NKJV

On occasion, it is essential for me to communicate in "Christianese" to make a point and this is one of those times. When I say "Body of Christ", that is Christianese for "the church". I am not talking about the building, but the assembly of individuals in the building and in an even wider sense, all Christians in the world. Just as a nose is a specialized ingredient to the whole being, so is each person uniquely gifted to fill a certain role in this "body". When all the parts of your own body are doing their job well, we say your body is "healthy". Likewise, when each individual is using his/her gifts to the benefit of the whole body, the church is healthy.

Discord within the body is detrimental. Let me explain. Do you realize that every time you eat a meal, you hold a potentially deadly weapon in your hand? What if you were eating a meal and your hand staged a coup against the brain? Well, obviously your hand is not suited to manage all the processes of your body like the brain is, so your body would die. In that case, it would be better to remove your hand - as it has become cancerous to the rest of the body. In this manner, God, in His divine wisdom, established an order within the church that enables each one of us to minister our gifts in the manner best suited for us and for the body. If you operate outside of your gifts, you are going to be frustrated. If you do not use your gifts at all, it will not only be frustrating, but you will also be in sin.

James 4:17 "Remember, It is sin to know what you ought to do and then not do it." NLT

When everyone uses their talents and gifts to serve one another, it is a beautiful thing. The body functions the way it should and the Gospel message of Jesus Christ goes forth. I am thankful for everyone who so generously gives of their time and their finances here at The Bridge. We have been extremely effective in reaching the world, and I look forward to engaging even more people as effective parts of this body.

Life Lesson: We all play a different part in the Body of Christ.

Dear Father,

Thank You for blessing me with Your Word. I want whatever You want to do in my life. I desire to use the talents and gifts You have given me for the purpose of edifying others and building up the church. Lord, I want to put off the fear of man, insecurities or whatever else would keep me from obeying and serving You. In Jesus' name, Amen.

JULY 8
REBEL OR RADICAL?

2 Kings 24:1-2

"In his days Nebuchadnezzar king of Babylon came up, and Jehoiakim became his vassal for three years. Then he turned and rebelled against him. And the LORD sent against him raiding bands of Chaldeans, bands of Syrians, bands of Moabites, and bands of the people of Ammon; He sent them against Judah to destroy it, according to the word of the LORD which He had spoken by His servants the prophets."
NKJV

I've heard many people refer to Jesus as a rebel. He was anything but a rebel. He was radical - but never a rebel. Had Jesus been rebellious, He would have been sinful. Jesus humbled and submitted Himself to God, to men, and to government.

Romans 13:1-2 "Let every soul be subject to the governing authorities. For there is no authority except from God, and the authorities that exist are appointed by God. Therefore whoever resists the authority resists the ordinance of God, and those who resist will bring judgment on themselves."
NKJV

The Bible informs us that God Himself places all authority and we should submit to authority. In 2 Kings, we see the fulfillment of seeds that were planted years before. God does not honor rebellion. He honors obedience. Each one of us has rebellion in our hearts. We have a choice. We can honor God with our obedience or allow rebellion to rule our lives. Either way we reap a harvest.

Galatians 6:7 "Do not be deceived, God is not mocked; for whatever a man sows, that he will also reap." NKJV

The harvest we reap not only affects us, but also affects our families, friends, employers and more. If we reap a harvest of blessings from God, those around us get to enjoy blessings. If we reap a harvest of bad consequences, those around us suffer along with us. Examine what is going on in your life, in your family, in your employment. Look at the faces of your family and friends and consider the question - Have you or are you sowing good seeds?

Life Lesson: Be very careful with your rebellion or anyone else's.

Dear Father,

Thank You for Your Son Jesus. Because of His submission before You, I have the gift of eternal life. Just as Jesus submitted Himself to You, I also submit myself to You. Help me to sow seeds of the Spirit rather than seeds of the flesh. Lord, let no rebellion rule in my heart and empower me to be a blessing to those I love. In Jesus' name, Amen.

JULY 9
TIGGER

Romans 12:11
"not lagging in diligence, fervent in spirit, serving the Lord;"
NKJV

I have spoken in the past about being a spiritual 'Eeyore' versus being a spiritual 'Tigger'. Eeyore, from the old Winnie the Pooh children's novels, is an old gray donkey who mopes about saying such bright and cheery things as, "We can't all, and some of us don't. That's all there is to it," and "When someone says 'How-do-you-do', just say you didn't." Tigger, on the other hand, is a spring-tailed ball of enthusiasm that is always bouncing about and throwing himself into life with gusto.

There are Christians that go about their lives as spiritual Eeyores. Don't do that! These folks mope about with all the enthusiasm of a concrete block serving their risen King as if to seem spiritually burdened, but they really come across as spiritually lacking. Now, now, Pastor David...you're just getting off on a tangent. If you are truly spiritual, you will be suffering...after all, we are called to take on the attitude of Christ in 1 Peter 4, right? Well, yes, that is correct, but let me ask you...What do you think is the attitude of Christ?

Jude 24 "Now to Him who is able to keep you from stumbling, and to present you faultless before the presence of His glory with exceeding joy," NKJV

John 15:11-12 "These things I have spoken to you, that My joy may remain in you, and that your joy may be full." NKJV

Friend, if you think your spiritual mope will make others want to come to eternal life in Christ, you are sadly mistaken. People want to be happy and seek joyful fulfillment in their lives. If they observe you, Christian, flogging yourself with pity, they will not want what you have. Jesus in His earthly ministry attracted crowds. There was something about Him that they wanted...the joy of living completely and totally for God. Got joy?

Life Lesson: We should be passionate about our spiritual lives.

Dear Father,
Thank You for Your gift of eternal life. Lord, please forgive me for the times I mope around meaninglessly. I know it is not being a good witness to the lives of others. Give me the power to stand joyfully in the Spirit expectantly grasping all life in Christ has to offer. In Jesus' name, Amen.

JULY 10
DRIFTWOOD

2 Kings 25:8-10

"And in the fifth month, on the seventh day of the month (which was the nineteenth year of King Nebuchadnezzar king of Babylon), Nebuzaradan the captain of the guard, a servant of the king of Babylon, came to Jerusalem. He burned the house of the LORD and the king's house; all the houses of Jerusalem, that is, all the houses of the great, he burned with fire. And all the army of the Chaldeans who were with the captain of the guard broke down the walls of Jerusalem all around." NKJV

After years of slowly drifting away from the Lord, we reach this sad chapter in the history of Israel. The first temple is destroyed, the walls are broken down and the city of God, Jerusalem, is sacked.

Recently, our President made the decision not to participate in the National Day of Prayer and prior to that, he had declared that the United States was not a Christian nation. Maybe those things were shocking to many, but it really was just recognition of the obvious. The United States has forgotten her Christian heritage. The decline of our country's heritage didn't happen suddenly; rather it had been a gradual decline, with consequences ever increasing in severity.

We cannot lay all of this at the feet of our elected officials. Let us look at ourselves. Friend, have you drifted? Did you once have daily devotions and memory verses? Do you attend church like you once did? Was there a time when you were faithful in tithing? What about the spiritual stewardship over your wife and children? Take a moment and reflect. Where have you drifted? Where have you allowed concessions to creep in? Be careful friend. When we drift from God, we also drift from His protection and provision. Our concessions yield a much bigger crop than we realize...perhaps spanning many generations. What is the spiritual legacy you will be handing to those who follow you? These are weighty things, but we must not back away from them. This nation is made up of individual families each serving someone or something. It starts in our homes. If we commit to honoring God in our homes and serving Him, God will place His hand of blessing back on us.

Psalm 33:12 "Blessed is the nation whose God is the LORD, The people He has chosen as His own inheritance." NKJV

Life Lesson: When we drift from God, we also drift from His protection and provision.

Dear Father,

Thank You for loving me and my family. Please forgive me for concessions I have made. Lord, help me to be a strong spiritual leader for my family and reclaim spiritual ground I have handed over to Satan. I pray for our President and all of our government officials. Grant them wisdom and place Godly men and women in their lives who will not shun from speaking into their decisions. In Jesus' name, Amen.

JULY 11
WHAT ARE THE EXCEPTIONS?

Romans 13:1
"Let every soul be subject to the governing authorities. For there is no authority except from God, and the authorities that exist are appointed by God."
NKJV

There are some verses that I love and others that, quite frankly, disturb me. All of scripture is given for our instruction.

2 Timothy 3:16-17 "All Scripture is given by inspiration of God, and is profitable for doctrine, for reproof, for correction, for instruction in righteousness, that the man of God may be complete, thoroughly equipped for every good work." NKJV

We aren't to observe some scripture and then sweep others under the rug. In Romans 13, we are instructed to be subject to authority - but what is the limit? What are the exceptions? There is something very telling about ourselves in the moment we read this verse. We try to think about what the exceptions could be. I know you did - I did too. I do not like paying taxes. I can't drive 55! When this scripture was written, the Roman government was pretty messed up. Nero was the Emperor and he would torture Christians – even burn them alive as living candles to illuminate his garden. Yet Paul says, we should submit to every ordinance. Jesus could have summoned legions of angels, yet He submitted to Pilate. David had several opportunities to take Saul out and rightfully claim the throne, but he didn't. Certainly, there are times when civil disobedience is called for, but those times are rare. If the government told me I could not teach the Bible anymore, I would be in jail! OK, that's an extreme circumstance but the truth is that when we submit, we honor God. Is there an area of your life where you harbor rebellion? Take some time and seek the Lord about it. What is He telling you?

Life Lesson: We should submit to authority.

Dear Father,
Thank You for giving us Your Bible. Lord, if there is any place in my life that I am being rebellious or harboring a rebellious attitude, please reveal it to me. Please teach me to be in submission to the authority you place over me. In Jesus' name, Amen.

JULY 12
ONE OF A KIND

1 Chronicles 1:50-54
"And when Baal-Hanan died, Hadad reigned in his place; and the name of his city was Pai. His wife's name was Mehetabel the daughter of Matred, the daughter of Mezahab. Hadad died also. And the chiefs of Edom were Chief Timnah, Chief Aliah, Chief Jetheth, Chief Aholibamah, Chief Elah, Chief Pinon, Chief Kenaz, Chief Teman, Chief Mibzar, Chief Magdiel, and Chief Iram. These were the chiefs of Edom."
NKJV

Remembering where you came from and where you are going makes up your individual one-of-a-kind testimony. There is power in the testimony of your life. Revelation 12 talks about believers overcoming by the blood of the Lamb and the word of their testimony. So what if your past does not include the seedier things of life - the Bible is clear that we were all on a death row sentence. Jesus died on the cross for your sins. Through His grace and the faith-gift of God, He saves you. Now, you are a child of God - a priest and a king. There are two people in the Bible who are called both a priest and king - Jesus and you. Now, you are saved and will spend eternity with God. Friend, in a world that is wracked with fear and uncertainty, people need to hear your testimony. Share it and talk about it. Share not in a prideful or bragging way, but out of the joy of your heart. Your testimony could be the very thing that leads someone else to come to Jesus. It might be what they have been waiting for.

Life Lesson: Remember where you came from, who you are and where you are going.

Dear Father,
Thank You for the gift of Your Son. I am so grateful for the grace and mercy You have given me. Lord, I want to be a vessel used to glorify Your name. Give me the boldness to share my testimony without fear and uncertainty. Give me the spirit of humility so that I may be used to minister in the lives of others. In Jesus' name, Amen.

JULY 13
LOVE DEBT

Romans 13:8
"Owe no one anything except to love one another, for he who loves another has fulfilled the law."
NKJV

The law tells us not to do anything bad. Love says to do something good. We are all in love-debt to one another. When does it end? Never - We should always owe one another love.

Matthew 22:37-40 "Jesus said to him, "'You shall love the LORD your God with all your heart, with all your soul, and with all your mind.' This is the first and great commandment. And the second is like it: 'You shall love your neighbor as yourself.' On these two commandments hang all the Law and the Prophets." NKJV

God is the initiator. "We love Him because He first loved us" (1 John 4:19). Now, it's our turn to be initiators of love - love starters. Love is a commitment. Do things that demonstrate your love for others. Help others rack up their love-debt. Look at everything you do and question whether it's out of love. You might find you need to make some adjustments. Let's kick Christianity up a notch and take following Jesus and loving people to a whole new level.

Life Lesson: We should love one another.

Dear Father,
Thank You for Your love, for Your grace and for Your mercy. Lord, You freely give these things to me. Help me to also be quick to show love, grace and mercy to others. Please forgive me for times when I have hoarded Your love to myself instead of opening it up to others. In Jesus' name, Amen.

JULY 14
GOD CHOOSES PEOPLE

1 Chronicles 2:1-2
"These were the sons of Israel: Reuben, Simeon, Levi, Judah, Issachar, Zebulun, Dan, Joseph, Benjamin, Naphtali, Gad, and Asher."
NKJV

Here we have a list of the twelve tribes of Israel. Almost every time the twelve tribes are listed, either they are in a different order or a tribe is left out. Why? I do not know. I could speculate, but it is just that... nothing conclusive. I am glad there are mysteries in the Bible. I am happy that not everything is spelled out. I love the treasure hunt! When God reveals something new to me that had previously been hidden, it is just an awesome moment.

Proverbs 25:2 "It is the glory of God to conceal a matter, But the glory of kings is to search out a matter." NKJV

Although I love the search, I understand that I do not have to know 'why' because it is God's prerogative. The same goes with the people God uses. I do not always understand how or why God is using a certain person in ministry, but He does not have to explain it to me. There is a great mystery in our free will and God's predestination. How does it work? I do not know and I am fine with that. Does it worry you? If it does, here is the solution... abide in Christ. If you abide in Christ, you do not have to worry. Abide in Christ and let God do the rest. Then, my friend, God will use you in mighty ways that will amaze you.

Life Lesson: God chooses people.

Dear Father,
Thank You for choosing me to know and experience Your grace. I thank You for the opportunity to live in Christ and I look forward to those things You have planned for me... even the things that are yet a mystery. I do not know what those things are, but I do know that they are good. Thank You. In Jesus' name, Amen.

JULY 15
RAISING CHILDREN

1 Chronicles 3:1-3
"Now these were the sons of David who were born to him in Hebron: The firstborn was Amnon, by Ahinoam the Jezreelitess; the second, Daniel, by Abigail the Carmelitess;2 the third, Absalom the son of Maacah, the daughter of Talmai, king of Geshur; the fourth, Adonijah the son of Haggith;3 the fifth, Shephatiah, by Abital; the sixth, Ithream, by his wife Eglah."
NKJV

David had eight wives, twenty-one children, ten concubines and their children. That is a lot of children with a lot of responsibility. Although David was an incredible military leader, he was not a very good leader with his children. There are several instances recorded in the Bible where David should have disciplined his children, but he did not. We see the fruit of his slack in discipline with his son, Absalom, who led a rebellion against David.

Friend, Christian families are under attack. Your home is a battleground for Satan. He does not bother with the crack houses or bars because there is no struggle there - he has won those fronts. He wants to infiltrate Christian homes and cause strife and division. He wants to subvert and destroy what God has ordained. This is why it is so important that we look to God for help in raising and disciplining our children. It is time for men to take a stand and be spiritual leaders in their homes. Satan likes nothing more than to find a Christian home with a weak spiritual leader. Father - Mother - that means, if you have slacked off in attending church or neglected your prayer and devotional time, you have placed your family in the line of fire. But wait, you may ask. If I do these things, does that mean that we are safe from attack? Absolutely not! It does mean, however, that you and your family's foundation are strong for when the attack does come. Take a moment to pray. Are you being the strong spiritual leader in your children's lives? Are you attentive to what they are doing and who they are friends with? Are you paying attention to what the Holy Spirit is telling you about your children? If you are not certain, you need to ask God to point out the areas where you are slack.

Life Lesson: We should ask for God's help in raising and disciplining our children.

Dear Father,
Thank You for the salvation of Your Son Jesus. Lord, I give all praise and glory to You for my family. Bless my family. Help me to lead my family with a strong foundation, and help me to lead my children to You. Lord, give me courage when situations within my family are difficult. Help us to be long-suffering and gentle toward one another and fill us with your Spirit of peace and love. In Jesus' name, Amen.

JULY 16
DOES IT MATTER?

Romans 14:1
"Receive one who is weak in the faith, but not to disputes over doubtful things."
NKJV

A few years ago, there was this argument about "WWJD - What would Jesus drive?" Would He drive an SUV or a golf cart? The whole thing was laughable, but the sad part was that it created a distraction from the message of the Gospel.

There are always going to be people who just want to argue. From Bible versions to the style of worship music, from spiritual gifts to the day of the week you worship, there is always some point of contention that they want to focus on. What gets forgotten in the argument? The very thing we are called to do - be salt and light - show the world Jesus. Do not play that game. Do not waste time with petty arguments.

Titus 3:9-11 "But avoid foolish disputes, genealogies, contentions, and strivings about the law; for they are unprofitable and useless. Reject a divisive man after the first and second admonition, knowing that such a person is warped and sinning, being self-condemned." NKJV

Some things are very clear from scripture and well... some things are not. How we are saved is very clear. The kind of car to drive is not in the scriptures. We should major on the majors and minor on the minors. Christians love to argue about the Bible. I wonder why that is? Could it be that it distracts them from the parts of the Bible that convict them? Friend, in love, if you are one of these people, you need to go to God and refocus on what is important.

Life Lesson: We should not waste time arguing about stuff that really doesn't matter.

Dear Father,
Thank You for the salvation of Your Son Jesus. Lord, help me to not engage in divisive conversation or arguing. I recognize that petty disagreements and arguing can drive a wedge between me and others. More importantly, I realize that my bickering can confuse those who do not already know You. I ask You to forgive me for the times I have not been sensitive to this. Help me to start fighting for the souls of the lost by laying down my disagreements at Your feet. In Jesus' name, Amen.

JULY 17
WHERE'S YOUR CONFIDENCE?

Philippians 3:3
"For we are the circumcision, who worship God in the Spirit, rejoice in Christ Jesus, and have no confidence in the flesh,"
NKJV

How often have you heard this – "As you know, the good book says, 'God helps those who help themselves.'" No, it does not! Nowhere in the Bible do we read this statement! In fact, the Bible tells us we should reject selfishness and serve others. We should lay aside our own wants and desires and seek the Lord's will in our life.

Psalm 118:8 says, "It is better to trust in the LORD than to put confidence in man." NKJV

Where do you place your confidence? Do you find yourself placing your hope in people or in God?

Life Lesson: We should trust in the Lord for our help.

Dear Father,
Thank You for Your Son, Jesus. Lord, I do not want to have any confidence in my flesh. I humbly come before you and admit that I have been selfish. Give me the strength to place my hope in You daily. In Jesus' name, Amen.

JULY 18
IMITATE ME?

Romans 14:7
"For none of us lives to himself, and no one dies to himself."
NKJV

Kids... I could probably end this devotion after that one word because we all know how kids imitate what they see around them. I will never forget one time, when I was driving in traffic, and someone cut in front of me. From the back seat of the car I hear, "Idiot." My kids were riding in the back seat of the car with me. Where do you think they learned that? They learned that through observation. It would be great if it were just our kids, but it goes deeper than that. You see, your friends, your co-workers, your neighbors, people you don't even know are watching your reactions. When they see a follower of Jesus who is sold out for Christ, living free of legalism and bondage of the world, they are drawn to Jesus. When they see a follower of Jesus living for 'self' and the world, they have no problem rejecting Jesus because it allows them to play the hypocrite card.

Our lives affect people in ways we may never know. The words we speak, the places we go and the things we watch all reap something. What is the harvest of your life?

Life Lesson: Our lives influence others, so we should not just do whatever we please.

Dear Father,
Thank You for loving me. Thank You for Your grace and mercy. Lord, I am sorry for the times I have not used good judgment around friends or family. Give me the wisdom and discernment to live my life as a disciple of Christ. Help me be the hands and feet of Your Word. May I represent You in all the things I say or do. In Jesus' name, Amen.

JULY 19
WHO IS AFFECTED?

1 Chronicles 4:10
"And Jabez called on the God of Israel saying, "Oh, that You would bless me indeed, and enlarge my territory, that Your hand would be with me, and that You would keep me from evil, that I may not cause pain!" So God granted him what he requested."
NKJV

It is a fact. Sin always brings sadness. Someone is going to suffer for your sin. Oh yeah, you will certainly suffer, but what about those around you? They are affected by your sin. If you have a picture of your spouse or kids, pull it out and look at it. Is it worth it? That little piece of leaven that you have tucked away in some secret place... what is it worth to you? Your spouse is affected by it. Your children are affected by it. Your household could be facing devastation and destruction like you never thought possible. Sin has brought down whole kingdoms, and it can certainly bring down your house. What do you do? How do you stop? Pray to God and confess. Seek biblical counseling from your church. Faithfully attend teachings and serve at your church.

Hebrews 12:1 "Therefore, since we are surrounded by such a huge crowd of witnesses to the life of faith, let us strip off every weight that slows us down, especially the sin that so easily trips us up. And let us run with endurance the race God has set before us." NLT

Life Lesson: Sin always brings sadness.

Dear Father,
Thank You for loving me. Please forgive me for the times I have allowed my flesh to govern my way of thinking. Forgive me where I have imposed suffering upon others. I want my life to be a living testimony to my family, friends and co-workers. Nothing is more important to me than living out Your Word in my life. Give me the power to choose carefully how I live out my daily walk. In Jesus' name, Amen.

JULY 20
ACCOUNTABILITY

Romans 14:12
"So then each of us shall give account of himself to God."
NKJV

This is a humbling verse. Here's another one:

James 3:1 "My brethren, let not many of you become teachers, knowing that we shall receive a stricter judgment." NKJV

I am accountable to God. As a teacher, I am accountable for every word I speak, every thought and every action... I am accountable to God. Spiritual leaders such as, pastors, elders, teachers, husbands and parents are accountable to God. Do you fall into one of these categories? Be humbled if God has placed you as a Godly influence in someone's life. Make sure you have Godly influence in your life. I have Godly men around me that have the ability to speak into my life. We all need that. If you are missing that, maybe you need to put yourself in a place where you have accountability with others. One of those places is serving at church alongside others who will hold you to your Christian walk. Who are the spiritual leaders in your life?

Life Lesson: Each one of us will give an account of our lives to God.

Dear Father,
Thank You for loving me. Thank You for the gift of Your Son. Lord, forgive me for not being discerning in my actions or in the words I speak. Give me the discernment and wisdom to make the godly decisions You have entrusted to me. In Jesus' name, Amen.

JULY 21
PERFECT PEACE

James 3:17-18
"But the wisdom that is from above is first pure, then peaceable, gentle, willing to yield, full of mercy and good fruits, without partiality and without hypocrisy. Now the fruit of righteousness is sown in peace by those who make peace."
NKJV

There is a special peace that can come only from the Lord. You probably remember what you felt like as a child after watching a creepy movie and later that night when you sheepishly peered around every dark corner. It brought up a fear of what's around the next turn, didn't it? Did you carry that fear into your adult life... would you admit it if you did? We all have our moments when things are going wrong and we think about how much worse it could get... instead of thinking on the One in Whose loving grip we endure. In the absence of trust in God we are left with a fear of life.

Isaiah 26:3 "You will keep in perfect peace all who trust in You, whose thoughts are fixed on You! Trust in the LORD always, for the LORD GOD is the eternal Rock." NLT

Do you have peace... or do you go about life anxiously awaiting the next problem or conflict? In light of Isaiah 26:3 what should you do? How do you demonstrate your trust in God? Do you demonstrate it by talking to Him in prayer (Philippians 4:6-9; Hebrews 4:16)? Do you demonstrate it by seeking godly counsel (1Timothy 3:16-17; Proverbs 13:10)? Do you place your next step firmly in His hands (Proverbs 3:5-6; 16:3)?

Life Lesson: Peace is not the absence of conflict but the presence of God.

Dear Father,
Thank You for loving me. Thank You that I cannot be removed from the promise of Your Salvation. Show me how to live in the peaceful comfort of Your hands. I give to You my fears and my circumstances. Help me to trust in You with all my heart. In Jesus' name, Amen.

JULY 22
ENCOURAGE OTHERS

Romans 14:19
"Therefore let us pursue the things which make for peace and the things by which one may edify another."
NKJV

Have you ever seen two kids building sandcastles together in the sand? Usually, one of the kids likes to build while the other one comes by and stomps it... especially if they are siblings. One builds up and the other takes joy in tearing down. Why? Mostly, it is for the reaction. Christians can do this as well. Worship music, food, dress, Bible translation... all of these are minor issues that many love to argue. What does it do? It distracts from the Gospel.

Doing things just to offend or argue is wrong. God is at work in our lives... at different speeds and at different times. "I get it, why don't you get it?" That is a prideful statement. It is quite probable that another brother or sister "get's it" in other ways better than you do. That is how it works... we fit together and cause each other to grow. Going to or serving in church but being prideful and snooty about it - God's not interested. The church is made of individual people with individual gifts and no one person is the whole church. We should build one another up and in turn, we will be encouraged as well. What if the church at large really did Romans 14:19? Let's start and see.

Life Lesson: We should encourage others.

Dear Father,
Thank You for loving me. Thank You for the many individual gifts that make up the body of Christ. Lord, help me to put off disagreements and value others. Forgive me when I have caused division and strife. Give me the spirit to be a blessing to someone else today. In Jesus' name, Amen.

JULY 23
FULL IMPACT

1 Peter 2:1-3
"Therefore, laying aside all malice, all deceit, hypocrisy, envy, and all evil speaking, as newborn babes, desire the pure milk of the word, that you may grow thereby, if indeed you have tasted that the Lord is gracious."
NKJV

Perhaps one of the most under-valued parts of the missionary, C.T. Studd's story is how he came to know the Lord. His father was converted when a friend took him to hear D.L. Moody speak in London in 1877. C.T. and his two brothers were converted when a traveling preacher stayed with his family as he was passing through. His father's friend had no idea that taking C.T.'s father to hear D.L. Moody would open the door to lead C.T. to the Lord. That visiting preacher had no idea that C.T. would eventually leave everything to go be a soul winner in China, India and Africa. When people told C.T. he had done enough and should go back home, he'd say, "God has called me to go, and I will go. I will blaze the trail though my grave may only become a stepping stone that younger men may follow."

We don't know the full impact we have on others. Every day we leave some kind of impression on others. We are God's representatives on earth, and we bear the responsibility to live in such a way as to leave others craving Jesus. Whether we have that kind of impact on others is, in many ways, up to us. You know yourself and have a pretty good idea of what people see in your life (and they do see - more than you realize). People are watching and listening. People are forming opinions about our Lord based on what they see in our lives. Let's commit ourselves to have the kind of impact that friend and traveling preacher had on C.T. Studd and his family. Never underestimate the impact you have on this world.

Life Lesson: "If Jesus Christ is God and died for me, then no sacrifice can be too great for me to make for Him." - C.T. Studd

Dear Father,
Thank You for loving me. Thank You that You have chosen me to be Your vessel to make an impact in the lives of others. Lord, help me to live my life in a way that honors You and does not confuse others about the Truth of Your Word. I want my life to be a testimony of Your grace, Your goodness and Your mercy. In Jesus' name, Amen.

JULY 24
OTHERS

Romans 15:2
"Let each of us please his neighbor for his good, leading to edification."
NKJV

Be honest...how often do you think about others ahead of yourself? If you are completely honest, your answer is probably "not often." Jesus, in His ministry, was completely others centered. Everything He spoke and did was for the edification of others. The world we live in is completely focused on 'self', and Christians have bought into it. Jesus, on the other hand, said:

Mark 8:35 "For whoever desires to save his life will lose it, but whoever loses his life for My sake and the gospel's will save it." NKJV

Jesus should be our model for living. We should be like Jesus and be 'others centered' and 'others focused'. We should give our lives away. It is the key to life and what Jesus told us to do. Like a lost key, many Christians will look past it without picking it up. Gandhi once said, "I like your Jesus...I don't like your Christians." If the church at large would live out what we say we believe, this world would be a different place and people would be clamoring for Jesus. Is Jesus your model for living? What do you need to change in your life to accurately portray a life sold out for Jesus?

Life Lesson: We should be spiritually concerned and caring with one another.

Dear Father,
Thank You for Loving me. Thank You for looking past my faults and failures and giving Your life away for me. Lord, I know sometimes I am too preoccupied with 'self' and I am sorry. Give me the passion to give my life for others. Help me to be a walking testimony of Your Truth so 'others' can know the grace, peace, comfort and hope I have found in You. In Jesus' name, Amen.

JULY 25
BATTLE

1 Chronicles 5:24
"These were the heads of their fathers' houses: Epher, Ishi, Eliel, Azriel, Jeremiah, Hodaviah, and Jahdiel. They were mighty men of valor, famous men, and heads of their fathers' houses."
NKJV

We are in a battle. It's all around us. Your family, friends, Pastor and church are in the battle. The enemy of your soul is out to divide and destroy, and if you allow your guard to drop, you will fall victim to his perilous plans. Satan is not stupid. He is going to go after those on the fringe of fellowship. Like a lion that picks off the young, the sick and the weak, he is watching to see who wanders outside the flock. Be mindful of yourself, your family and friends. Is someone lagging behind? Now is the time to encourage them to get back into the flock. Are you wandering? Friend, you are in danger of being picked off. Don't let that happen!

Life Lesson: We are in a battle over our souls and the souls of those we love and care about.

Dear Father,
Thank You for loving me. Lord, give me the wisdom and discernment to recognize when I have dropped my guard. Help me to encourage my family, friends and co-workers in the midst of trouble. When the battles come, help me to find rest in you. In Jesus' name, Amen.

JULY 26
NAMES OF GOD

James 5:4
"Indeed the wages of the laborers who mowed your fields, which you kept back by fraud, cry out; and the cries of the reapers have reached the ears of the Lord of Sabaoth."
NKJV

Who better to go to with our troubles than One who can truly help? All of your pains and all of your sorrows - take them to Jehovah Rapha, the LORD who Heals you. All of your worries and anxiety - take them to Jehovah Shalom, the LORD of Peace. All of your insufficiencies and all of your lacking - take them to El Shaddai, the All Sufficient One. When you are fearful of what the world holds, go to Jehovah Nissi, the LORD is my Banner. When you are lonely and all alone - know Jehovah Shammah, The LORD is There. When you are wandering and lost, wait for Jehovah Raah, the LORD my Shepherd. When you stumble or fall go to Jehovah M'kaddesh, the LORD who makes You Holy. Who are these? These are One, Elohim, God - Creator and Keeper of Covenants. The One who says, "and lo, I am with you always, even to the end of the age" (Matthew 28:20). Your Heavenly Father loves you and will never leave or abandon you.

Proverbs 18:10 "The name of the LORD is a strong tower; The righteous run to it and are safe." NKJV

Life Lesson: Make your request known to God.

Dear Father,
Thank You for loving me. You are my LORD who is my hope and strength. In my weakness and helplessness, give me a sense of Your presence. It is only through Your perfect love I can find rest. When I am brokenhearted Lord, help me to remember to draw close to You and have trust in Your protecting love and strengthening power. In Jesus' name, Amen.

JULY 27
HE'S THE SAME

Colossians 1:10
"that you may walk worthy of the Lord, fully pleasing Him, being fruitful in every good work and increasing in the knowledge of God;"

I relish the opportunities to see how the Lord is expressing Himself in the lives of the Assisting Pastors here at The Bridge and receive from them. What? You mean the Senior Pastor can receive from the Lord through the Assisting Pastors? Yes sir - that is exactly what I mean - and you will receive through them, too. God's Word does not return void and the same Holy Spirit that speaks through me speaks through them. Now, let me share something I received through one of our Assisting Pastors last night.

This is a Bible teaching church. We will never have service and read through a book other than the Bible. I've heard people say that they've learned more in three months here than in three years somewhere else. That is due to our verse by verse and chapter by chapter approach to the Bible. All that we are learning is not to make us better, smarter, more well adjusted. It is to please God. We are learning about God and how to follow Jesus. We are learning about characteristics we should see in our life to please God. That is what this is all about.

Revelation 4:11 "You are worthy, O Lord our God, to receive glory and honor and power. For you created everything, and it is for your pleasure that they exist and were created." NLT

Every time we live for our own pleasure sooner or later we will come to regret it. That is because our lives are meant to please God and not ourselves. It is a good thing to pray that we live a life that is pleasing to Him.

Life Lesson: Our goal is to please God.

Dear Father,
Thank You for loving me. Thank You that through Your Son I have forgiveness of my sins. Fill me with the knowledge of Your will with all wisdom and spiritual understanding. Help me to live my life pleasing to You and be fruitful in every good work. Lord, I surrender my life to Your will. In Jesus' name, Amen.

JULY 28
JESUS CAME FOR EVERYBODY

Romans 15:8-9

"Now I say that Jesus Christ has become a servant to the circumcision for the truth of God, to confirm the promises made to the fathers, and that the Gentiles might glorify God for His mercy, as it is written: 'For this reason I will confess to You among the Gentiles, And sing to Your name.'" NKJV

It is good to be reminded that Jesus came for everybody. The next-door neighbor who mows his lawn at 6am; Jesus came for him. The drug dealer on the street corner; Jesus came for her. The murderer, the newborn baby, the single mother and the person who cut you off in traffic; Jesus came for all of them. Jesus came for the Jew and He came for the Gentile. Don't be selfish. Treat others like you would treat Jesus.

Matthew 25:40 "And the King will tell them, 'I assure you, when you did it to one of the least of these my brothers and sisters, you were doing it to me!'" NLT

So, now let's make it more personal because, friend, Jesus came for you. Do you realize that? It doesn't matter where you've been or who you've been because Jesus knows who you are and He loved you so much that He died for you. God has invested an eternity in you... All of history is leading up to this moment where you realize that forgiveness is just one prayer away.

Romans 10:13 "For 'Everyone who calls on the name of the LORD will be saved.'" NLT

Life Lesson: Jesus came for everybody.

It's not an exclusive offer. You are in if you ask to be...it's that simple. All you have to do is ask. Why don't you take that moment right now? If you would like to ask Jesus to be your Lord and Savior (or if you have wandered, off and want to come back), please pray something like this...

Dear Jesus,
Thank You for loving me. Thank You for dying on the cross for my sins, rising again from the dead and breaking the bonds of sin over me. I have sinned. Please forgive me. Please give me the ability to live for You all the days of my life. In Jesus' name, Amen.

JULY 29
HOSPITAL OR MAUSOLEUM?

1 Chronicles 6:57-60
"And to the sons of Aaron they gave one of the cities of refuge, Hebron; also Libnah with its common-lands, Jattir, Eshtemoa with its common-lands, Hilen with its common-lands, Debir with its common-lands, Ashan with its common-lands, and Beth Shemesh with its common-lands. And from the tribe of Benjamin: Geba with its common-lands, Alemeth with its common-lands, and Anathoth with its common-lands. All their cities among their families were thirteen."
NKJV

Jesus equated hating someone with murder because murder is what lurks in the heart of all who hate. Jesus also equated lust with adultery because adultery is what lurks in the heart of all who lust. It is a heart issue. Without physically committing murder, we have still done so because it is in our heart. Sin has many tentacles and it will find its way into all the cracks we leave open in our lives. Who can say they have never hated? Who can say they have never lusted, lied or stolen? We all need a refuge.

It has been said that the church is a hospital for sinners and not a mausoleum for saints. The perfect church does not exist because all churches are made up of people and all people have sinned (Romans 3:10, 23). The church is a refuge where murderers, adulterers, liars and idolaters come to the One who can forgive our sins, Jesus. When the church puts on an air of righteousness and unobtainable holiness, we cease to be a refuge and become a mausoleum instead.

Hebrews 6:18 "So God has given us both his promise and his oath. These two things are unchangeable because it is impossible for God to lie. Therefore, we who have fled to him for refuge can take new courage, for we can hold on to his promise with confidence." NLT

Life Lesson: The church should be a city of refuge. This church should be a city of refuge.

Dear Father,
Thank You for loving me. Thank You for providing Your Son as a refuge for my sins. Lord, I need You. Through You, I can lay down the chains of my past and lay hold of the hope You have set before me. Help me to be strength to others. Give me the ability to use my gifts and talents to draw others closer to You. In Jesus' name, Amen.

JULY 30
REMEMBER

Romans 15:15
"Nevertheless, brethren, I have written more boldly to you on some points, as reminding you, because of the grace given to me by God"
NKJV

Satan loves to remind us of our past sins and failures. He finds great pleasure in bringing up things that God has long forgiven us of. Revelation 12:10 refers to Satan as the "accuser of our brethren." That's what he does, but not because he's really got anything on us. If you have accepted Jesus as your Lord and Savior, the Bible tells us that your sins have been separated from you as far as the east is from the west (Psalm 103:12). So, what does it profit the enemy to bring up what you've been forgiven of? He wants to distract you from following Jesus. If he can get you to listen to his accusations, maybe he can shame you into believing that you've crossed some line of forgiveness that doesn't exist. That is his game and he is betting that he can pull you into it. Remember the words of 1 John 1:9...

"If we confess our sins, He is faithful and just to forgive us our sins and to cleanse us from all unrighteousness." NKJV

Has Satan distracted you from following Jesus? Don't believe his lies, and friend, in love, you need to quit listening to your enemy. You have got a great future ahead of you. Satan, on the other hand... well...his future is not so good because he will be thrown into the lake of fire. He will be destroyed. He knows it. So, the next time the enemy tries to remind you of your past, remind him of his future.

Life Lesson: We often forget what we should remember and remember what we should forget.

Dear Father,
Thank You for loving me. Thank You for the forgiveness of my sins. I rejoice in knowing the future that lies ahead of me is so much better than the past that is behind me. In Jesus' name, Amen.

JULY 31
LEGACY

1 Chronicles 7:20-22
"The sons of Ephraim were Shuthelah, Bered his son, Tahath his son, Eladah his son, Tahath his son, Zabad his son, Shuthelah his son, and Ezer and Elead. The men of Gath who were born in that land killed them because they came down to take away their cattle. Then Ephraim their father mourned many days, and his brethren came to comfort him."
NKJV

What a legacy to leave behind. Ephraim's sons were killed stealing cattle. I remember seeing a series of commercials on television for Tombstone brand frozen pizzas. The commercial that I remember most is a gangster scene. The commercial opens at the shipyards on a foggy night. A well-dressed man is in cement shoes, about to be thrown into the river. A gangster says to the man, "So, Tony, it's nothing personal. Before we get started, what do you want on your tombstone?" Tony smiles and then replies, "Pepperoni and sausage." Obviously, Tony was distracted from the seriousness of the situation. It was life or death, and he is thinking about pizza. It is funny because it is absurd, yet so many of us go about life ignoring the obvious fact that someday we are going to die. We may have made some poor choices in life, but the one we don't want to get wrong is whether we have accepted Jesus. I have done some difficult funerals. I have done some funerals where we just did not know if the person was saved or not. Why is that? Shouldn't someone have known? Their lives did not demonstrate their salvation, so questions lingered.

What do you want people to say at your funeral? Do you want them to feel like they have to lie? Do you want them to skirt around the obvious? Or... do you want to leave a legacy that inspires people to follow Jesus? Should the Lord tarry, we will each have a funeral. Will those you leave behind be saying, "See you later" or will they be saying "Goodbye?"

Life Lesson: Live the way you want to be remembered.

Dear Father,
Thank You for loving me. It is through Your Son, Jesus that I am an adopted child of God, and I am so grateful. Lord, I want to live out my life as an inspiration to others. May my life demonstrate the love and Truth of Your Word. Empower me Lord, to make the most of the time You have given me. In Jesus' name, Amen.

AUGUST 1
FRUIT INSPECTING

1 John 2:15
"Do not love the world or the things in the world. If anyone loves the world, the love of the Father is not in him."
NKJV

These are days of self-deception and lies. These are times marked with focus on 'self'. Many are deceived and many Christians have clothed themselves with a candy coating of worldliness. The average American spends 142 minutes a day watching television. By age 65, you will have spent nearly 9 years of your life, watching television. Sticky sweet idolatry marked with slogans such as "A diamond is forever", "Because you're worth it" and "Have it your way", proclaimed hourly to wide-eyed zombies ready to toe the line of "in". It is no wonder so many have bought into the lie.

Have you bought in to today's "self-worth" mentality? A good way to tell is to examine the fruit in your life. Good fruit comes by love for God and love for others. Bad fruit is the product of concentrating on 'self'. Be discerning about the fruit in your life. There is great potential for every child of God to bear awesome fruit. What are your priorities? Whom do they point to? Do they point to you, or do they point to Jesus?

Life Lesson: You cannot fake fruit.

Dear Father,
Thank You for loving me. Thank You for dying for me so that I can be forgiven. Lord, help me not to live a life of deception, but rather strive to live and walk in the Holy Spirit always showing my 'fruit'. In Jesus' name, Amen.

AUGUST 2
LOVE GOD, LOVE PEOPLE

Mark 8:34-35

"When He had called the people to Himself, with His disciples also, He said to them, "Whoever desires to come after Me, let him deny himself, and take up his cross, and follow Me. For whoever desires to save his life will lose it, but whoever loses his life for My sake and the gospel's will save it."

NKJV

There is a whole lot of 'self' going on in the world today. "What is in it for me?" is a question we ask ourselves more often than we realize or would ever probably admit. The world media today would have us believe that to make a real impact on this world; we need to take care of ourselves first. It is selfishness justified with a loss of cabin pressure mentality. What is that you ask? You know how aircraft stewards will announce that in the case of a loss of cabin pressure an oxygen mask will drop from the ceiling. What do they tell you next? They tell you to place the mask on yourself before helping anyone else...including your own children! That is the mentality that we tend to have in life. If I do not help myself first, how can I help others? "I need to win the lottery so that I can give to someone else." "I would be glad to help except the NCAA Championship is on TV." "Sorry, that's my dinner time." What self-serving excuses do you make to avoid sacrifice? That mentality is so not Jesus.

Jesus says we are to lay down our lives, actually denying ourselves, in order that we may place others first. Jesus told us to take up our cross, knowing full well that His cross was a literal instrument of sacrifice...the means by which He would give His own life for you. I will bet that championship game seems less significant in light of His sacrifice.

Life Lesson: Loving God and loving people - leaves no room for our self.

Dear Father,
Thank You for loving me. Thank You for dying for me. I want to live as Your vessel to share the Gospel with others. Lord, I have been selfish with my time. Help me to deny myself and place the needs of others first. Allow me the opportunity to make a 'missional' impact on the lives of others and the world around me. In Jesus' name, Amen.

AUGUST 3
REACH OUT

Romans 15:20-21

"And so I have made it my aim to preach the Gospel, not where Christ was named, lest I should build on another man's foundation, but as it is written: 'To whom He was not announced, they shall see; And those who have not heard shall understand.'"
NKJV

I advise my church congregation to be careful about inviting individuals from other churches or fellowships. If they are starving for the Word of God, then invite them. When someone is happy and called to be where they are, please do not invite them or at least pray before you do. Like Paul, I do not want to build on another man's foundation.

There are so many people in the world who are not saved and are headed, frankly, for a terrible end. You should invite them to church! Go out and find people who are not in fellowship or not saved and reach out to them. We are to be fishers of men not keepers of the aquarium.

Matthew 28:18-20 "And Jesus, walking by the Sea of Galilee, saw two brothers, Simon called Peter, and Andrew his brother, casting a net into the sea; for they were fishermen. Then He said to them, "Follow Me, and I will make you fishers of men." They immediately left their nets and followed Him." NKJV

How great is your desire to see people saved? It seems crazy for me to put together a sentence like that...think about the absurdity. How great is your desire TO SEE PEOPLE GET SAVED? Suppose you are out for a day of fun on the lake. From your boat, you and a friend notice someone in the water in distress. Would your friend need to turn to you to ask if you want to help save the person? I hope not. Every second that goes by, someone, who has never called on Jesus for salvation, dies. That is every second. If you do not have a desire to see others saved, friend, in love, you need to consider your own standing in Christ. Are you the one in the boat or the one going under?

Life Lesson: The Church should be reaching out to those who don't know and those who have never heard.

Dear Father,
Thank You for loving me. Motivate my heart in grace to reach those who do not know You Lord. Help me to live everyday as an active witness for You. Give me the desire and attitude of personal involvement to be Your vessel to spread the Gospel. In Jesus' name, Amen.

AUGUST 4
EXCUSES, EXCUSES

Jeremiah 1:6-7
Then said I: "Ah, Lord GOD! Behold, I cannot speak, for I am a youth." But the LORD said to me: "Do not say, 'I am a youth,' For you shall go to all to whom I send you, And whatever I command you, you shall speak."
NKJV

God knows everything about us... what we've done, what we will do - it's a hard thing to really grasp. In spite of this, He still wants to use us. Many times God's plan for our lives does not jive with our own plan for our lives. What do we do then? Jeremiah wanted God to accept the excuse that he's too young and inexperienced to do what God has called him to. God, on the other hand, knew exactly what Jeremiah was capable of. He chose Jeremiah not because of what Jeremiah wanted to do, but because of what He could do through Jeremiah.

Have you been handing God excuses? Lord, I know You want me to do this but... How can you say Lord and but in the same sentence? You can't, friend. It's one or the other. Either He is Lord of your life or He isn't and if you are throwing out excuses not to do what God has asked you to do, maybe you need to consider just who is Lord of your life?

Life Lesson: God's will leads to blessing; our selfish will leads to destruction.

Dear Father,
Thank You for loving me. Forgive me for times when I've given you excuses instead of hearing, believing and doing. Please show me areas of my life where I am saying "but" to You. In Jesus' name, Amen.

AUGUST 5
WAITING ON GOD'S TIMING

Romans 15:28-29
"Therefore, when I have performed this and have sealed to them this fruit, I shall go by way of you to Spain. But I know that when I come to you, I shall come in the fullness of the blessing of the gospel of Christ."
NKJV

God is a blessing God. He desires to grant favor to His children. At the same time, we have our own free will, which God will not violate. Sometimes, we cheat God of the ability to bless us when we selfishly and stubbornly force our own way. The Lord's clock does not abide by our calendar. As much as we want things to run according to our own design, God's blueprint is much better. There is an order to things that God has established. He created all the gears, cogs and wheels of life that we do not understand.

Paul had desired to go to Rome but he knew that his trip would be much more profitable in the Lord's timing. He had learned to wait on God's timing and not force it on his own. Sometimes, we have to wait on God. Sometimes, we may know what God has called us to do, yet we know it is not yet time. When we wait on the Lord to say when the time is right, we can know it is going to be an incredible ride! It might not be easy, but it will be good. If it is easy, be careful. Satan will do everything he can to oppose God's plans, and if you are not facing opposition, you may want to pray to see if you are indeed walking in God's timing.

Life Lesson: If we wait upon the Lord and His timing, it is going to be good.

Dear Father,
Thank you for the love, grace and mercy that You extend to me day in and day out. Thank You for Your goodness; for Your kindness. Thank You for the incredible plans You have for my life. Please lead me into and through them in Your timing and not in my own. In Jesus' name, Amen.

AUGUST 6
SOON ENOUGH

1 Chronicles 9:22-24

"All those chosen as gatekeepers were two hundred and twelve. They were recorded by their genealogy, in their villages. David and Samuel the seer had appointed them to their trusted office. So they and their children were in charge of the gates of the house of the LORD, the house of the tabernacle, by assignment." NKJV

Samuel, the prophet and spiritual leader of Israel, started out as a doorkeeper. In fact, it was during this time serving as a doorkeeper that he heard God's call (1 Samuel 3). God looks for those who are faithful in small things to serve Him in big things. Jesus spoke about this in the parable of the five talents in Matthew 5, and it is something seen repeatedly in scripture. David is another great example. He was faithful in caring for his father's flock. It was from that place of service that he was called by God to tend all of Israel as king.

Where are you serving God? Are you serving at all? Do you want to skip the floor sweeping or bathroom cleaning and go straight to teaching or leading worship? Friend, you may be able to force your way into a leadership position, but if it is not by God's calling, you are going to be miserable. God looks at the heart and calls leaders who have servant's hearts. If you want to serve in your true calling, then serve faithfully where He has you and listen - soon enough, like David and Samuel, you too will hear the call of God.

Life Lesson: In the church, leaders should always be servant leaders.

Dear Father,
Thank You for loving me. Thank You for Your grace and Your mercy. Lord, it has become clear that I have not been fully ready to assume the tasks You have called me to do. Help me to take a step toward a new beginning in my life. Drive me closer to You, and lead me down the path of Your choice. As I look back on my life, I see where I have been afraid to take a step of faith. Help me to recognize my true gifts and talents. Use me as Your vessel to accomplish Your purposes. In Jesus' name, Amen.

AUGUST 7
TRUE FRIENDS

Romans 16:3-4
"Greet Priscilla and Aquila, my fellow workers in Christ Jesus, who risked their own necks for my life, to whom not only I give thanks, but also all the churches of the Gentiles."
NKJV

Paul not only won souls but also made friends. Throughout his ministry, Paul demonstrated great kindness toward others and exhorted others to treat one another well. He gathered around himself some true friends... friends who were not only willing to exchange kindness one-for-one with him, but they were willing to lay down their time, finances and even lives sacrificially to help Paul. These were not 'here today gone tomorrow friends,' but were true friends in every meaning of the word. We should be like that with one another.

I am reminded of a story about a young Private First Class in the United States Army during the brutal fighting of World War II. In the midst of a skirmish, the unit had been forced to retreat due to heavy gunfire and was pinned down in the trenches. His best friend had been hit in the exchange and the unit retreated so fast he was left behind lying in the field. The young soldier could see his friend and began to climb out of the trench to get him. His Sergeant stopped him saying, "Son, your friend is gut shot. That means he is going to die. There is nothing you can do for him, and if you go out there, you will die as well. We do not need to lose two soldiers today." The private looked his Sergeant in the eye, set his jaw and scrambled out of the trench. Reaching his buddy, he too took a bullet in the belly but managed to pull his friend back to the trench. His buddy was dead. The Sergeant looked at his friend and looked at the private and said, "Son, your friend is dead and now you are going to die. Was it worth it?" The young soldier looked down at his own wound then looked up and said, "Sir, yes sir, it was worth it, because when I got there, my friend looked at me and said, 'I knew you would come.'"

Church is not a building; it is a group of people who are serving side by side in the army of God. Sometimes we get wounded, and sometimes we see another get wounded. The battles can be heavy and at times, the potential for hurt can be great. Are you the kind of friend that soldier was?

Life Lesson: We should want to treat other people better than we do now.

Dear Father,

Thank You for loving me. Thank You that Your love was so great for me that You died for me. Lord, give me the courage to step into the gap for others. Putting aside all fear and selfishness, allow me the opportunity to come along side of someone in their time of need. In Jesus' name, Amen.

AUGUST 8
EXCUSES

1 Chronicles 10:2
"Then the Philistines followed hard after Saul and his sons. And the Philistines killed Jonathan, Abinadab, and Malchishua, Saul's sons."
NKJV

The books of 1 & 2 Samuel and 1 & 2 Chronicles parallel one another. It has been well observed that 1 & 2 Samuel are man's perspective of these events while 1 & 2 Chronicles are God's perspective. Most of the book of 1 Samuel (man's perspective) chronicles the life of Saul, but in 1 Chronicles (God's perspective) the life of Saul takes up just one chapter. Now, Saul was the first king of Israel. In man's eyes he was an important man, but not in God's eyes. When we first meet Saul in 1 Samuel, he is hunting after his father's donkeys, which he had lost. That is not a good indication of Saul's character. Later on in 1 Samuel 13, we see Saul offering a burnt offering on his own.

1 Samuel 13:11-12 "And Samuel said, "'What have you done?'" Saul said, "When I saw that the people were scattered from me, and that you did not come within the days appointed, and that the Philistines gathered together at Michmash, then I said, 'The Philistines will now come down on me at Gilgal, and I have not made supplication to the LORD.' Therefore I felt compelled, and offered a burnt offering." NKJV

Saul is coming up with excuses and throwing blame for what he did wrong. He was not a priest and sinned by offering the sacrifice on his own. When Samuel confronts Saul about it, he begins making excuses.

We are all fallen people. When we are approached with our own wrong doing, our first instinct is to cast blame and find excuses. How often do our apologies include reasons (because) and excuses (but)? Friend, when you mess up and need to apologize, just apologize. Don't take from your apology by adding anything to it. Don't try to find excuses for your wrong doing.

Life Lesson: Do not find excuses for your wrong doing.

Dear Father,
Thank You for loving me. Lord, I need Your forgiveness. Thank You for forgiving me. Please stop me when I try to make excuses for my sins, and help me to be quick to apologize to others. In Jesus' name, Amen.

AUGUST 9
ROLL CALL

Romans 16:5-6
"Greet my beloved Epaenetus, who is the firstfruits of Achaia to Christ. Greet Mary, who labored much for us."
NKJV

One of the things that makes The Bridge different from most other churches, is we have no formal membership. I do not see it in the Bible, and I believe that membership tends to be more of a barrier anyway. Membership means somebody has to decide who is in and who is out. I am not going to do that.

So, what makes someone a part of The Bridge? It is really quite simple. It's getting involved and doing something. You see, whether your name is on some membership roll or not, doesn't mean squat if you are not involved. Let me throw this example your way and see if it makes sense. At the end of a play, who do you see on stage taking a bow? Here is a hint: It is not the audience. It is the actors and actresses. When you watch the credits at the end of a movie, who do they list? Here is another hint: it is not the audience. It is everyone who actively played a part in making the film. If you are an active part of this church, then guess what? Here is a hint: you are not the audience. That's right; you are an active participant or component of this mighty work of God. But that is not all. Oh, no... there is much more to it. There are benefits to "participation" such as a changed life, a deeper relationships with others and protection from the enemy. It is an important day in the life of a believer when they begin to step out and serve God and others. Real growth begins to happen and soon you realize that not only has your relationship with others deepened, but your relationship with God has as well. That is not just this church. I'm not saying you have to come to this church to have a deeper relationship with God. Serve wholeheartedly at the church you attend and prepare to be blown away by what happens.

Life Lesson: Serving in ministry with someone provides a great foundation for a deeper relationship.

Dear Father,
Thank You for loving me. Thank You for Your Son, Jesus, that I can know the ONE true relationship. Lord, I find at times it is difficult to share my life with others. Help me to share my life with others, as well as to give and receive love in those relationships. Empower me with the boldness to step out and serve alongside them. In Jesus' name, Amen.

AUGUST 10
TOGETHER

1 Chronicles 11:7
"Then David dwelt in the stronghold; therefore they called it the City of David."
NKJV

For four hundred years, from Joshua to David, Israel had never captured Jerusalem. Throughout this time, the nation of Israel was fractured and fragmented. Bickering and controversy kept the kingdom from being completed. With a king submitted to God, they were able to realize the potential that did not exist until unity was established. The capture of Jerusalem was the choice crop of coming together as one.

The "church at large" is extremely impaired. Bickering and arguments rage over ridiculous and inconsequential things. Some churches and denominations have determined a completely different direction by disregarding the ways of God in exchange for traditions, rituals and the wisdom of man. I wonder where the world would be right now if churches, instead of choosing conflict, chose to cooperate. Would slavery and starvation be a problem in the world? Would poverty be so pronounced in the world and would there be anyone who has yet to hear the Good News of Jesus Christ?

Let's bring this down to a personal level. What if each one of us decided to lay aside our differences and petty arguments and join with one another to serve God? No doubt, the world would be changed. Let's do it! Choose to change the world by starting in your home, your neighborhood and your city. We can accomplish so much more when we join together.

Life Lesson: We accomplish so much more when we fight together.

Dear Father,
Thank You for loving me. Lord, I want to set aside arguments and differences that hinder me from sharing Your Word to lost souls. Lord, unite the church to become members with one heart and mind. Allow me to join with all my brothers and sisters in Christ to do battle together, arm in arm, to change the world. In Jesus' name, Amen.

AUGUST 11
DIVISION

Romans 16:17-18
"Now I urge you, brethren, note those who cause divisions and offenses, contrary to the doctrine which you learned, and avoid them. For those who are such do not serve our Lord Jesus Christ, but their own belly, and by smooth words and flattering speech deceive the hearts of the simple."
NKJV

David's son, Absalom used to sit at the city gate and pitch malcontent about his father's leadership. Under the guise of juicy news or the old Christian standby, "won't you join with me in prayer about...," Absalom cast division to the people. The accusations were twisted misrepresentations of truth meant to fuel anger and discontentment. In the harvest of his contempt, a lot of people were hurt and the perseverance of the state was tested.

Later, and only thirty years into the creation of the church, Paul would spend a lot of time battling those who sought to cause division and disruption in the church. Today, church leaders have to spend time preventing or fixing the damage of division. This is valuable time not spent reaching people with the Good News of Jesus Christ, and that is just what Satan wants. If the enemy of our souls can inspire division among the Body, he can distract servants of the Lord from what they should be doing.

People who cause division are never acting on behalf of God. Gossip and division only hurt the Work of God. Note the people you know who are divisive, and avoid them. It's not often we are told in the Bible to avoid specific individuals, but we are told to avoid those who cause division. Friend, in doing so, you will save a lot of heartache and a lot of pain.

Life Lesson: Stay away from divisive people.

Dear Father,
Thank You for loving me. Thank You for wrapping me in Your robe of righteousness. Lord, I want to be a lover of the Word. Give me a hunger to know the Bible and give me wisdom to recognize the counterfeit. I ask for Your strength and discernment to recognize the battles that Satan orchestrates. I choose... to serve only You. In Jesus' name, Amen.

AUGUST 12
ABOVE AND BEYOND

1 Chronicles 12:33-34
"of Zebulun there were fifty thousand who went out to battle, expert in war with all weapons of war, stouthearted men who could keep ranks; of Naphtali one thousand captains, and with them thirty-seven thousand with shield and spear;"
NKJV

In 1972, NASA launched a space probe, Pioneer 10. The primary mission of this satellite was to reach Jupiter, photograph the planet and its moons, take measurements and beam data back to earth. For 1972, this mission was deemed a very ambitious plan. Prior to this, no satellite had made it beyond Mars. Pioneer 10, however, didn't know that. Over the next 20 plus years, Pioneer 10 kept plugging away, traveling more than 6 billion miles by 1997. The satellite passed Saturn, Uranus, Neptune and Pluto continuing out into the unknown reaches of our galaxy. That whole time, Pioneer 10 kept beaming back data with only an 8 watt transmitter...the equivalent power of a child's night light.

Pioneer 10 defied all expectations of failure and plugged along doing its job in a way that exceeded its creator's expectations. Too many times, I've seen Christians step up to serve the Lord, and when adversity hit, they quit. They decide they are not qualified or they don't have the power or the energy. Yet, as Christians, we have within us the dynamite power of the Holy Spirit and the promise of Jesus that "With men this is impossible, but with God all things are possible" (Matthew 19:26). Forget about adversity. God's got it covered. Let's do our jobs above and beyond. Let's step up and serve our King. Failure is not an option.

Life Lesson: You should be committed in your service to the Lord.

Dear Father,
Thank You for loving me. Thank You that my past is pardoned and my future is secure! Lord, give me determination and ambition to step out and serve. Help me to make a difference in the church and in the lives of others. Empower me Lord, to answer the call to do battle. May I never be satisfied to just coast along, but to be actively involved in reaching lost souls. I am a disciple of Christ! In Jesus' name, Amen.

AUGUST 13
GOD IS A KEEPING GOD

Romans 16:25
"Now to Him who is able to establish you according to my gospel and the preaching of Jesus Christ, according to the revelation of the mystery kept secret since the world began"
NKJV

There is great comfort in this, friend. Our God is a keeping God. He may keep some secrets but He also keeps His promises. His faithfulness is without end. God establishes us as His children according to the generous outpouring of His love through Jesus Christ. He keeps us secure in His hand from which no power can snatch us away.

John 10:27-30 "My sheep hear My voice, and I know them, and they follow Me. And I give them eternal life, and they shall never perish; neither shall anyone snatch them out of My hand. My Father, who has given them to Me, is greater than all; and no one is able to snatch them out of My Father's hand. I and My Father are one." NKJV

Where man fails to keep promises made to God, our Father never fails in His promises to us. He establishes us and won't let go. What have you promised God that you have neglected to do? While you are less than faithful to the Lord, He is ever faithful to you. Don't you think you owe Him more of a commitment than that? The things we do reflect the commitments we honor. Would your family say you were committed to serving God? What about a stranger?

Life Lesson: God is a keeping God.

Dear Father,
Thank You for loving me. Thank You for the forgiveness of my sins. I want Your fresh mercy and grace. Lord, I am available to do the work You have called me to do. Help me, Lord, to share the simple Truth of Your Word with others. In Jesus' name, Amen.

AUGUST 14
GOD HAS BLESSED YOU

1 Corinthians 1:5
"…that you were enriched in everything by Him in all utterance and all knowledge,"
NKJV

There's a story of a young man, just out of High School, who approached his father about a graduation gift. "Dad," he said while pointing to a car in a magazine, "This car is what I want. It would be the best graduation gift you can give me." The father looked at his son, gave him a hug and took the magazine and put it on his desk. A few weeks later, father and son met together at a favorite restaurant. Dad said, "My boy, I'm proud of you. I've got something for you and it's the best present I could ever give you." The son could hardly stop from grinning because he just knew his dad was going to pull out a set of keys. Instead, his father placed an old, worn Bible on the table. "Son, this is my Bible. It's meant everything to me and I know it will to you as well. I want you to have it." His son looked at the Bible, visibly disappointed. He took his eyes off his father, shook his head and left the restaurant, leaving his father and the Bible behind. Years passed with no communication between the two. Then one day, word came that his father had passed away. The son returned to his father's home to settle the estate. As he looked through his father's desk, he noticed the Bible sitting in its own spot beside a picture of him and his father in happier times. He picked the Bible up and as he did, a piece of paper fell to the ground. Looking closer, he realized it was a dealer's check for the car he had wanted. It had been tucked inside the Bible that his father wanted to give him so many years ago.

Friend, you and I are so blessed, and the crazy thing is we usually don't even notice it. We are just like the son in this story who didn't realize the blessings that were already his. Friend, don't overlook blessings because you are focused on what you don't have. You know how many people in this world wish they were able to live the way you do? Even in hardship and pain, you are blessed because you are an heir through Jesus to the riches of our Father in Heaven. God has blessed you, my friend. Give Him thanks and praise.

Life Lesson: God has blessed you, give Him thanks and praise.

Dear Father,
Thank You for loving me. Thank You for the gift of salvation. Lord, I know at times I do not recognize the day to day blessings around me. I humbly give thanks for You and all that You have done for me. Help me to put my focus and trust in You and not on myself. I recognize that all blessings come from You. I ask You to give me faith to see You in everything and everybody. Thank You, Lord. In Jesus' name, Amen.

AUGUST 15
LEAVE YOUR ME

Acts 6:1

"And in those days, when the number of the disciples was multiplied, there arose a murmuring of the Grecians against the Hebrews, because their widows were neglected in the daily ministration." KJV

In Acts chapter 6, we see an interesting transaction between the Apostles and some disciples regarding a situation in the early church. The gist of the situation was that the Greek widows felt discriminated against and that special favor was being shown to the Jewish widows. The Apostles realized that they could not continue in the calling the Lord had given them and take care of the minutia of church affairs. The answer was to allow faithful men who had demonstrated their heart for God and love for others to be servant leaders over the people. But, what brought this situation to a head? People focused on themselves.

Many problems that creep up in the church are the result of our focus getting off God and being placed on self. When that happens, things get out of kilter in our following Jesus. We cannot follow Jesus and be focused on self. This is true individually, but also on a church wide basis. An inward focused church is a selfish church. To follow Jesus we must be focused on Jesus. When that happens, it's like a dam breaks allowing incredible works of love to flow unhindered in our lives. That, my friend, is God's model for the church, loving God and loving others.

Life Lesson: Leave your ME at the door.

Dear Father,

Thank You for loving me. It was Your great love for me that kept You on the cross. In light of that, I am humble. I admit, many times, I take my eyes off of You and focus on situations and circumstance around me. Give me the strength to draw my focus back to You. Empower me with a passion to share my love with others. In Jesus' name, Amen.

AUGUST 16
BASIC INSTRUCTIONS BEFORE LEAVING EARTH

1 Corinthians 1:9
"God is faithful, by whom you were called into the fellowship of His Son, Jesus Christ our Lord."
NKJV

There are a lot of people who want to tell you about how to be a Christian. Bookstores are replete with how-to books, iTunes is full of podcasts and television is brimming with programs. It's enough to make one think that being a Christian is something really complicated. Friend, don't be distracted by instructions and manuals. Put away the books and open your Bible. Close your eyes, and talk to God. Open your ears to God and not to your iPod. Allow Him to lead your heart. Christianity is not about rituals or traditions. It's about Jesus. Don't let the world take the place of Jesus in your life, and if you do, take comfort because He remains faithful. He starts the good work in you, and He completes it. Not you, Him.

Philippians 1:6 "And I am sure that God who began the good work within you will keep right on helping you grow in his grace until his task within you is finally finished on that day when Jesus Christ returns." TLB

You cannot be secure in yourself. If you have accepted Jesus as your Lord and Savior, your salvation is a gift. It's a gift God places in you that produces works demonstrating whose child you are. You had nothing to do with it, but Jesus...He had everything to do with it. You are secure in Christ and that's important because Jesus is soon coming. Live for God. Do all you can to know Him and follow Him, then trust Him with everything.

Life Lesson: Jesus is coming soon.

Dear Father,
Thank You for loving me. Thank You for the forgiveness of my sins and being a keeping God. Please change me from the inside out. I trust that You will complete a good work in me. As I look at today's events, I see Your coming is drawing near and I am comforted. But Lord, when I look around me, there are so many who don't yet know You. Lord, challenge me to get serious and see that no one is left behind. In Jesus' name, Amen.

AUGUST 17
LIVE YOUR FAITH

1 Chronicles 14:3-7
"Then David took more wives in Jerusalem, and David begot more sons and daughters. And these are the names of his children whom he had in Jerusalem: Shammua, Shobab, Nathan, Solomon, Ibhar, Elishua, Elpelet, Nogah, Nepheg, Japhia, Elishama, Beeliada, and Eliphelet."
NKJV

David, while an incredible man of God, was not the father he should have been. In several places in scripture, we see where he did not discipline his kids the way he should have. Additionally, the fact that he took many wives, in violation of God's command (Deuteronomy 17:14-17), shows that what he lived out in public he may have skimped on in his own home. God blessed David in spite of multiple marriages, but he had many problems because of it.

This is not only true for David, but probably true in so many ways for each and every one of us. It's quite easy to cover up for deficiencies at work or with friends, but deficiencies are often very evident in family life. Don't believe me? Ask your spouse.

Being a spiritual leader in your home means more than issuing orders and doling out discipline. It also means being the first to repent and apologize when you get things wrong or lose your temper. That's not easy to do. Your family is learning from you. To little eyes, the things you do or don't do speak just as loudly as the things you say. Show your family a life submitted and poured out to God and they will follow in the path you blaze.

Life Lesson: Live out your faith at home.

Dear Father,
Thank You for loving me. I am so grateful that You care to help me when I call on You in the midst of my battles. Please help me not to pretend that all is O.K. to everyone else. You see my brokenness, my sin and my shame. Lord, I am running to You right now. I have been so beat up lately. Lord, I want to be real and honest. I want to demonstrate true spiritual leadership in my home and in the workplace. Please be strong in my life. Restore my brokenness and help me develop a dependence on You, Lord. Empower me to live my life demonstrating Your love to others. In Jesus' name, Amen.

AUGUST 18
DIVIDED WE FALL

1 Corinthians 1:10
"Now I plead with you, brethren, by the name of our Lord Jesus Christ, that you all speak the same thing, and that there be no divisions among you, but that you be perfectly joined together in the same mind and in the same judgment."
NKJV

This is true in marriage, family, workplace and church. We all have some kind of problem in the realm of our relationships. Maybe you went into a relationship thinking that you were 100% in agreement about everything. I'm sure that bubble was quickly burst. It's rare to have absolute agreement between two people much less between hundreds or even thousands.

When you work through differences, you build a stronger relationship. Many times, when a marriage hits a rough patch, there is a freshening of the relationship. It's like hitting the reset button on a game console - suddenly things are working again.

Disagreements can also be distractions, especially within the church. How do you keep a church from reaching others with the Gospel of Jesus Christ? You create division among the members. How many churches has Satan rendered ineffective because he was able to generate dissension? Christians are easy prey when the trap is baited with prideful prejudice over unimportant matters. Division hurts Jesus and the cause of Christ.

Life Lesson: When we come together, we create problems. When we work together to solve them, we become stronger people and stronger in the Lord.

Dear Father,
Thank You for loving me. Thank You for forgiving me. Help me not to be argumentative. Lord, I want to reach people with the Gospel of Jesus Christ. Give me the wisdom and discernment to recognize division and live a life reaching out to others in unity. Thank You for Your glorious salvation and a life forever changed. In Jesus' name, Amen.

AUGUST 19
WALK IN YOUR CALLING

1 Chronicles 15:2
"Then David said, None ought to carry the ark of God but the Levites: for them hath the LORD chosen to carry the ark of God, and to minister unto him forever."
KJV

Do you know God has a special calling on your life? You can run from that calling, like Jonah, or you can embrace it, like David. Give yourself to the Lord and walk in your calling. Don't look at someone in their calling and grow envious. Your calling is special and unique to you and only you can fill that role. How did David know the right path to his calling? He read and studied God's Word. David served God where God had him, even when it was difficult and dirty. He was open to receiving from others who also were passionate about God...and he got it right.

Perhaps, you don't know what your calling is; that's okay, but allow God to show you your calling. Don't just sit around and wait for an answer. There is something we are all called to do and that is to serve God. Serve Him right where He has you. At The Bridge, everyone (even pastors) started out cleaning toilets. It was in the midst of cleaning that many were called to be staff members, team leaders, deacons, elders and pastors. Friend, it's in the midst of faithful serving (obedience) that God will reveal your calling.

Life Lesson: God has a special calling and purpose for each person.

Dear Father,
Thank You for loving me. Lord, help me to be set apart and think differently from the world. Please show me Your plan for my life and give me a boldness to walk in the unique call You have for my life. Lord, fill me with an indescribable joy. In Jesus' name, Amen.

AUGUST 20
CHANGES

1 Corinthians 1:15
"...lest anyone should say that I had baptized in my own name."
NKJV

Paul, in writing this letter to the Corinthians, dealt with division inside the church. Any idea you may have that church is a perfect place is shattered the moment you walk through the door. It was the same in the early church. We all bring something valuable to the church, but we also, because we are sinful people, add to the problems.

In this letter, Paul takes on people's attitudes; their way of thinking. Do we need to be challenged today? Absolutely we do. Being saved does not mean we're done being changed. We continue to be changed, and as we are, our ideas and concepts of what it means to be a Christian are challenged. God wants to adjust our attitude and if we are truly honest with ourselves, we are desperate for that change.

Life Lesson: God wants to adjust your attitude.

Dear Father,
Thank You for loving me. Thank You for Your Son Jesus who died for me so I could have life more abundantly. Lord, I confess to You that I am struggling. I have been looking to the world for answers rather than depending on You. I surrender my heart to You, Lord. Help me to make the changes You want for me. In Jesus' name, Amen.

AUGUST 21
QUIT CLAIM DEED

Genesis 1:1
"In the beginning God created the heavens and the earth."
NKJV

Everything we need to know about money and possessions can be wrapped up into the very first verse in the Bible. If we understand that God created everything and owns everything, then we can understand that our possessions are on loan from God. We are stewards of these things. The Bible holds over 2,300 verses relating to finances and stewardship. In fact, Jesus spoke more about stewardship of money than He did about both Heaven and Hell combined. Obviously, it's important. Why is that?

Matthew 6:21 "For where your treasure is, there your heart will be also." NKJV

Who or what has your heart? That's the issue. God enjoys blessing us with things we can enjoy. The problem is, we get turned around and start to love the gift more than the Giver. When that happens, God has to remove this new idol from our lives. Friends, enjoy the things God has blessed you with, but remember Who your provider is and love Him.

Life Lesson: There is a fundamental connection between your relationship with God and how you use money and possessions.

Dear Father,
Thank You for loving me. Thank You for providing Your Son, Jesus, to die for me. Lord, I thank You that You are also faithful to provide for my needs. Everything I have and all that I am is because of Your loving desire to have a relationship with me. I know at times I can get my focus off You and on the material things of the world. Help me to see the bondage of debt and become the Godly steward of Your possessions. In Jesus' name, Amen.

AUGUST 22
FOOLISHNESS?

1 Corinthians 1:18
"For the preaching of the cross is to them that perish foolishness; but unto us which are saved it is the power of God."
KJV

There are many websites, books, movies and other things portraying the message of the cross as foolish. People pursue legal action to remove the cross and its meaning. Why? The cross offends those who do not want to hear the message. Jesus Christ came and died for our sins, and that's offensive?! Yes, we are all sinners. "Well, that is just so judgmental." No, friend, it's the truth. People don't want to hear it. Jesus and the cross demand that we admit our failings. We cannot admit we are sinners and yet cling to our pride.

Pride feels so good, doesn't it? "Look at me. I am a self-made man. Come and be amazed by my shiny pride." No friend...You are an incomplete and malfunctioning created being without Jesus in your heart. In spite of your pride, He stands knocking and waiting for you to open the door and ask Him in. It's an incredibly simple plan that requires an incredibly simple response of child-like faith and a King David sized heart of boldness.

Life Lesson: The fact people think we are foolish is evidence that they are perishing.

Dear Father,
Thank You for loving me. Thank You for the invitation of the cross. I know my sins have separated me from You, Lord. I ask that You forgive me of all of my sins. Give me the power to live for You all the days of my life. Thank You that You have made my relationship with You so simple. In humble faith, I give You my weaknesses and flaws and ask that Your glory be revealed in me. In Jesus' name, Amen.

AUGUST 23
THE WHOLE ME

1 Chronicles 16:3
"And he dealt to every one of Israel, both man and woman, to every one a loaf of bread, and a good piece of flesh, and a flagon of wine."
KJV

We have a tendency to compartmentalize our lives don't we? We find ourselves saying, "This part of my life belongs to my family, this other part belongs to my job, and I've set this part aside for God."

That sounds very religious and sacrificial but should *Melekh HaOlam* (Hebrew for the King of the Universe), our Creator, Lord and Savior, be relegated to a portion of your life? That's not sacrifice. Sacrifice occurs when we lay down our whole life for God, not a portion of it. But, you may ask, "How do I know when I'm giving too much?" Friend, you will never out give God.

When we sacrifice for God, He always meets our needs. There is a blessing in giving our lives to God that cannot and does not come in any other way. Don't hold back. Give your whole life to God. I'm reminded of the story of a man, of little means, sitting in a church pew as the offering plate was passed. When the usher reached him with the offering plate, the man motioned for the usher to lower the plate. The man motioned again and again until finally, the plate was on the floor, at which point, the man stepped into the plate and said..."This is all I've got, but He's got all of me."

So, tell me friend. Does He have all of you?

Life Lesson: We should offer God our lives not just pieces of it.

Dear Father,
Thank You for loving me. Thank You that Your mercy endures forever and is available to me. Lord, I need your mercy and grace right now. I confess to You that I have not always given You all my life. Lord, I want to give You ALL of my life, not just a portion. I surrender my life to You. Forgive me for losing focus. I want to worship You. In Jesus' name, Amen.

AUGUST 24
TELL YOUR GOD STORY

1 Corinthians 2:1
"And I, brethren, when I came to you, came not with excellency of speech or of wisdom, declaring unto you the testimony of God."
KJV

The power of your testimony is not in how well you speak or how you couch the details. It's not in the clothes you wear or in worldly prosperity. The power of your testimony is in God and the lengths He went to make you right with Him. Your testimony is your walk with Jesus now. That's why it's so precious. People don't see who you were, but they do see who you are.

There is power in your story. It is the "I used to be but now I'm..." God story. People need to hear it. There is no issue you need to work through first. You will always be working through issues and if you are waiting to be perfect, have the Bible memorized or have a refined Christianese vocabulary filled with ten syllable words, you will be with Jesus before you ever share your story. That would be a shame. How many can be reached through the hearing of your testimony? I don't know and neither will you unless you step out, uncomfortable or not, and share. Do you want to find out?

Life Lesson: Tell people your God story often.

Dear Father,
Thank You for the simple story of Your Son, Jesus, who died for me so I could be forgiven. Lord, thank You, that in Your love, You offer me Your grace and mercy. Give me the strength not to drift in sharing the simple message of Your story. In boldness to glorify You, allow me the opportunities to tell others my story. In Jesus' name, Amen.

AUGUST 25
FEED THE WORLD

1 Chronicles 17:6
"Wheresoever I have walked with all Israel, spake I a word to any of the judges of Israel, whom I commanded to feed my people, saying, Why have ye not built me an house of cedars?"
KJV

God has commanded leaders to feed His people. There are Christian ministries designed to meet the physical needs of people. That's great; there are so many people on this planet in the grip of poverty and starvation. The desire to meet these physical needs is a demonstration of a hunger and a thirst for righteousness. It is a desire to see this world as God truly intended and created it. There's only one problem...What about the spiritual needs of people?

Some of these ministries meet both the physical and the spiritual needs and that is how it should be. That's why it is our mission to Reach and Teach. Not only do we meet someone's physical needs, but we also meet spiritual needs through the faithful verse by verse teaching of the Bible. We provide real, hands-on discipleship in action.

People are hungry for the Word of God, and in a time and place where there is a church building on every corner, I am amazed at how rare it is to find expositional teaching.

Amos 8:11 "Behold, the days come, saith the Lord GOD, that I will send a famine in the land, not a famine of bread, nor a thirst for water, but of hearing the words of the LORD." KJV

Is there a famine of the Word of God on this earth? I believe there is and it is time for Christians everywhere to step up and make the change happen according to the abundant sufficiency of our Lord.

Now is the time to feed the starving people of this world. Are you with me? Don't miss it. There will be a blessing for all who lock arms in this wave of change. If you hesitate you could miss it. Come on, let's change the world.

Life Lesson: We should desire to feed the local community and the world the life-changing Word of God.

Dear Father,

Thank You for loving me. I am so humbled by Your invitation to use me in building Your kingdom. Lord, I am not worthy. Who am I to serve in this glorious plan? Looking back at my past, I am gripped in my fear to step out at times. I desire to live Your will for my life. Lord, empower me to respond to Your invitation. Help me to become a kingdom builder. Use me to reach others so they can know You. In Jesus' name, Amen.

AUGUST 26
BE REAL

1 Corinthians 2:3
"I was with you in weakness, in fear, and in much trembling."
NKJV

Paul is being very honest in this verse. He is not trying to make himself look better than he really is. He isn't covering up his weakness. In fact, in 1 Timothy 1:16, Paul proclaims that he is an example of God's longsuffering. He is not a perfect man but a perfect example of God's loving kindness, grace and mercy.

At times, Christians act like we don't have any problems. One problem with this is the impression it gives to those who don't know Jesus. They see Christians pretending they are not messed up and assume that since they still struggle with problems, they don't belong in church. In doing so, are we proclaiming God's goodness or our own?

We need to proclaim God's goodness by being open about our problems and proclaiming that it is the goodness of God that saves! That's being real. It's real life, demonstrating the real love and real hope of the real God. In your weakness, the Good News of Jesus Christ is made strong.

Life Lesson: We should be real with people and not portray some 'False Spirituality'.

Dear Father,
Thank You for loving me. Thank You for the forgiveness of my sins and for giving me the opportunity to experience life more abundantly. Lord, thank You for revealing Yourself to me through Your Word. Lord, I want the offer of joy, hope and peace that only You can give. In Jesus' name, Amen.

AUGUST 27
LIVING OUT POWER

Ephesians 2:10
"For we are His workmanship, created in Christ Jesus for good works, which God prepared beforehand that we should walk in them."
NKJV

Many assume that "ministry" is something exclusively for pastors or "people with a calling." That sort of thinking, while probably propagated in part by pastors, is simply not true. Every disciple of Christ is called to minister. What is ministry? Ministry is serving. Good works, while not the source of salvation, are for all Christians to walk in. Its boundaries are not defined by length, height, width or depth, but by need. Wherever people are, there is need. Ministry can be challenging to our flesh because ministry requires us to deny "self." We make it complex to justify the excuse, "I'm just not ready."

God equips and preordains us for works He has specifically prepared for us. Not only are the works set aside specifically for us, but we are uniquely created for them. As a result, we find ourselves without excuse. What excuses have you made not to serve others? God has set the bounds of ministry and given every Christian a call to actively love others. God tests the hearts of His servants so that we can be conformed to the image of His Son. Are you up for the challenge?

Life Lesson: Challenges while we serve God do not mean we aren't called. Don't quit.

Dear Father,
Thank You for loving me. Thank You for sending Your Son to set me free. I know You have a plan for my life and trust that You will complete a good work in me. Lord, lay it on my heart daily to share with others about Your love. In all my shortcomings, empower me with strength to press on and challenge me to live in the attitude and nature of You. In Jesus' name, Amen.

AUGUST 28
GO BACK TO WHAT YOU KNOW

1 Corinthians 2:9-10
"But as it is written:
'Eye has not seen, nor ear heard, Nor have entered into the heart of man. The things which God has prepared for those who love Him.' But God has revealed them to us through His Spirit. For the Spirit searches all things, yes, and the deep things of God."
NKJV

I have many times heard pastors teach verse nine but fail to move on to verse ten. When one teaches only verse nine, it gives the impression that we cannot know what God has prepared for us. But continue to verse ten, and we learn that we do have access to the mysteries of God through His Holy Spirit. God has not left us stranded on the rusty and rickety old bridge of uncertainty.

When we are not sure of things or circumstances, we should go back to what we do know. Remind yourself..."God, I know You love me. I know my sins are forgiven. I know You will use all things for my good. I know You have a plan for me."

The moment we realize God loves us and has forgiven us, other mysteries of life don't have to strike fear in our hearts. Instead, we can boldly step out into those things He created for us to do. When God reveals Himself to us, He gives us the responsibility to share Him with others.

Life Lesson: When you are not sure of things or circumstances, go back to what you do know.

Dear Father,
Thank You for loving me. Thank You for Your kindness and grace to reveal Yourself to me. Lord, draw me close to You and show me Your plan for my life. Give me the strength to share Your simple message to reach others. In Jesus' name, Amen.

AUGUST 29
BATTLES

1 Chronicles 18:1
"After this it came to pass that David attacked the Philistines, subdued them, and took Gath and its towns from the hand of the Philistines."
NKJV

Jesus promised that there would be trials and trouble for those who follow him. Paul referred to Christians as "soldiers of Christ." Because Satan has set himself against the Lord, it stands to reason that as a soldier of Christ, you are in the battle. You cannot be active in the battle and be seated on the sidelines. There are no couches on the front lines; only foxholes and fighters are found there.

David was not hiding and asking God to keep him safe. He understood there were battles in his life. Instead, David was praying and stepping out in faith. God wants to keep us and give us the victory. Sometimes, we think the worst thing that could happen is to fail. In Christianity, the worst thing is failing to try. God has declared victory in your life. Friend, don't argue with God about it...live it! Be victorious.

Life Lesson: A life of faith is a battle.

Dear Father,
Thank You for loving me. Thank You for Your Word and the desire to use me as a vessel to bless others. Lord, empower me with boldness to put Your kingdom first. I don't want to be a spectator in the battle. I want to see lives changed for Your glory. Help me to step out and be a kingdom builder. In Jesus' name, Amen.

AUGUST 30
TELL SOMEONE

1 Corinthians 2:14
"But the natural man does not receive the things of the Spirit of God, for they are foolishness to him; nor can he know them, because they are spiritually discerned."
NKJV

The Lord wants to reveal Himself to people; His goodness to people that don't know Him. Unless God reveals Himself to someone they won't get it. The fact that we get it is not because we are so wise but because God has shown us. He opens our hearts to His Word... It's His gift by grace through faith and not by our own works.

Ephesians 2:8-9 "For by grace you have been saved through faith, and that not of yourselves; it is the gift of God, not of works, lest anyone should boast." NKJV

The world tries to separate man from God. When modern man tries to explain God from worldly perspectives, it ends up in a foolish mess. The cross is foolishness to those who don't understand. People cannot "get it" until God reveals it to them. Does this mean we should quit sharing and just let people figure it out themselves? Of course not! Our calling is to share and leave the rest up to God.

If your motivation in sharing the Gospel is to have people accept Jesus, then you will become discouraged. If your motivation is obedience to God, then when someone accepts Jesus, you get to revel in the joy of obedience. It's an obedience issue and not a quota to be met. When God shows up, things happen! Share with expectation and know that whether someone accepts Jesus or not, you are a faithful steward of the love of Christ.

Romans 10:14 "But how can they call on him to save them unless they believe in him? And how can they believe in him if they have never heard about him? And how can they hear about him unless someone tells them?" NLT

Life Lesson: God wants us to reveal His goodness to people that don't know Him.

Dear Father,

Thank You for loving me. Thank You that in Your vastness as creator of the heavens and earth, You desire to know me. You call me to share with others. Lord, give me the mind of Christ so that I may see You and myself more clearly than I ever have. In your grace and mercy, I am comforted to know that You have offered me forgiveness. Empower me the with a passion to tell others about You so I can reveal Your glory. In Jesus' name, Amen.

AUGUST 31
HE WHO HAS EARS

Matthew 13:9
"He who has ears to hear, let him hear!"
NKJV

A parable is an earthly story with a heavenly meaning. Jesus would often teach a moral truth by connecting natural things to make incredible spiritual points. Too often; however, the people did not want to hear the Truth He brought. Jesus was fond of saying, "He who has ears to hear, let him hear!" Obviously, God gave us ears for listening. Do we always? If we were honest with ourselves, we would have to say no.

"The teaching was on point today" or "I just wasn't feelin' it today"...Things overheard from people leaving countless churches across this land. Why do we come to church? Is it to grade the teacher? Is it to evaluate the effectiveness of the teaching? No. We come to church to hear from God.

The Apostle John wrote that the same Holy Spirit that instructs the teacher also instructs the Christian. The Bible tells us that scripture is *God-breathed*, and it is a *discerner* of the heart's intentions which does not return void (doesn't fail) (1 Timothy 3:16-17; Hebrews 4:12; Isaiah 55:11). So, whose fault is it when we go to church, listen to a teaching from the Bible, and don't receive? Here's a hint: It's not the teacher, it's not the Bible and *it's not God*. That's right. It's our own fault. We don't hear because we don't like the challenge.

We should never walk away from a Bible teaching church (no matter who the teacher is) without realizing a change or recognizing a step we need to take. Make it your personal commitment to find the life-challenge, the *life lesson* within each teaching and apply it to your life. Share it with a friend or a family member. Ask them to hold you accountable for making that change.

James 1:25 "But he who looks into the perfect law of liberty and continues *in it*, and is not a forgetful hearer but a doer of the work, this one will be blessed in what he does." NKJV

Life Lesson: We should do the Bible not just hear the Bible.

Dear Father,

Thank You for loving me. I know I am incapable of paying the debt for my sins. Thank You for providing Your Son, Jesus, to pay that debt. I am grateful that You delight in having a relationship with me. Lord, help me to apply Your Word in my daily life and live out a life of peace and faith. In Jesus' name, Amen.

SEPTEMBER 1
CHANGES

1 Corinthians 3:1-2
"And I, brethren, could not speak to you as to spiritual people but as to carnal, as to babes in Christ. 2 I fed you with milk and not with solid food; for until now you were not able to receive it, and even now you are still not able;"
NKJV

Paul has written that there are two kinds of people; believers and unbelievers. Now he writes of two kinds of believers, mature or immature (carnal).

Carnal is from the word, Carna, which means flesh. You have an old nature and a new nature. Your old nature is carnal. You have probably heard the word Carnival (Carna Vale) which literally means farewell to the flesh. Originally, parties were held before the week of Lent to usher in this time of dying to the flesh. Mardi Gras, a much less spiritual party celebrated in New Orleans and other places around the world started in this way.

God is in the process of changing us. The way we grow in God is by doing the things He has told us through His Word.

1 Peter 2:2 "...as newborn babes, desire the pure milk of the word, that you may grow thereby," NKJV

Jesus told us that, "Man shall not live by bread alone but by every word that proceeds from the mouth of God" (Matthew 4:4). It would seem that Jesus placed great importance on His followers learning the scriptures.

As we read and draw our nourishment from God's Word, we begin to grow in our new nature. Our lives begin to reflect changes by saying "yes" to the Holy Spirit. We are being conformed to the image of Jesus. Personal time in the Bible, in prayer, in faithful attendance of a Bible teaching church are all indications of spiritual maturity and are all important for our continued spiritual growth. Do you see these things in your life? Take a close look ...maybe even ask a friend or family member. Are these things apparent in your life? God does not want us to remain babes in Christ, but to enjoy the full blessing of walking in His will.

Life Lesson: God is in the process of changing us.

Dear Father,

Thank You for loving me. Thank You for Your desire to use me in the Harvest. Lord, I know I have made excuses and yet You and Your Word are still willing to guide me even in my selfishness. Thank You for teaching me. Forgive me for any envy, strife or division I have caused. I desire to know more and more of You. Thank You for loving me and for having a great plan for my life. In Jesus' name, Amen.

SEPTEMBER 2
COMFORT

1 Chronicles 19:2
"Then David said, "I will show kindness to Hanun the son of Nahash, because his father showed kindness to me." So David sent messengers to comfort him concerning his father. And David's servants came to Hanun in the land of the people of Ammon to comfort him."
NKJV

One of the great joys of being a Christian is bringing comfort to others. Sometimes though, it feels like the weeds of our own bad decisions choke out our ability to do so. Sure, we must deal with earthly consequences of our sins, but that in no way prohibits us from being able to show God's peace to others. In the throes of our own pain, we are comforted with God's words saying:

Romans 8:28 "And we know that all things work together for good to those who love God, to those who are the called according to His purpose." NKJV

Because of our past experiences, we are uniquely qualified to minister to others. According to the Bible, God has specific plans for our lives (Jeremiah 29:11; Ephesians 2:10). Our Father God carries the title of "Father of mercies and God of all comfort" (2 Corinthians 1:3). He is training us to be comfort for others.

2 Corinthians 1:4 "...who comforts us in all our tribulation, that we may be able to comfort those who are in any trouble, with the comfort with which we ourselves are comforted by God." NKJV

So friend, don't count yourself out of ministry because of your mistakes or your past. The same merciful embrace God gave you in your day of distress could become the hug you share with others in their day.

Life Lesson: We should seek to comfort others.

Dear Father,
Thank You for loving me. Thank You for the grace You give me. Help me not to carry around the woundings of my past, but to lay them down at Your feet. Lord, I want to extend the same grace You have given me to others. I need You. Please work in my life and in my heart. I surrender it ALL to You. In Jesus' name, Amen.

SEPTEMBER 3
LOST SOMETHING?

1 Corinthians 3:9
"For we are God's fellow workers; you are God's field, you are God's building."
NKJV

God blesses our acts of service. God fills us and prepares us for service. God doesn't act for vanity; instead, He is purposeful in everything He does. You, my friend, are a part of God's plan and purpose. You are the breathing, walking and talking result of His Word. God's Word will not return void. This means that when God invests in you, He expects multiplication of return. That's not self-serving. Our salvation is a gift from God. What we do with our lives after that is our gift back to God.

Genesis 22:8 "And Abraham said, "My son, God will provide for Himself the lamb for a burnt offering." So, the two of them went together." NKJV

There are rewards stored up in heaven for your serving. It is by God's grace, you are allowed into heaven (Ephesians 2:8-9). Once there, you will be rewarded or not rewarded for your serving. Intentions will not be rewarded.

It goes even beyond that. Do you know someone who is not serving? If so, then you are accountable, in love, to call them on it. Appeal to them. Perhaps due to your boldness to hold them accountable, they will not stand before Jesus with a heart full of intentions and hands full of air.

Life Lesson: We will all give an account of what we did or did not do for the Lord.

Dear Father,
Thank You for loving me so much and being so good to me. Lord, I want to give You my life. I want to give back to others because You have blessed me so much. I am sorry I haven't been as kingdom-minded as I should have been. Help me to store up heavenly rewards. Help me to be a world-changer and to make a difference. In Jesus' name, Amen.

SEPTEMBER 4
ARE YOU READY?

1 Corinthians 3:13
"...each one's work will become clear; for the Day will declare it, because it will be revealed by fire; and the fire will test each one's work, of what sort it is."
NKJV

I fondly remember my youthful days at the beach running back and forth with the meter of the waves. Seashells were joy-finds that held mysteries of the deep, willing to whisper their secrets to the ears of children open to being amazed. How many sandcastles did I build too close to the pounding of the surf only to watch them wash away as the tide crept in. Even the most glorious, well built castle eventually crumbled.

We all face days of testing.

Sometimes, our perspective is diminished by dependence on our own understanding. In the light of eternity, our understanding is the sloppy sand mortar of childhood castles. In the light of eternity, there is a day coming when you will give an account to Jesus for the impact you had or did not have in life.

"I can't do this," "I don't have the time," "I don't have the money," or "I'm afraid." These, my friend, are the grains that make up failure. God created you for boldness and for Kingdom moments. You were not created for timidity or fear. You were created for victory and eternal rewards. One day all you see will be destroyed and all you will be left with is what you sent before you. The tide is coming in. Are you ready?

Life Lesson: Live, in the light of eternity.

Dear Father,
Thank You for loving me. Thank You for speaking to me through Your Word. Lord, I get distracted so easily at times. I want to accomplish all of what You have called me to do, and leave an eternal impact on others around me. Help me, Lord, to let go of things and make decisions to live for You. I want to live my life in the light of eternity. In Jesus' name, Amen.

SEPTEMBER 5
ARE YOU A SIDELINER?

1 Chronicles 20:1
"It happened in the spring of the year, at the time kings go out to battle, that Joab led out the armed forces and ravaged the country of the people of Ammon, and came and besieged Rabbah. But David stayed at Jerusalem. And Joab defeated Rabbah and overthrew it."
NKJV

Being on the sideline is a battleground, not a playground. It's a dangerous place to just hang out there. In an early battle of the Civil War, many of Washington DC's elite gathered around the battlefield to picnic as they watched the battle play out before them. To their horror, the Union Army was defeated and began to retreat. In the mass hysteria, they were hindered by civilians fleeing from the battle; they realized they had become targets. What if those prideful elite had been in the battle instead of gathering around their picnics?

When Christians laze about doing nothing or seek their own rather than the good of others, not only do they hinder their own blessings, but they hinder the blessing of others. The laziness among the church is even more horrifying because it puts others in harm's way.

Do you understand the power that God has given us as a group for the Kingdom? Are you on the sidelines or in the trenches with the army? A team or an army is a powerful thing. Be part of the team. Don't be picked off of the sideline. Go in a blaze of glory fighting on the front lines with the best of the battle.

Life Lesson: Being on the sidelines is a dangerous place for a Christian.

Dear Father,
Thank You for Your goodness and mercy. Thank You that I am in a battle and that You have allowed me to see the victories! Lord, help me to realize that I am not alone in my struggles. I know You are with me and you have surrounded me with others who are there for me. Thank You for that. Help me to wage a mighty war and fight for the souls who are lost. Strengthen me with determination to do battle for those who have no hope and who do not yet know You! Lord, give me determination and ambition to answer to the call to do battle. In Jesus' name, Amen.

SEPTEMBER 6
NEED WISDOM?

1 Corinthians 3:19
"For the wisdom of this world is foolishness with God. For it is written, "He catches the wise in their own craftiness"
NKJV

People search the stars and nature and according to the Bible (Romans 1), God does express Himself in His creation. Seeking the face of God in His work is appropriate, but do not forsake unity of fellowship in church (Hebrews 10:25). God has designed the church to meet the needs of the world, both spiritually and physically. The church should not meet these needs in the ways or wisdom of the world. It is when we seek man's wisdom that we fall into error; when we accept man's knowledge over God's wisdom.

What God calls wisdom and what the world calls wisdom are two very different things. The world looks to academia for wisdom. That is a trap. Pride loves the appearance of wisdom, but it is always rooted in self-deception. The wisdom of God; however, is viewed as foolish to the world.

Proverbs 3:5-8 "Trust in the LORD with all your heart, And lean not on your own understanding; In all your ways acknowledge Him, And He shall direct your paths. Do not be wise in your own eyes; Fear the LORD and depart from evil. It will be health to your flesh, And strength to your bones." NKJV

So, where do we find true wisdom? My friend, it's in the Bible. Search within those pages and find that God promises to give you wisdom. The Bible, above all other books, can be trusted. The difference is the Author. Walk in the wisdom of God's book and you will walk in the intentions of God for your life.

Life Lesson: To be truly wise, read and apply the Bible in your life.

Dear Father,
Thank You for loving me. Thank You for Your grace and mercy. Lord, You know my thoughts. You know that I want to be made well and victorious in my struggles. At times, I know I have listened to the wisdom of the world rather than trusting in You. Empower me to rely on You. I know I have made mistakes. Thank You for Your forgiveness and revealing Your love toward me. In Jesus' name, Amen.

SEPTEMBER 7
LIFE OUT LOUD!

Matthew 6:1
"Take heed that you do not do your charitable deeds before men, to be seen by them. Otherwise, you have no reward from your Father in heaven."
NKJV

Worship is so much more than the music and singing that come before a teaching. Worship is a lifestyle. It's a decision to walk a path that most people will not walk. It is self-denial as a way of life; putting God and others before you. Worship is intentional and is expressed in praise, admiration, joy, love, mercy, forgiveness, giving and serving. It is doing the things that God has told us to do.

Sometimes, worship can be uncomfortable, and other times, it's grimy and dirty. Sometimes, it is dangerous. Jesus was the example of worship lived out loud and as we follow Him, we should reflect His life to others.

Worship is telling others about Jesus and showing them the goodness of God. Worship is our commission, from Jesus, to show and tell the world the Good News of Jesus Christ. Are you a worshiper?

Life Lesson: Jesus should be the central focus of worship.

Dear Father,
Thank You for loving me. Thank You for allowing me to worship You. Lord, I want to live out my life as an expression to others of Your grace and mercy. I want to be sold out for You to serve others regardless of how uncomfortable it may feel. I want to accomplish all of what You have called me to do, and leave an eternal impact on others around me. Help me to do this. In Jesus' name, Amen.

SEPTEMBER 8
THIS 'OAR' THAT

1 Corinthians 4:1
"Let a man so consider us, as servants of Christ and stewards of the mysteries of God."
NKJV

In this verse, the Greek word huperetes (translated as minister) means under-oarsman. Under-oarsmen were men who worked under the main deck of a rowing boat. (As seen in Viking movies) A minister is a servant. The under-oarsman doesn't know where the boat is going, but continues to row until he reaches the final destination. He has an oar, and he knows what to do with it. You, my friend, have been handed an oar...

"What oar," you may ask? The oar of salvation. You are a steward of the mysteries of God. As Paul mentions, you are a living epistle (2 Corinthians 3:1-2). The message you send each day you live your life has the power to lead someone else from death to life. God has invested in you expecting a return. I look around here and see hundreds of people who contain this message. Many are rowing while some are sitting idle expecting others to do the rowing. Take a moment and reflect...What are you doing with your oar?

Life Lesson: Our lives may be the only Bible someone ever reads.

Dear Father,
Thank You for loving me. Thank You for the gifts, talents and resources You have given me. Lord, I have been blessed by You. Help me to lay down my fears. I know I am not living for Your Kingdom as I should. I have complained and been ungrateful for the blessings You have given me. Forgive me. Forgive me for being so distracted by what others are doing and not focusing on the gifts You have given me. I want to give all of my life. Empower me to be a mighty person of valor. In Jesus' name, Amen.

SEPTEMBER 9
FRIEND OR FOE?

1 Chronicles 21:3
"And Joab answered, "May the LORD make His people a hundred times more than they are. But, my lord the king, are they not all my lord's servants? Why then does my lord require this thing? Why should he be a cause of guilt in Israel?"
NKJV

We have a real enemy. Satan is not the ambivalent deviled-ham-can cartoon he has tricked people into thinking he is. He wants to take you out. He will do whatever he can to derail you in serving God. Your adversary, Satan, operates in the darkness of selfishness and pride, and he will try to get you to do the same. When you walk in generosity, kindness or blessing others, you walk in the Spirit.

For reasons we don't know, David wanted to number the people of Israel. Surely counting people is not the sin, but the motive of David's census was. We see Joab, David's friend, warning David against his decision. Had David heeded to his friend's warnings, many lives would have been spared.

Proverbs 27:6 "Faithful are the wounds of a friend, But the kisses of an enemy are deceitful." NKJV

Are you willing to speak into the life of a friend? Are you willing even when it's uncomfortable or difficult? Do you love your friends? People who always speak easy-pleasy things to you may not have your best interest in mind. Are you willing to hurt a friendship to prevent a friend from falling into Satan's trap? Are you willing to allow a friend likewise to speak hard things to you?

Life Lesson: Our real friends will warn us when they think we are doing something wrong.

Dear Father,
Thank You for Your grace and mercy. Lord, I recognize that I am in a real battle and I have messed up. I have opened the door to the plagues in my life and hurt others and myself. Help me to put away all selfishness and pride. Lord, I do not want to live my life blaming others or making excuses for decisions I have made. Lord, forgive me. Thank You for Your Word. Thank You for speaking to me and giving me victory through the blood of Your Son, Jesus. I am so grateful that my sin does not have to count me out. Strengthen me with determination to fight in the battle for the souls of others around me. In Jesus' name, Amen.

SEPTEMBER 10
GIFT RAP

1 Corinthians 4:7
"For what gives you the right to make such a judgment? What do you have that God hasn't given you? And if everything you have is from God, why boast as though it were not a gift?"
NLT

"Well, if it were me, I wouldn't have done it like that." "Why does he do it that way?" "What's up with that?" God has uniquely gifted you in special ways because He has special things for you to do. Enjoy the calling God has gifted you with, but be careful where your eyes wander. It can be easy to begin coveting another's gifts. Be careful of that, my friend. When we get wrapped up in envy, we can neglect our own calling, thus pridefully telling God that He gave us the wrong gifts. Ask yourself, on who does pride misplace your reliance? Pride is a dangerous thing and it has wrecked many a man despite the best intentions.

Romans 12:3 "Because of the privilege and authority God has given me, I give each of you this warning: Don't think you are better than you really are. Be honest in your evaluation of yourselves, measuring yourselves by the faith God has given us." NLT

So, how do you explore your gifts? You won't unearth much sitting on your couch. Jump in and serve others! Through serving, you will begin to identify those things God has equipped you to do. As you use your gifts, you will discover and develop skills you didn't know you had. Gifted musicians spend hours practicing; the more you use your gifts the more gifted you become. Are you faithfully using your gifts?

Life Lesson: We have all been given gifts by God. We should develop our gifts for the glory of God and to bless others.

Dear Father,
Thank You for loving me. Thank You for uniquely gifting me with talents and resources. Lord, I want to use my gifts for You. I want to experience the joy You have for me. Lord, I know I have been ungrateful for the gifts You have given me. Forgive me. Forgive me for being so distracted by what others are doing and not focusing on what You have blessed me with. I offer You all of my life. In Jesus' name, Amen.

SEPTEMBER 11
THE GREAT PHYSICIAN

1 Chronicles 13:3
"...and let us bring the ark of our God back to us, for we have not inquired at it since the days of Saul."
NKJV

Today, on September 11, we remember lives taken by terror and heroes who fought valiantly to preserve our freedoms. The recent years have brought recession and financial ruin to many - a financial pain to all. Across the world, people are dying from curable and easily treated viruses and diseases that by no means should claim lives. In this day and age and perhaps as much as ever, we need to seek God's wisdom. We need our elected officials to seek God's wisdom and to be surrounded by Christian men and women who will speak bravely into situations.

If a Nobel Prize Winner came to you and said he wanted to spend some time to teach you certain things that only he knows, wouldn't you invest in that relationship? What if you were suffering from an incurable disease and a world renowned physician told you he knew of an easy cure and would like to share it with you. Wouldn't you listen to him right then and there?

James 1:5 "If any of you lacks wisdom, let him ask of God, who gives to all liberally and without reproach, and it will be given to him." NKJV

Well, the almighty, all-powerful Creator of everything, God, wants to spend time with you to tell you about His plans for your life and about His cure for an incurable disease called sin. Have you invested in the relationship with Him? Have you taken the time to listen to what He has to say to you? Have you read His book? Will you?

Life Lesson: We should seek God for more wisdom.

Dear Father,
Thank You for loving me. Thank You for the cost that You paid on my behalf for my sins. Lord, I come boldly to the throne of Your grace and ask You to forgive me afresh. In the presence of You Lord, I ask that You alter me and make me different. Lord, give me a passion to know Your Word so that I can intimately know Your will for my life. I ask You for wisdom and discernment. Grant me the strength to apply this wisdom each day to my own life. In Jesus' name, Amen.

SEPTEMBER 12
NEVER MIND THE KIBBLE

1 Corinthians 4:10
"We are fools for Christ's sake, but you are wise in Christ! We are weak, but you are strong! You are distinguished, but we are dishonored!"
NKJV

We see each other one way but God sees us another way. We are all a work in progress...God's work in progress. We all need God to show us who we really are. Let Him work, friend. Don't be preoccupied with yourself. Instead, consider the people around you. We all have blind spots but through God's spirit, God's Word and the fellowship of others, we can see ourselves more clearly. When we can truly see ourselves the way God sees us we can then see others the way God sees them. That's a challenge isn't it? People can stink, especially when they are not like you.

Get this...you're trotting through life just fine until Mr. Skunk enters the picture. Eventually, you learn to tolerate Mr. Skunk, but one day you find him eating out of your food dish! It's your food dish and it's your kibble!

Get out!

It is hard to love people, but that is what you are called to do. You are to love and bless those who cramp your style. You are to rise above the ways of the world and take a higher path of faith. Respond with love and power and not hate and weakness. God will empower you to take the high road. "That skunk ate my kibble," you might respond. Love the unlovable! Bless him. Ask God to bless him. Do this and fulfill your freedom from the ways of this world.

Life Lesson: We need God's help to see things clearly.

Dear Father,
Thank You for this day. Thank You that You desire me to see things more clearly. Lord, I want to see myself as You see me, and I want to see others the way You see them. Lord, help me. I am sorry for being judgmental and hard-hearted. Forgive me. I ask You to bless others who have wounded me. I am ready to let grudges go. Lord, I thank You for Your goodness and mercy. Empower me with strength and open my eyes to see You, Lord. In Jesus' name, Amen.

SEPTEMBER 13
WHEN GOD SAYS NO

1 Chronicles 22:5
"Now David said, "Solomon my son is young and inexperienced, and the house to be built for the LORD must be exceedingly magnificent, famous and glorious throughout all countries. I will now make preparation for it." So David made abundant preparations before his death."
NKJV

This is such an important ministry lesson. David, one of the greatest kings and one of the greatest leaders of Israel, asks God to allow him to build the temple, but God told him no.

Nobody wants to be told no.

David proves the greatness of his leadership by setting aside his wants and begins to help. Instead of complaining, David begins to prepare so Solomon can build the temple.

Sometimes, God says no.

Sometimes, though we have the grandest of plans and the purest of hearts, God says "no" to our plans. What should we do then? Should we grumble and whine? Of course not! God wants us to help one another to build His kingdom. We should take joy in helping those who God has chosen. Kingdom builder's work together in the roles God has uniquely gifted to each, and by such, live up to their God-given utmost potential... And God smiles.

Life Lesson: We are to help others build the kingdom of God as well. Kingdom builders are not concerned with who gets to do what; just that it is getting done.

Dear Father,
Thank You for loving me. Thank You for Your Word and for giving me the opportunity to be a kingdom builder. Lord, I desire to be used in whatever capacity You would have me to serve. Help me to recognize the gifts and talents You have equipped me with and give me a boldness to put Your Kingdom first. I don't want to be a spectator in the Kingdom. I want to be a world-changer. In Jesus' name, Amen.

SEPTEMBER 14
LOVE A CRITIC

1 Corinthians 4:14
"I do not write these things to shame you, but as my beloved children I warn you."
NKJV

A battleship was on exercise at sea in bad weather. The air was thick with fog and the ship's captain was on the bridge. Just after dark, the lookout spotted a light on the starboard side. The captain asked if it was steady or moving. The lookout replied the light was steady, meaning they were on a direct collision course with the other ship. The captain ordered the lookout to signal the other ship...

"Change course 20 degrees. We are on a collision course."

The signal came back "Advisable for you to change course."

The captain signaled "I am a captain. Change course 20 degrees."

"I am a seaman second class. You had better change course 20 degrees" came the reply.

The captain was furious. He sent back, "I am a battleship. Change course!"

Back came the signal, "I am a lighthouse."

The captain changed course.

Everyone likes to be praised. The warm-fuzzy praise strokes our pride just the right way. The danger is that we start to pay more attention to the praise than to criticism. Praise is fine, but criticism offers something better ... the opportunity to change course from catastrophe. Are you open to criticism or do you prefer praise?

Life Lesson: Sometimes, we would rather be ruined by praise than be saved by criticism. That can be deadly.

Dear Father,

Thank You for loving me. Thank You that You speak to me through Your Word. Thank You for Your forgiveness of my sins. I am so grateful that there is a hope and a future in You. Help me to not become prideful of what You are doing through my gifts and talents. Lord, help me to be a kingdom-builder and a world-changer. In Jesus' name, Amen.

SEPTEMBER 15
HIS WORKMANSHIP

Ephesians 2:10
"For we are His workmanship, created in Christ Jesus for good works, which God prepared beforehand that we should walk in them."
NKJV

The other morning I left my wife with a list of things we needed for the garden. I knew she would be out to purchase groceries, and it's only a small hop from the grocery store to the hardware store. Later, when I arrived home from church, she had purchased those items. At some point during the day, she confidently went into the store to make those purchases because she knew there was money in the bank to cover the expense. She was empowered and she knew it.

We see clearly in Ephesians 2:10 that God has planned out, in advance, works which we are to walk in. We can be confident in His plans for our life because He has given us the power to walk in His plans. He tells us He has given us the power to live out His will. It's up to us to go where that knowledge takes us.

Matthew 28:18-20 "And Jesus came and spoke to them, saying, 'All authority has been given to Me in heaven and on earth. Go therefore and make disciples of all the nations, baptizing them in the name of the Father and of the Son and of the Holy Spirit, teaching them to observe all things that I have commanded you; and lo, I am with you always, even to the end of the age.' Amen." NKJV

This may mean taking the Gospel to your family or it may be taking the Gospel to another country; it might be taking the Gospel to your community. Whatever it looks like, it is living out the very Gospel that saved you...A powerful expression of God to the world.

Life Lesson: If we have given our life to God, He has given us the power to live for Him.

Dear Father,
Thank You for loving me. Thank You for desiring to have a relationship with me. Lord, I want to walk in Your power. Give me the strength to submit to You and put You first in my life. Thank You for being so patient with me. Help me to fall in love with You. In Jesus' name, Amen.

SEPTEMBER 16
BE AUTHENTIC

1 Corinthians 4:19
"But I will come-and soon-if the Lord lets me, and then I'll find out whether these arrogant people just give pretentious speeches or whether they really have God's power."
NLT

With the introduction of social media, a lot of claims get thrown around. Unfortunately, very little proof exists to back up most of the claims. It's easier than ever to puff yourself up and make yourself look better than everyone else.

Christians that have been in church learn to speak what I call "Christianese." "I've been washed in the blood of the Lamb," you might hear. That's all fine and dandy until you start to hide behind the jargon. The real test of your faith is the action behind it... not what you say.

James 2:18 "Now someone may argue, 'Some people have faith; others have good deeds.' But I say, 'How can you show me your faith if you don't have good deeds? I will show you my faith by my good deeds.'" NKJV

James went on to write that, "faith without works is dead" (James 2:20). What about you? Does your track record prove your faith without the hype? Talk is cheap and it doesn't blaze trails. Christians willing to get down in the dirt and minister are the ones who forge roads of reconciliation. There's a world in need of Jesus and I'm not content to just talk about it. Won't you work with me?

1 Corinthians 4:20 "For the Kingdom of God is not just a lot of talk; it is living by God's power." NLT

Life Lesson: We should have creeds and deeds.

Dear Father,
Thank You for showing Your love for me by dying on the cross for my sins. Thank You for the glorious opportunity to choose You. Lord, Your Holy Spirit draws me to You, and I am so grateful that You love me that much. Help me to not just talk about my faith, but to show my faith by serving others. Lord, help me to be a kingdom-builder and a world-changer. I choose life... I choose blessing... I choose You. In Jesus' name, Amen.

SEPTEMBER 17
FENCE-SITTING OR WORLD-CHANGING?

1 Chronicles 23:3
"Now the Levites were numbered from the age of thirty years and above; and the number of individual males was thirty-eight thousand."
NKJV

"You talk too much about serving," Pastor David. Perhaps you've thought something like this before. Well yes, I do talk about serving but only when it comes up in scripture. That's the beauty of teaching verse by verse. I don't get to pick my pet topics. I teach what appears in the scripture as we come to it. Even though serving comes up a lot in scripture, I also teach on many varied topics as they come up. So... if serving is a theme that keeps getting stuck in your craw, then friend, in love, perhaps the Holy Spirit is trying to tell you something?

God has called you to serve and has set you apart for special use. He has uniquely gifted you with talents and gifts to serve and be a blessing to others.

Ephesians 4:11-12 "And He Himself gave some to be apostles, some prophets, some evangelists, and some pastors and teachers, for the equipping of the saints for the work of ministry, for the edifying of the body of Christ," NKJV

Ministry is the responsibility of God's people. We get the incredible opportunity to serve God together in this place and across the world. The choice is yours. Fence-sitter or world-changer... Which will you choose?

Life Lesson: We have the incredible opportunity to serve God together.

Dear Father,
Thank You for loving me. Thank You that although You know my past mistakes, You would still ask me to help serve in Your kingdom. Lord, I don't want to be a spectator. Help me to step outside of myself and be a world-changer. I want to help build the kingdom of God and live a life poured out in service to You. Thank You for calling me Your redeemed, Your chosen generation. I choose to live in the fullness of life You have for me. In Jesus' name, Amen.

SEPTEMBER 18
MORAL COMPASS

1 Corinthians 5:1
"It is actually reported that there is sexual immorality among you, and such sexual immorality as is not even named among the Gentiles-that a man has his father's wife"
NKJV

Jeff Foxworthy once quipped, "You might be a redneck if...your state's got a new law that says 'when a couple gets divorced, they are still legally brother and sister.'"

According to 1 Corinthians 5, if someone is introducing their momma and their girlfriend to you and there is only one lady standing there...yeah...there's a problem.

Hopefully, you have never come across that but more and more all you have to do is glance at the front page of the local daily to see just how disoriented and off-course humanity has become. Some people try to convince themselves that they ultimately cannot know right and wrong. That, my friend, is false. Even children know the difference between right and wrong. After a while, repetitive sin and sinful thoughts become adoptive behavior, and the heartache from willful sin begins to wane. Sin is still sin. We need to recognize that there are moral absolutes.

We shouldn't expect someone, who does not know the Lord, to abide in the moral absolutes of the Bible... but Christians have no excuse. We know what is right, and when we are confused, we have God's instructions of what we should do. Something as simple as a compass will lead a whole fleet of ships to their destination. The Bible is the Christian's moral compass. When the Bible tells us not to do something, it is because God loves us enough to tell us what will hurt us. He will instruct us the right way to go. I love my own kids, teach them to do right and discipline them when they disobey. How much more so our Father in Heaven who loves us? No matter how much I love and discipline my children, they still have to make the decision to be obedient.

So, how would you finish this sentence, "You might be a child of God if ...?"

Life Lesson: If you are a follower of Jesus, then your moral absolute compass is the Bible.

Dear Father,

Thank You for loving me. Thank You for inviting me to come to you. Lord, through Your Word, You warn me of what is right and wrong. I desire to respond to You. Because of Your mercy, love and grace, I can give You my broken dreams and struggles. Thank You for accepting me where I am, but not leaving me there. Lord, help me to live in the fullness of my new nature. I want to be a kingdom-builder and a world-changer. In Jesus' name, Amen.

SEPTEMBER 19
ARE YOU WISE?

Proverbs 12:1
"Whoever loves instruction loves knowledge, But he who hates correction *is* stupid."
NKJV

Each week when this church comes together, I instruct you in righteousness through God's Word. A beautiful thing happens when I teach verse-by-verse through the Bible. I hit all the points of instruction and not just my favorite topics. This is a very balanced approach that ensures you will receive the full counsel of God.

Have you ever been in a teaching and it feels like I'm speaking directly to a situation in your life? It's not me. Your wife didn't call and tell me your struggles. We are just there in scripture. That's God speaking to you through His living, powerful and cut-to-the-heart-of-the-matter Word. Heed His counsel, my friend, and you are wise. It means you are loved. Take heart, beloved of the Most High God, the Lord loves you too much to leave you where you are.

Life Lesson: Be open to rebuke and correction from God's Word.

Dear Father,
Thank You for loving me. Thank You for speaking directly to me through Your Word. Lord, I desire to follow You. Because of Your mercy, love and grace, I am blessed. Please protect my days and draw me closer to You. In Jesus' name, Amen.

SEPTEMBER 20
TAINTED TESTIMONY

1 Corinthians 5:6
"Your glorying *is* not good. Do you not know that a little leaven leavens the whole lump?"
NKJV

I've heard many well meaning people share fifty-eight minute testimonies on the blood and guts of their life before Christ, and then two minutes on the beauty of their walk with Jesus. Friend, don't do that! Don't glorify the past while playing down the future. Don't let your sin steal the glory from God—In your testimony and in life.

If you glorify your past sin, guess what will happen when you are eventually tempted? You will begin to reason about the size of the sin. "It's just a little sin," you might say. You are a living testimony. My friend, a little bit of leaven will violate your entire life if you let it in. Guess what then happens to your testimony?

Life Lesson: Bragging about your sin is wrong.

Dear Father,
Thank You for loving me. Thank You that even though I have done wrong things, You invite me to come to You. Lord, I come to You afresh and ask that You forgive me of my sins. Give me the power to live for You, and help me to walk in the newness of life. I choose to be a kingdom-builder and a world-changer. In Jesus' name, Amen.

SEPTEMBER 21
TIME FOR CHANGE

Psalm 24:1
"The earth is the Lord's, and everything in it. The world and all its people belong to him."
NLT

Psalm 146:8
"The LORD opens the eyes of the blind. The LORD lifts the burdens of those bent beneath their loads."
NLT

There was a time when "seasons of plenty" meant storehouses were flush with favor and plans were put into place for meager months. Today, people have fallen into the trap of expecting things now for less work. For a while these expectations were met. But times have turned tough, and the debt that was racked up in the pursuit of pleasure has doubled back baring greedy teeth. What you do with the blessings God gives you directly affects how God is able to bless you in the future.

Luke 16:11 "And if you are untrustworthy about worldly wealth, who will trust you with the true riches of heaven?" NLT

God allows you to make your own choices and God looks for good stewards to bless. He wants His investment to yield a good return. What's your track record with finances? Be honest with yourself, this could change your life. Debt is bondage. If Jesus set you free from bondage, why then do you seek it out? Once free, no slave places the shackles of tyranny back on themselves. Why keep going back to debt? If you continue, there will come a day when debt will become your master.

Life Lesson: You want God to bless you? Then be a better steward of what He has already given you.

Dear Father,
Thank You for loving me. Forgive me where I have not been a good steward over the things You have provided. Help me to be a better steward of my time, resources and talents. Lord, protect me from my foolishness and bad choices. Empower me to be a blessing to others. In Jesus' name, Amen.

SEPTEMBER 22
DON'T LOSE HEART

Habakkuk 3:1-2
"A prayer of Habakkuk the prophet, on Shigionoth. O LORD, I have heard Your speech *and* was afraid; O LORD, revive Your work in the midst of the years! In the midst of the years make *it* known; In wrath remember mercy."
NKJV

Babylon was about to take Judah; Babylon, who's gates must have bulged with wickedness, more so than all of Israel. Habakkuk couldn't understand how God could use evil in the lives of the righteous to produce His good purposes. You've probably had the same question.

It is so difficult to understand how God, in His sovereignty, is able to use bad things to produce good results - yet He does. Do you ever look back at the potholes of your life and realize God was at work? It's so much easier to comprehend God's work in your life looking back than when in the midst of trials, yet we should be confident that God is ultimately in control.

Psalm 20:7 "Some *trust* in chariots, and some in horses; But we will remember the name of the LORD our God." NKJV

It is so hard not to place our trust in man's wisdom - man's creations and power - our assumptions. Yet there is One who calls it all foolishness. When troubles come where do you place your trust? Your actions reveal it. Where do you go? The Bible, prayer, godly counsel - these are the refuge of those who place their trust in God. Faith is not only what you believe in, it's what you put your trust in. When in the midst of trials, know that God is with you. Don't lose heart!

Life Lesson: Faith isn't just what you believe in; it's what you put your trust in.

Dear Father,
Thank You for loving me. Thank You for who You are and for Your love, grace, and mercy. Lord, I am so grateful You are patient with me. I thank You for all the things you have so freely given to me. Lord, there are things in my life that I need to change. It's not easy to trust sometimes, and I am sorry. Help my doubt. Help me to keep my eyes on You. Empower me through my trials and uncertainties to trust in You. I submit my life to You wholeheartedly. In Jesus' name, Amen.

SEPTEMBER 23
GOD'S WILL, GOD'S WAY

Luke 9:2
"He sent them to preach the kingdom of God and to heal the sick."
NKJV

What is God's will for your life? That's the ten thousand dollar question, isn't it? Well, it's really very simple. You see, many times when we ponder God's will for our lives we get very self-focused and miss the point. God's will for our lives isn't so much about us as it is about Him. Living for God, is that so hard for us to do after He died for us?

God revealed His will for all through His Son, Jesus. Through repentance and forgiveness we can live a life of service and sacrifice. It is God's will for you to love others and be a living testimony to the world. Do you have a concern, care and compassion for a world of people dying without Jesus? God's will for your life is to lead others to salvation in Jesus. Be a steward of the Gospel by sowing into the lives others, and you will see God's will in action in your life.

Life Lesson: It is important to know God's will for your life.

Dear Father,
Thank You for loving me. I am so grateful that You did not leave me to live my life on my own. Thank You for having a plan for my life and revealing it through Your Word. Lord, I confess that I have tried to live my life my own way, and I am sorry. I want Your will for my life. Lord, help me to live out the plan You have for me. I give You my life...to do Your will...in Your way. In Jesus' name, Amen.

SEPTEMBER 24
IT'S ME

1 Corinthians 5:9-11
"I wrote to you in my epistle not to keep company with sexually immoral people. Yet I certainly did not mean with the sexually immoral people of this world, or with the covetous, or extortioners, or idolaters, since then you would need to go out of the world. But now I have written to you not to keep company with anyone named a brother, who is sexually immoral, or covetous, or an idolater, or a reviler, or a drunkard, or an extortioner—not even to eat with such a person." NKJV

Seinfeld made light of the classic break up line, "It's not you, it's me." Maybe you've been handed that line before, but you know what? There's some truth behind it. Deep inside, you know it's the sin inside you. Relationships are complicated. They are complicated even more by the sin in your life. Are there rocky relationships in your life? Own the problem; look at yourself.

Whether at work, home or church, relationships are everywhere, and you are to be stewards of them. Relationships can promote your walk with Jesus or they can derail you - if you allow it. You are called to love the unlovable, but there are times when you will have to decide which relationships are healthy and which relationships are not. A relationship that is promoting you to sin and wander from your walk with Christ is not a good relationship.

There are some who think that if they get away from other people they will get away from the sin that's in the world. Convents, monasteries and the like have all been built with this mindset. That's not a solution. This only walls them in with their own sin while denying the world the "salt" in their lives. Jesus told you to be the salt of the world. You know what salt does? It makes people thirsty. You are to make this world thirst for a relationship with Jesus. If you withdraw from the world, this doesn't happen.

You are a steward of the life God has blessed you with. Whether you participate in wrong activities or not the decision is yours to make. God has called you, Christian, to be active in other's lives and a part of that is confronting sin, with a heart of love. When this fails to happen, everyone gets hurt; feelings get bent, anger festers, and relationships become whack. Confrontation is uncomfortable. It's not fun. But love requires us to step beyond the bounds of comfort because we love others. This, my friend, is the calling of all Christians ... to be leaders in the world.

Life Lesson: Our main problem is the sin inside us not the people around us.

Dear Father,

Thank You for loving me. Thank You for the forgiveness of my sins. Even though I have done wrong things, You ask me to come to You. It is through Your payment for my sins that I can come to you in repentance. Lord, I am sorry. I ask that You help me to own up to the things I try to hide from You. Empower and equip me with the knowledge or Your will for my life. Lord, give me the power to live for You, and help me to walk in the newness of life. I choose to be a kingdom-builder and a world-changer. In Jesus' name, Amen.

SEPTEMBER 25
UNEQUALLY YOKED

Ezra 4:1-2

"Now when the adversaries of Judah and Benjamin heard that the descendants of the captivity were building the temple of the LORD God of Israel, they came to Zerubbabel and the heads of the fathers' houses, and said to them, "Let us build with you, for we seek your God as you do; and we have sacrificed to Him since the days of Esarhaddon king of Assyria, who brought us here."
NKJV

There are many who claim to be Christians, but a glance into their lives and an examination of the fruit of their lives, reveals evidence contrary to the claims. Many times I have, in marriage counseling, seen one spouse surprised to discover that the other is, in fact, not a believer. As crazy as it sounds, it happens a lot! I've seen Christians team up with business partners whom they believed to be Christian only to later discover that they are not. God has been quite clear that it is not in the best interest of Christians to partner with non-Christians.

2 Corinthians 6:14-15 "Do not be unequally yoked together with unbelievers. For what fellowship has righteousness with lawlessness? And what communion has light with darkness? And what accord has Christ with Belial? Or what part has a believer with an unbeliever?" NKJV

You should not be unequally yoked with an unbeliever. Why? Well, think of a yoke around the necks of two oxen. Why is it there? That's right...it ensures that they each go in the same direction. What direction? Well, without someone leading the team, the pair will go in the direction of the strongest ox. In a marriage between an unbeliever and a believer, the relationship will go in the direction of the unbeliever. In business, don't expect a non-Christian partner to operate within the Godly principals of your convictions.

Does this mean we are to separate ourselves from other people who do not know Jesus as their Lord and Savior? No, absolutely not. We are to be involved in life with them in order that we might tell all and lead some to salvation. Their lives, however, are not to dictate our lives and their yoke is not to be ours. When you take up the yoke of a non-believer, you will put down the yoke of Jesus.

Matthew 11:28-30 "Come to Me, all you who labor and are heavy laden, and I will give you rest. Take My yoke upon you and learn from Me, for I am gentle and lowly in heart, and you will find rest for your souls. For My yoke is easy and My burden is light." NKJV

Life Lesson: Be careful who you team up with.

Dear Father,

Thank You for loving me. Lord, I have been so distracted with the things of this world. I have been complacent and self-centered. I know I am not worthy of anything Lord, but through Your Grace and Your Spirit, You empower me to do great things. Help me to live a life that is surrendered and walk in Your will for my life. In Jesus' name, Amen.

SEPTEMBER 26
DROP IT

1 Corinthians 6:4-6

If you have legal disputes about such matters, why go to outside judges who are not respected by the church? I am saying this to shame you. Isn't there anyone in all the church who is wise enough to decide these issues? But instead, one believer sues another-right in front of unbelievers!" NLT

A large number of lawsuits will be filed this year in state courts throughout the United States. The statistic is somewhere in the ballpark of 15 million lawsuits. That is one new lawsuit every two seconds or one lawsuit for every 12 adults in America. Truly, that is a large number of lawsuits!

I believe it all began in 1992 when a U.S. woman sued McDonald's, after being burned with a coffee purchased at the famous fast-food restaurant. Everybody laughed about it, until she received 2.9 million dollars as compensation. The frivolousness of this is obvious even to the least discerning, yet we consistently allow these suits to move forward and even reward those who file them. What a laughing stock. That's precisely the impression when the church gripes and complains against itself. It's been said that the Christian army is the only army in the world that shoots its own wounded. How many times in the past decade have we seen Christian leaders fall only to have the rest of Christians pounce on them like hungry jackals? The answer is pretty much every time. Instead of seeking to restore the fallen, they are cast aside by the church. The church is the body of Christ...every member is important.

So then, why do Christians seek non-Christian counseling? Why do Christians pursue and even pay for secular (worldly) advice? Well, I think a huge part of it is that Christians know what answer they will receive from Christian counselors and that's not what they want to hear. They seek out someone who will give them the answer they want to hear. Don't do that. Seek out Biblical counsel and heed it. First, pray and read your Bible. If you do not receive your answer, speak with an Elder or Pastor at your church. But, if you do that, honor the time that they spend seeking the Lord for your counsel and heed it. It could be that, indeed, you were wronged by another Christian. It could be that you could see some kind of victory in a secular court. What harm will it do to the body of Christ? What impression will non-Christians looking in get from your actions? Sometimes, you may have to just let an issue drop for the good of the whole body.

Life Lesson: We should try to work out our differences with other Christians, if needed, with spiritually mature people.

Dear Father,

Thank You for loving me. Thank You that even though you did nothing wrong, You were willing to suffer for my wrongdoings. I am the one who deserves what You have received for me. Through Your sacrifice, my sins are forgiven. Thank You for taking my punishment so I could be declared innocent. Help me to walk in the joy, peace and grace that You extend to me and give me the power to be a kingdom-builder and a world-changer. In Jesus' name, Amen.

SEPTEMBER 27
TO READ OR NOT TO READ

1 Chronicles 24:1-2
"Now these are the divisions of the sons of Aaron. The sons of Aaron were Nadab, Abihu, Eleazar, and Ithamar. And Nadab and Abihu died before their father, and had no children; therefore Eleazar and Ithamar ministered as priests."
NKJV

One of the hallmarks of The Bridge is a commitment to teaching the Word of God verse by verse and chapter by chapter. I've said this before...one of the best things about teaching through the Bible verse by verse is that nothing is missed. You wouldn't read a book by skipping the beginning and reading the middle, to the back and to the beginning again would you? No, certainly not. So, why do so many pastors teach the Bible that way? The Bible is the full counsel of God. When pastors pick through the Bible and choose the things they want to teach, it does a disservice to the body of Christ. Think about it. God tells us...

2 Timothy 3:16-17 "All Scripture is given by inspiration of God, and is profitable for doctrine, for reproof, for correction, for instruction in righteousness, that the man of God may be complete, thoroughly equipped for every good work." NKJV

If God gave His Inspired Word to equip you for the task He's placed before you, then what an unprofitable servant you would be to teach or instruct only part of His Word. If God holds me accountable as a teacher of His Word, I want to be able to say that I taught the entire Bible, not just part of the Bible.

So, if you listen to the teachings here at The Bridge, you are receiving the full counsel of God. What are you doing with it? Are you picking and choosing what you want to receive? I can only teach the Bible. I cannot make you do the Bible. That's your choice. My prayer is that you experience the complete joy that comes from applying the doctrine, reproof, correction and instruction in righteousness you receive from the Bible.

Life Lesson: To live spiritually fruitful lives we should read and apply all of God's Word, not just selected parts.

Dear Father,

Thank You for loving me. Thank You for desiring to have a relationship with me. Thank You that You chose me not because of what I have done, but in spite of what I have done. I am grateful You give me a choice and Lord, I choose You! Lord, empower me to receive Your Word and experience all that You have for me. I am adopted, I am yours, and I am a child of God. In Jesus' name, Amen.

SEPTEMBER 28
CAN I BE A CHRISTIAN AND...?

1 Corinthians 6:9-10
"Do you not know that the unrighteous will not inherit the kingdom of God? Do not be deceived. Neither fornicators, nor idolaters, nor adulterers, nor homosexuals, nor sodomites, nor thieves, nor covetous, nor drunkards, nor revilers, nor extortioners will inherit the kingdom of God."
NKJV

I was in a music store one day to pick up some items for the church. While I was there, I overheard another man who was also purchasing some items for his church. The language he was using was peppered with profanity. I looked at him and asked if he was a Christian. He rebutted, "Of course I am...I'm an American." This was one of the few times I've been left speechless. He was already out the door before I thought of what to say. With a changed heart should come a changed life. In his letter to the Galatians, Paul puts it this way...

Galatians 5:13 "For, brethren, ye have been called unto liberty; only use not liberty for an occasion to the flesh, but by love serve one another." NKJV

Jesus went through incredible suffering and pain so that you could be free from the bondage of sin. We should never use freedom as occasion for sin.

You have probably heard the Christian life described as a "walk". That's because it's not just a onetime decision and then life carries on as usual. It's a complete change, a new way, a new path and a new walk. A decision to follow Jesus, by definition, means leaving the path you were on for a new one. A life that has not taken on new direction is not changed and may not be saved.

Psalm 119:59 "I thought about my ways, And turned my feet to Your testimonies." NKJV

Life Lesson: When we decide to follow and serve Jesus, we decide to do certain things or try not to do certain things.

Dear Father,

Thank You for loving me. Thank You for allowing me the opportunity to make choices. Lord, I choose to have a relationship with You. Thank You for Your Spirit that draws me closer to You. Through Your loving grace and mercy, I have the power over my guilt, my sins, my shame and the world. Empower me to overcome areas that are holding me back and to be free through the Truth of Your Word. I want to experience the abundant and blessed life that you have gifted to me - I am a kingdom-builder and a world-changer. In Jesus' name, Amen.

SEPTEMBER 29
WORSHIP

1 Chronicles 25:1
"Moreover David and the captains of the army separated for the service some of the sons of Asaph, of Heman, and of Jeduthun, who should prophesy with harps, stringed instruments, and cymbals. And the number of the skilled men performing their service was:"
NKJV

There are actually seven different Hebrew words for our one English word for 'worship'.

1. YADAH - yaw-daw - to worship with the extended hand.
2. TEHILLAH - teh-hil-law - to sing, a song or a hymn of praise
3. BARAK - baw-rak - To kneel or to bow. To give reverence to God as an act of adoration.
4. HALAL - As in Hallelujah meaning Praise the Lord Hallel meaning praise and Jah meaning God. (this word appears over 110 times in the OT) to be clear (orig. of sound, but usually of color); to shine; hence, to make a show, to boast; to rave;
5. TOWDAH - to-daw - To give worship by the extension of the hand in adoration or agreeing with what has been done or will be.
6. ZAMAR - zaw-mar - To sing with instruments. To make music accompanied by the voice.
7. SHABACH - shaw-bakh - to address in a loud tone, a loud adoration, a shout! Proclaim with a loud voice, unashamed, Shout to the Lord.

Worship is not only what happens in music during the service; it's a lifestyle. It's a song in your heart as you go about your day-singing praises to the Lord. Worship includes music but is also all kinds of things outside music; reading your Bible, giving thanks, giving financially to the kingdom, prayer and so much more. Worship is making God and His kingdom number one in your life and priorities.

Worship is giving thanks when things are going well. Worship is praising God regardless of your circumstances in the midst of trials. Sometimes, it is not easy. We will not always 'feel' like worshiping God, and it is then we are reminded we worship Him because He is worthy. Worship is a battle, and it is the battle cry of the Christian.

Worship pleases God. When you live out your life day in and day out walking in worship, it will change your life. Take just a few minutes right now, loved one, and worship Him and give thanks. Do you have a roof over your head? Thank Him. Do you have food to eat? Give Him praise. Are you in the midst of trials or tribulations? Thank Him that one day those trials will end.

Life Lesson: God is worthy of all of our worship.

Dear Father,

Thank You for loving me. Thank You for Your Word and the opportunity to sing praises to You! Lord, I lift my eyes to the heavens and recognize Your goodness. Help me to get into the habit of worshiping You in the good times and the bad. I sing praises of Your loving grace and mercy, and lift my voice to You because You are always worthy to be praised. In Jesus' name, Amen.

SEPTEMBER 30
SHINE ON

1 Chronicles 26:12
"Among these were the divisions of the gatekeepers, among the chief men, having duties just like their brethren, to serve in the house of the Lord." NKJV

Will you shine or will you rust? Time does interesting things to us, our relationships and our bodies. We seem to have this notion that time will always help us sort things out and that somehow, it helps our priorities to rise to the top and solves our problems. Friend, it really doesn't. We think that time heals all wounds and yet time can often wound all our heals. We have to decide on a daily basis what is important. Is God important to you? If God is important to you, then His Kingdom priorities become your priorities. When we say we are following Jesus, this should describe an active and ongoing relationship with Jesus. If we make the daily decision to follow Him, if we decide daily that Jesus is important, over time, He becomes more important. He will be important enough to take the time and make the effort to serve Him in the house of the Lord. Jesus said we are the light of the world. Actually, He said YOU are the light of the world. As you serve God, your light shines. Check out these verses.

2 Corinthians 4:3-4 "If the Good News we preach is hidden behind a veil, it is hidden only from people who are perishing. Satan, who is the god of this world, has blinded the minds of those who don't believe. They are unable to see the glorious light of the Good News. They don't understand this message about the glory of Christ, who is the exact likeness of God." NLT

Matthew 5:14-16 "'You are the light of the world. A city that is set on a hill cannot be hidden. Nor do they light a lamp and put it under a basket, but on a lampstand, and it gives light to all who are in the house. Let your light so shine before men, that they may see your good works and glorify your Father in heaven.'" NKJV

Daniel 12:3 "Those who are wise will shine as bright as the sky, and those who lead many to righteousness will shine like the stars forever." NLT

When Charlie, in the movie "Willy Wonka," does the right thing, Willy Wonka says, "So shines a good deed in a weary world." Friend, serve God and let your light shine in a cold, dark and hurting world. As your light shines, it will change your life, the world and give spiritual light and sight to your family, friends and loved ones. So your call... shine like the stars forever or rust like a bucket. You are called to shine. Shine on loved one, shine on...forever.

Life Lesson: It is when we give our lives to the work of the kingdom that we shine the brightest.

Dear Father,

Thank You for loving me. Thank You for the opportunity and reminder to shine for You. I want to give my life away and shine like a star in the night sky. Empower me with Your strength to encourage, pray, support, serve, love and give to others. I want to do all I can to reach all I can - I want to be a kingdom builder, a world-changer and a light to the world. I choose to let my good works shine and serve in the house of the Lord. In Jesus' name, Amen.

OCTOBER 1
THE HARVEST AWAITS

1 Chronicles 27:1
"And the children of Israel, according to their number, the heads of fathers' houses, the captains of thousands and hundreds and their officers, **served the king** in every matter of the military divisions. These divisions came in and went out month by month throughout all the months of the year, each division having twenty-four thousand." NKJV

I am amazed each time I think about what God is doing here at The Bridge. What started as a family home Bible study has grown to over two thousand in weekly attendance! In addition to this, the verse by verse teaching is now broadcast all around the world on TV, radio, and the Internet in an ever-increasing number. All of this is possible in part because of the people who humbly and faithfully serve in this place, perhaps like you—thanks.

Matthew 25:23 "His lord said to him, 'Well done, good and faithful servant; you have been faithful over a few things, I will make you ruler over many things. Enter into the joy of your lord." NKJV

Christians should desire to serve God and be a worker in the harvest. If you're serving God as He tells you in His Word, then God will bless your obedience. You should be ambitious for the kingdom, not for position, prestige or power. Each person has been uniquely gifted to serve. Friend, that means you have been gifted to actively serve alongside others in the body of Christ. Making up excuses as to why you cannot serve God indicates a heart issue. Please read Luke 9:57-62. Do you make excuses or make time to serve the King? Ask yourself, "What do I place first in my heart?" Is it your job, family or finances? God should be your first priority. You should be others-centered rather than self-centered. The Holy Spirit, in the life of the believer, can accomplish anything. Jesus gave us a life-changing message, but without workers in the harvest, those who need to hear cannot and will not hear the Good News.

Matthew 9:37-38 "Then He said to His disciples, "The harvest truly is plentiful, but the laborers are few. Therefore pray the Lord of the harvest to send out laborers into His Harvest." NKJV

Friend, let me challenge you today to think about where your heart is. Do you have a passion that drives you to serve Him and others? Are you fulfilling God's purpose for your life? When you look over your life, will you be able to say, "I poured my life into what mattered most?" Your time is so valuable. Make a decision about what is worthy of your time.

Life Lesson: We should all desire to serve God and to be workers in the harvest.

Dear Father,

Thank You for loving me. Thank You for inviting me to sit at Your feet. Lord, You are so willing to forgive me, and I thank You. Thank You for the unique abilities and talents You have given me and I want to give them back to You. I want Your blessings to overflow upon me and through me. I want to give my life away. Empower me with Your strength and courage to serve You and others. I want to be a kingdom-builder and a world-changer. In Jesus' name, Amen.

OCTOBER 2
WHO WAS JESUS?

Luke 5:19-26
"And when they could not find how they might bring him in, because of the crowd, they went up on the housetop and let him down with his bed through the tiling into the midst before Jesus. When He saw their faith, He said to him, "Man, your sins are forgiven you." And the scribes and the Pharisees began to reason, saying, "Who is this who speaks blasphemies? **Who can forgive sins but God alone?"** But when Jesus perceived their thoughts, He answered and said to them, (What did we say, what did He not say) "Why are you reasoning in your hearts? Which is easier, to say, 'Your sins are forgiven you,' or to say, 'Rise up and walk'? But that you may know that the Son of Man has power on earth to forgive sins" - He said to the man who was paralyzed, "I say to you, arise, take up your bed, and go to your house." Immediately he rose up before them, took up what he had been lying on, and departed to his own house, glorifying God. And they were **ALL** (disciples, friends, enemies, etc.) amazed, and they glorified God and were filled with fear, saying, "We have seen strange things today!" NKJV

The Bible mentions several people involved in the death, burial and resurrection of Jesus Christ. This is something that you rarely, if ever, find in fairy tales and folklore. You find Mary Magdalene, Joseph of Arimethea, James and John, the sons of Zebedee, and five hundred other witnesses. Either this was the most cleverly concocted hoax ever perpetuated on the world even fooling Roman politicians and Jewish spiritual leaders, or it really was the most pivotal event in human history.

Life Lesson: The life, burial and resurrection of Jesus are historically recorded events that would stand up in a court of law.

Matthew 28:5-7 "But the angel answered and said to the women, "Do not be afraid, for I know that you seek Jesus who was crucified. He is not here; for He is risen, as He said. Come, see the place where the Lord lay." **NKJV**

The intriguing thing to note is that how you look at this tells how you look at heaven, hell, life, death, faith, love and forgiveness. There were five hundred witnesses and some of them were famous. There was overwhelming and undeniable proof!

Millions of lives today have changed because of this, including mine. The calendar itself forever changed with the birth and death of Jesus (BC and AD). The church would forever after worship on Sunday. Are you are still waiting for more information? Friend, you have enough information to make an educated decision but it still requires a step of faith. Take the chance. I did. My life was forever changed for the better.

Dear Father:

Thank You for sending your son to die for me so that I could be forgiven and have new life. I ask You to forgive me of all of my sins. Lord, I have done wrong things, and I am sorry. Thank You for Your forgiveness. Please give me the power to live for You, all the days of my life. In Jesus' name, Amen.

OCTOBER 3
THE CHOSEN

1 Chronicles 28:1
"Now David assembled at Jerusalem all the leaders of Israel: the officers of the tribes and the captains of the divisions who served the king, the captains over thousands and captains over hundreds, and the stewards over all the substance and possessions of the king and of his sons, with the officials, the valiant men, and all the mighty men of valor."
NKJV

David was a poet, a warrior and an incredible leader. He was a man who had made mistakes, and yet people still followed him. In order for a church to perform its mission well, it must stand in unity with its leader. The body of Christ shouldn't be sitting on the bench but should be actively following God's plan. You should lay down your mistakes and shortcomings and begin pouring your life out in service to God as part of the team. Don't waste time wandering in the desert of your mistakes but discover God's plan and get back up again. He has chosen you right where you are to serve in His kingdom with other believers.

Deuteronomy 7:6 "For you are a holy people to the LORD your God; the LORD your God has chosen you to be a people for Himself, a special treasure above all the peoples on the face of the earth." NKJV

Just like David recognized God's hand and call on his life, you also were called. God chose you knowing everything you had ever done wrong--knowing all your strengths, weakness and past failures. He knew all those things and yet He still chose you. There are many reasons God should not have called any of us, but He did. God did not call you because of who you are but in spite of who you are. He then makes you a part of His kingdom and gives you an opportunity to respond to the call. Will you choose to follow His call? Will you be a spectator or a kingdom builder? You decide. Step out and be part of what God is calling you to do.

Life Lesson: It takes a team and a leader for a church to perform its mission well.

Dear Father,
Thank You for loving me. Thank You for the opportunity to choose You and Your plan. Thank You for giving me the power to choose. Lord, my choices affect the souls of men and women whose lives are eternally hanging in the balance of my decision to respond to your call. I want to give my life away and be a part of the team. At times, I lose my focus and follow my own plans. Empower me with Your strength and courage to pray, give, support, serve in Your kingdom. Whatever task at

hand, I want to be all I can to reach all I can—I want to be a kingdom builder, a world-changer. I am committed to be an active part in Your kingdom. In Jesus' name, Amen.

OCTOBER 4
LET YOUR LIFE SHINE

1 Corinthians 7:15-16
"But if the unbeliever departs, let him depart; a brother or a sister is not under bondage in such cases. But God has called us to peace. For how do you know, O wife, whether you will save your husband? Or how do you know, O husband, whether you will save your wife?"
NKJV

When you accept the grace of Jesus Christ and realize that it was your sins that nailed Him on the cross, your life changes. It is not a mental acquiescence but rather an active belief that affects the way you live. Your life should be moving toward Christ, letting go of the old and embracing the new. Friend, folks around you should see the fruit in your life. Do you pray, go to church read the Bible or fellowship with other believers? All fall short of the glory of God and none are righteous. It is because of Jesus that you can be declared innocent before a righteous and holy God.

You are saved by grace, and yet we are called to do good works. (Ephesians 2:8-10, NKJV)." When you asked Jesus to forgive you of your sins, something happens—a heart change. There is a desire in the new believer to move from decision, to confession and then to commitment. Jesus tells us not all that say Lord, Lord will be saved (Matthew 7:21, NKJV).

Romans 10:9-10 "that if you confess with your mouth the Lord Jesus and believe in your heart that God has raised Him from the dead, you will be saved. For with the heart one believes unto righteousness, and with the mouth confession is made unto salvation." NKJV

This is what it takes to be a believer. You cannot brag about something you have been given. Your salvation was paid for with a heavy price. He chose to die for you, for me and the sins of the entire world. What has the grace that you have been given done for those around you? There is an influence you give as you follow Jesus in your home, the work place and at school. May your life shine as you walk in a dark world and may you offer hope to those who do not know Him.

Life Lesson: The grace that does not change your life cannot save your soul.

Dear Father,

Thank You for loving Me. Thank You for Your patience, grace and mercy for me. Today, I want to refocus on my relationship with You. Lord, I have been burdened, weary and broken hearted. I thank You that You care for me so much that no matter how much I have messed up, You invite me to come to You. Help me to give my life away to be kingdom-builder and a world-changer. I choose the changed life You offer—a life lived for You. Through the Truth of Your Word, I am restored. In Jesus' name, Amen.

OCTOBER 5
NOTHING BUT THE TRUTH

Micah 2:1-2
"Woe to those who devise iniquity, and work out evil on their beds! At morning light they practice it, because it is in the power of their hand. They covet fields and take them by violence, Also houses, and seize them. So they oppress a man and his house, a man and his inheritance."
NKJV

In the verse above, we see those in power taking advantage of the people. The world believes that it is acceptable to take advantage of others for gain of position or authority. If you are a leader in the workplace, do you take advantage of the system to benefit yourself? Friend, let me make this more personal. Do you take advantage of your family, friends or co-workers for your benefit? When we get to know a person, we know how to set them off or manipulate them for what we want. That is ungodly and God does not bless the unbiblical practices of deception.

1 Corinthians 10:13 "No temptation has overtaken you except such as is common to man; but God is faithful, who will not allow you to be tempted beyond what you are able, but with the temptation will also make the way of escape, that you may be able to bear it." NKJV

Even in those times when it seems there is no other option but to bend the truth for your benefit - God provides a way out. Taking responsibility for your actions is an important characteristic of a Godly disciple. God will always honor you when you take responsibility for your mistakes, even when it's difficult. Live out the Biblical model that God entrusted to you in regards to your relationships even when it doesn't make sense.

In the end, it comes down to your making a decision about Jesus. How far will you follow Jesus in your relationships? Until it gets inconvenient-uncomfortable-what about when it becomes painful? Are you willing to follow the Biblical model all the way? What will you decide? Gain for yourself or lay your life down for the sake of the Gospel?

Life Lesson: One characteristic of a Godly leader is to do what is Biblical even when it causes personal hardship.

Dear Father:

Thank You for loving me. Thank You for continuing to do a work in my life. You have called me to live a disciple's life, and I choose to honor You in living out the model You have set before me. Lord, when things get tough and I mess up, empower me with courage and strength to live out Your Truth and encourage others. I am a Kingdom-builder and a world-changer. In Jesus' name, Amen.

OCTOBER 6
A LIFE WORTH LIVING

1 Corinthians 7:19
"For it makes no difference whether or not a man has been circumcised. The important thing is to keep God's commandments."
NLT

Friend, you have unique talents and abilities that God wants to use for His glory. Your act of love for God is expressed when you serve and keep His commandments. Don't be dissatisfied with your giftings, but obey God and walk in them.

Serving God with your gifts and obeying his commandments should be a high priority in the life of the believer. This is not to say that you are under the law, but because of His amazing love for you, you can respond in love by serving others with your talents. While you are not trying to earn your righteousness, you should desire to be obedient to Him. Not because you are earning your salvation but because you love Him.

1John 5:2-3 "By this we know that we love the children of God, when we love God and keep His commandments. For this is the love of God, that we keep His commandments. And His commandments are not burdensome." NKJV

You are to love God with all of your heart, soul and mind (Matthew 22:37). Serving and obeying God should not be burdensome because He loved you first. There are a lot of things I do not feel like I want to do, but because of my love and commitment to God I do them. When I take flowers to my wife, I do not do so because I am married. I do this out of love. In the same way, show your love and affection for God by being committed to witness, read the Bible, pray and love others.

Do you express your love to God by serving Him and others? Remember how God told us to discover a life worth living? Feel safe and secure in the arms of God's redeeming power and undeniable love. Step out in obedience to Him and share the hope and love of God to this cold, dark world that does not have anything worth living for and sure does not offer anything worth dying for.

Life Lesson: Serving and keeping God's commandments is not only a commitment but an act of love as well.

Dear Father,

Thank You for Your love that sets me free when I ask you to forgive me of my sins. Thank You for allowing me to come to You. Lord, I thank You for the talents and abilities You have given to me. Forgive me where I have envied someone else's gifts while neglecting to use my own gifts. Help me to be grateful for the call You have for my life so that I can discover purpose and meaning the way You intended. Lord, thank You for Your patience with me. Help me bring hope to a lost and dying world - to be a Kingdom-builder and a world-changer. In Jesus' name, Amen.

OCTOBER 7
BE AN EXAMPLE

Micah 3:1
And I said: "Hear now, O heads of Jacob, And you rulers of the house of Israel:
Is it not for you to know justice?"
NKJV

Today's society is fast paced and full of busyness. But what are we busy doing? Is it trying to live life with a mission to better ourselves? Any of us who have tried to live this kind of life know that we are never satisfied even when we achieve our goals. Friend, if we have a relationship with Jesus, is it not for us to know justice? If we claim to be a follower of Jesus, we have a responsibility to live a Godly life everywhere we go. God has showed us that life is not about us, it's about knowing Him, loving Him and loving others. If anyone should know that, it is the body of Christ—those who have been forgiven of their sins. Now that God has blessed us with His forgiveness, He desires that we share His love with others. The world needs us to be an example of living the Bible so that they too are drawn to Christ. They need answers, and for us to say we are "Christians" and live our life in pursuit of personal gain would only be a contradiction to who we say we follow.

2 Corinthians 13:5-6 "Examine yourselves as to whether you are in the faith. Test yourselves. Do you not know yourselves that Jesus Christ is in you? - unless indeed you are disqualified." NKJV

Friend, let's stand before God often, and ask Him to reveal things in our life that are not pleasing to Him. As we do that, the world will not have any stones to throw. They will be drawn to Jesus and living their life for Him just like we should.

Life Lesson: The world is looking for answers, not for hypocrites.

Dear Father:
Thank You for loving me. Thank You for forgiving me of my sins. Help me to live a disciple's life wherever I go. Please remove those things that are not pleasing to You so others are not confused. Thank You Lord, for using me to change lives for eternity just like you changed mine. I am a Kingdom-builder and a world-changer. In Jesus' name, Amen.

OCTOBER 8
FATHER KNOWS BEST

1 Corinthians 7:21-22
"Were you called while a slave? Do not be concerned about it; but if you can be made free, rather use it. For he who is called in the Lord while a slave is the Lord's freedman. Likewise he who is called while free is Christ's slave."
NKJV

We often think our circumstances in life are our problem. Whether it is our job, friends or family situations, we often think these are the source of our issues. Life can be uncomfortable at times, but friend, if you are a Christian, God has allowed circumstances in your life because he is forming Himself in you.

God is trying to help you in your circumstances and trials. By allowing you to go through difficult challenges in life, you can grow to be more like Him. Sometimes, trials can be painful. Is there anybody in your life that God is trying to use to remove what does not resemble Him in your life? You are precious to God and He loves you. He wants to grow you through your challenges. As you mature in the Lord, you should ask Him what He wants you to learn through them and change you.

Consider a clay pot. The potter forms the clay to create a beautiful masterpiece. Once he forms it, he fires the clay to make it hard and usable for the tasks for which it was created. What if the potter pulled the clay out too soon? It would be half-baked and the clay pot could not be usable. The potter would then have to break the pot, re-wet it, form and fire it again. Life is a lot like this clay pot. Who wants to be a half-baked Christian? When we do not learn a lesson that God is trying to perfect in us, we have to go through it again and again until He forms Himself in us.

Philippians 1:6 "being confident of this very thing, that He who has begun a good work in you will complete it until the day of Jesus Christ;" NKJV

Friend, God has called you to serve Him. He is using your circumstances to free you from the bondage of the shame, guilt and sin that separates you from Him. Whatever is going on in your life—trust Him! God is willing to do whatever it takes to reach you. He wants to set you free.

Life Lesson: Our circumstances are usually not the problem; it is our response or attitude to the circumstances that is the problem.

Dear Father,

Thank You for loving me. Thank You for the opportunity to go through circumstances and using them to form me to be more like You. Lord, You sentenced and punished Yourself for me so I could be forgiven. I thank You that You were willing to pay such a high price for me. I choose to walk in the incredible plans You have for me instead of the plans I have made. Help me to be faithful in the small things by listening to You. You are my hope, my love and my peace. Help me to hear Your voice and to discover my own call and adventure in life. In Jesus' name, Amen.

OCTOBER 9
THE CALLED

1 Chronicles 29:1-2
Furthermore King David said to all the assembly: "My son Solomon, whom alone God has chosen, is young and inexperienced; and the work is great, because the temple is not for man but for the LORD God. Now for the house of my God I have prepared with all my might: gold for things to be made of gold, silver for things of silver, bronze for things of bronze, iron for things of iron, wood for things of wood, onyx stones, stones to be set, glistening stones of various colors, all kinds of precious stones, and marble slabs in abundance." NKJV

David was an incredible leader and king. Although he had made mistakes, God called David a man after God's own heart (Acts 13:22). He chose to follow God with all of his heart regardless of his mistakes. Why would God call David this? When God forgives you, He chooses to forget your wrongdoings when you ask Him. Regardless of your shortcomings or wrongdoings, God has called you. God has called me to be senior pastor. With that responsibility, I have to make difficult decisions. The work ahead is enormous for the body of Christ. God chooses each of us to do certain tasks. If we choose to follow Him it works wonderfully. If we choose not to follow Him or His plan, it never works out well. God will not violate your freewill. God wants to bless you. He has called you to the work of the Kingdom so He can bless you and so you can be a blessing to others.

Friend, whatever your calling or gifting is, you should walk in it. You will have difficult decisions to make, and there will be distractions. Don't lose heart and keep your eyes on Jesus. When Nehemiah was building the wall, there were distractions. When Paul was on his mission, there were distractions. What you do for the Kingdom is not for man but for God. David wanted to build the temple but God said "no." Often the test of your submission to the work God has called you to comes when God says "no" or when a leader says "no." What do you do when you have a disagreement? What did David do? He didn't throw a tantrum or quit. Instead, he walked in his calling and helped get things ready for God's temple. Whenever you begin to complain or question God's choices, you get into trouble. Notice that David didn't give and serve halfheartedly - he did it with all of his heart. This shows his submission to the will of God. Friend, this same commitment should be in you. Your response in how you submit, serve, give of your finances and time, say a whole lot about your level of commitment to Him. No one else can make the choice for you. Will you choose to follow His call? Will you be a spectator or a Kingdom-builder? You decide. Step out and be part of what God is calling you to be. Discover the blessing of being a blessing.

Life Lesson: God chooses certain men/women for certain tasks.

Dear Father,

Thank You for loving me. Thank You for choosing me to work in Your Kingdom. I want to give my life away and be a blessing to others. At times, I get distracted and lose my focus on You. I am sorry. Empower me with Your strength and courage to walk in the tasks You have gifted to me. All that I have or ever will be comes from You. Thank You for Your blessings. I choose to fix my heart on you Lord. I give You my life, my talents and my giftings. Whatever task is at hand, I want to be a Kingdom-builder, a world-changer and a blessing to others. In Jesus' name, Amen.

OCTOBER 10
CAN I AFFORD TO COMPROMISE?

2 Chronicles 7:14
"if My people who are called by My name will humble themselves, and pray and seek My face, and turn from their wicked ways, then I will hear from heaven, and will forgive their sin and heal their land."
NKJV

In today's society, it can be difficult to live a life that calls for us to be different. We excuse away bad behavior and submit to pressures that weigh on us—and we compromise. We try to do things our own way and resist doing things God's way. Second Chronicles 7:14 says, If we seek Him humbly and turn from our wrongdoings we can have this intimate relationship with Him. If we disobey Him, our lives will be consumed with ruin (Zephaniah 1:1-6). God longs for us to be obedient and desires a deep relationship with us. While we cannot live a perfect life, we can set our heart and minds on God and seek Him.

Are you living on the fence? Have you compromised in your relationship with other Christians, in prayer or in time with Him and His Word? Are you willing to seek God and turn away from your own selfish ways? Friend, the day is drawing near when God will intervene in each of our lives. In our inability to offer Him anything, He still accepts you and me. God provides a way out through His Son, Jesus, as payment for our sins—for those who place their faith and trust in Jesus Christ.

What will you decide today? You can decide now to live for Him, sit on the fence or reject Him and spend eternity separated from Him. This is an act of your will and no one can make the decision for you. The time is now.

Life Lesson: The warning was for them, and it still applies to us today.

Dear Father,
Thank You for loving me. Thank You for the opportunity to examine my relationship with you. I have strayed, and I do not want to compromise my life anymore. I commit myself to you afresh... I admit that I am a sinner. I believe You died for my sins. I open the door of my heart and life to You. I receive You as my personal Lord and Savior. Right now, I ask for Your power to help me turn from my sins. Thank You for forgiving me and saving me. Help me to be a blessing to You and others with each day that You give to me. In Jesus' name, Amen.

OCTOBER 11
WHO'S ON FIRST?

1 Corinthians 7:32, 35

32 But I want you to be without care. He who is unmarried cares for the things of the Lord—how he may please the Lord. But he who is married cares about the things of the world—how he may please his wife. 35 And this I say for your own profit, not that I may put a leash on you, but for what is proper, and that you may serve the Lord without distraction."
NKJV

In the verse above, Paul is saying that whether you are married or unmarried you need to place God first in your life. If you make Him first, you will find life a joy and a blessing. If not, you are headed for trouble. What are your eyes on today? The answer tells a lot about what your priorities are. Often, we look around us and grow anxious of all our responsibilities. When we are anxious with the priorities of life, it should drive us to pray—drive us to Him! Sometimes, priorities take on different levels of importance at different times in life, but nothing should ever come before God in our lives.

What is first in your life right now? Is it your family, finances, spouse or career? Friend, if it is anything other than God, your priorities need to be reorganized. You have the power over your own will to choose. Choose God or don't choose God, but you are the only one that makes this decision. God has to be first today. It's a daily decision, and the reality is that if He is not first in your life, the rest of your life will lack peace and be chaotic. Is that what you want?

God has placed the desire in you to follow Him. So ask yourself some hard questions. Are you being distracted? Do you want to be filled with regret or will you make a decision to reap the peace, joy and blessing only He can give? Make Him number one and watch God pour himself out on you. He is waiting. Will you move?

Life Lesson: Married or unmarried, the important thing is to put God first in your life.

Dear Father,
Thank You for loving me so much that You give me chances to realign my heart and priorities. Thank You for telling me how life works and allowing me the opportunity to choose You. Please help me to get my priorities in order. I have been distracted and put other things before You. Remind me gently each day to make You first in my life today and always. I choose to serve You first—to be a Kingdom-builder and world-changer. In Jesus' name, Amen.

OCTOBER 12
SAVE YOURSELF THE HEARTACHE

Colossians 2:8
"Don't let anyone lead you astray with empty philosophy and high sounding nonsense that come from human thinking and from the evil powers of this world, and not from Christ."
NLT

Many of us know Jeremiah 29:11 and are often encouraged by the fact that God has a plan for our life, but then shortly we find ourselves pushing our agenda rather than submitting to His. We boldly stand up, puff out our chest and proclaim "I've got it God...I know you have a plan, but mine is better." Friend, we cannot run our life better than our Lord. In our hands, our lives will be filled with pain, heartaches and suffering. In the hands of God, we will find forgiveness, grace and love.

Unfortunately, the world does not realize this truth and often tries to replace God's way with its own. For instance, in Alabama, Utah and other states we find proms encouraging and even celebrating homosexual couples who attend. In schools around our country, students are taught that they are little more than evolved pond scum and that right and wrong are whatever you want it to be. These same schools then sit back in shock as students struggle with violence, suicide and STD's. There is a better way and that way is found in God's Word.

Friend, there is an amazing life out there waiting for you, but it comes when we submit to God's way rather than our own. In Christ, we can have life and have it "abundantly." Choose this moment to submit to God's plan. I promise - you won't be disappointed.

Life Lesson: Save yourself the heartache by submitting to God's preferred way.

Dear Father,
Thank You for loving me. Lord, forgive me for the times that I have chosen to go my own way rather than submit to You. I understand now that I was wrong and that Your way is far greater. Father, teach me through Your Word and fill me with the Holy Spirit that I might live a life completely dedicated and submitted to You. In Jesus' name, Amen.

OCTOBER 13
COUNTING SHEEP IS EXCITING

Colossians 3:15-17
"And let the peace of God rule in your hearts, to which also you were called in one body; and be thankful. Let the word of Christ dwell in you richly in all wisdom, teaching and admonishing one another in psalms and hymns and spiritual songs, singing with grace in your hearts to the Lord. And whatever you do in word or deed, do all in the name of the Lord Jesus, giving thanks to God the Father through Him."
NKJV

A few years ago, I played music and taught at a large church. It was a church of about 6,000 and it seemed like everyone was there that day. They walked me from the backstage to the stage to teach, share and play music. Many came forward, and in the end many asked Jesus to be their Savior. It was awesome. Then, I was escorted through a back hallway to a product table to sign CD's.

Later that evening, I reflected on the day and thought, "God, I didn't get to talk to the people that got saved." God reminded me that He had given me my life, and I had given that life back to Him. It was not my life but His life to do with as He saw fit to best serve people and the cause of Christ. If He wanted to open big doors and bless whatever ministry I was involved with, and if I had less time for myself, family or friends, that was His decision and not mine. I made that decision years ago and continue to walk in that decision. I love that so many have gotten saved and discipled through this ministry here at The Bridge. I do regret that one of the byproducts of the massive blessings He is pouring out upon us is not being able to sit around and just talk and share. It is God's choice and He has made it. There are lives at stake it's not about us, it's about Him.

Life Lesson: One thing that is constant in life is change.

Dear Father,
Thank You for loving me and desiring to use me. Remind me to reflect upon You daily and rejoice in the changes that You are making in my church and in me. Lord, lives of lost souls are hanging in the balance of my decision to fully serve You. Soften my heart and empower me boldly to serve you and influence others with your life-changing message. In Jesus' name, Amen.

OCTOBER 14
NEVER BEEN UNLOVED

Malachi 1:2
I have loved you," says the LORD. "Yet you say, 'In what way have You loved us?' Was not Esau Jacob's brother?" Says the LORD. "Yet Jacob I have loved;"
NKJV

At the time of Malachi, the people of Israel had a checkered past with God. There were times of celebration and victory as God brought them out of Egypt and established them in the Promised Land. There were also times of hardship and discipline when they were exiled from their land, often because of their idolatrous behavior. During all these times one thing remained the same—God still loved them and still called them His people.

The same is true today. We have all fallen short of the glory of God and His standard of perfection. We deserve nothing but punishment and yet God, who is rich in mercy, chooses to love us despite our past.

Ephesians 2:4-5 "But God, who is rich in mercy, because of His great love with which He loved us, even when we were dead in trespasses, made us alive together with Christ (by grace you have been saved)," NKJV

If you have asked God for forgiveness and know Jesus as your Savior, you are chosen by God. You are loved by the Creator of the universe. Not because of what you can do for Him, but because He chooses to love you. What an amazing God.

So friend, if you find yourself wrestling with circumstances that are difficult and feel like God has stopped loving you, come to Him today and know that you are loved.

Life Lesson: God loves you because He chooses to love you.

Dear Father,
Thank You for loving me. I know that I have sinned against you. Lord, forgive me of my sin and create in me a new heart that desires You. Father, help me understand the amazing love you have shown me on the cross and may it motivate me to serve You and serve others. In Jesus' name, Amen.

OCTOBER 15
DEFLATE

1 Corinthians 8:1

"Now concerning things offered to idols: We know that we all have knowledge. Knowledge puffs up, but love edifies."
NKJV

We've all been there. You find yourself standing face to face with someone who is absolutely certain that they know everything there ever was to know. In essence, they want to make sure you know all they know—and that's a problem. While knowledge is important and the knowledge of God's Word is vital to any Christian, we cannot let knowledge lead to pride. In fact, the more we learn about God, His grace and what He has done for us, it should lead us to humility and love—and deflate our pride.

Let me ask you friend. Has God's Word led you to love others? Do you read God's Word in order to know God more or so that you can win the next theological debate? Yes, we must know God's Word and it should be front and center in our life; however, it should lead to a life of love and not arrogance. Or, maybe you find yourself on the other side and you aren't in God's Word like you'd like to be. Friend, let me encourage you to pick it up and read it daily. Remember; take the time to read because He took the time to bleed.

Life Lesson: Bible knowledge should lead to love. Bible study should lead to Bible doing.

Dear Father,
Thank you for loving me and for your amazing grace. Thank you for giving me Your Word so that I may know You more. Teach me your ways and fill me with Your Spirit so that I can be used to reach others with the Gospel. In Jesus' name, Amen.

OCTOBER 16
TITHE TALK

2 Corinthians 9:6-7
"But this I say: He who sows sparingly will also reap sparingly, and he who sows bountifully will also reap bountifully. So let each one give as he purposes in his heart, not grudgingly or of necessity; for God loves a cheerful giver."
NKJV

Tithing; the sound of that word usually has one of two effects on people. We either rejoice at the thought of being able to give back to God or we cringe as we think about handing over "our" money. Of course, the idea that it is "our" money is the first problem.

Psalm 24:1 "The earth is the Lord's, and all its fullness. The world and those who dwell therein." NKJV

You see friend, all that you or I have is not our own. We have been given these things by our heavenly Father and He desires that we use them for His Kingdom. Most times this is done by giving to your local church so that God's Word can be taught and ministry can happen. Imagine if everyone in your church decided that they weren't going to tithe anymore. How would the church function? How would the services the church provides continue? Now imagine if everyone in the church tithed. Imagine the cities that would be impacted by the outreach and ministry. Imagine the missionaries who would be equipped with Bibles, medicine & other supplies. Imagine the Word of God being supported by the people of God impacting more people for God. Just Imagine.

Friend, are you partaking in this awesome opportunity to give to the work of the Lord? God has done so much for you—are you willing to sacrifice for Him?

Life Lesson: We should be faithful with whatever God has given us.

Dear Father,
Thank You for all that You have given to me. Lord, I desire to view my money, my family and my own life as a gift from You. Help me to focus on how I can better use those things for Your Kingdom. Fill me with Your Spirit so that I may give to you all I have, not grudgingly, but with a joyous heart. In Jesus' name, Amen.

OCTOBER 17
TIME WASTER

Titus 3:9
"Do not get involved in foolish discussions about spiritual pedigrees or in quarrels and fights about obedience to Jewish laws. These things are useless and a waste of time."
NLT

One of the songs we love to sing in our fellowship is titled "They will know we are Christians by our love". This song sums up how the world "should" view us as followers of Christ. Unfortunately, the world is more apt to recognize churches these days for their disagreements and backbiting, rather than their love.

Yes, as followers of Christ, we must stand up for the truth and present the primary issues of scripture with boldness and power. Issues like the virgin birth; salvation by grace alone through faith alone and the inerrancy of scripture are all key doctrines that must be upheld. Yet, we also must not be overwhelmed with secondary issues & foolish debates that lead to division. So you like pipe organ and a choir for worship? That's cool. Does that mean you can't fellowship with a guy who likes electric guitar & drums? Of course not! If he loves Jesus and you love Jesus then fellowship together in Christ.

Once we all quit wasting time arguing over the foolish things and begin loving one another, this world will take notice. Then we can point them to the One who loved us first.

Life Lesson: Don't waste time arguing about stuff that does not matter. By the way, most stuff does not matter.

Dear Father,
Thank You for Your love. Thank You for Jesus who showed that love by dying on the cross for my sins. Lord, help me to look beyond petty issues and foolish arguments so that I may show Your love to those around me. Fill me with Your Spirit so that I will be ready to stand for Your Truth and to share the love of Christ wherever I go. In Jesus' name, Amen.

OCTOBER 18
STUMBLING BLOCK

1 Corinthians 8:8-9
"But food does not commend us to God; for neither if we eat are we the better, nor if we do not eat are we the worse. But beware lest somehow this liberty of yours become a stumbling block to those who are weak."
NKJV

We are all different. This is true in our personalities, our life circumstances and our spiritual walks. At any given church, you will find both mature and immature believers. In 1 Corinthians 8, Paul is dealing with these two groups who were wrestling with eating meat sacrificed to idols. The mature believers knew that there was nothing evil about the meat itself, yet the less mature believers still did not think it was right. So what was a mature believer to do?

...Die to themselves and think of others first.

Paul challenges the mature believers to not fight over petty things but instead be willing to give up freedoms in order to keep a brother from stumbling. In fact, in verse thirteen he writes, "Therefore, if food makes my brother stumble, I will never again eat meat, lest I make my brother stumble." Paul is willing to give up eating meat for the sake of his brother. That is a great picture of sacrificial love. Whether it is alcohol, movies, music or even meat - are you willing to put it aside for the sake of your brother?

Life Lesson: Through love and knowledge, people who are stronger in the Lord should help each other and those who are weaker in the Lord.

Dear Father,
Thank You for Your love. I pray that You would help me to love others even if it means giving up something in my life. May the actions and words of my life point to You and You alone, causing no one to stumble. Fill me with Your Spirit so that I may be a beacon of light to this world. Thank You Lord for all that You are doing in my life to make me more like Jesus. In Jesus' name, Amen.

OCTOBER 19
ANCORA IMPARO

Micah 4:2

"Many nations shall come and say, 'Come, and let us go up to the mountain of the LORD, To the house of the God of Jacob; He will teach us His ways, And we shall walk in His paths.' For out of Zion the law shall go forth, And the word of the LORD from Jerusalem."
NKJV

In the last years of his life, Michelangelo was said to have scribbled "Ancora Imparo" in the margin of some of his work. These two words translate to "I am still learning" and show that even a brilliant man like Michelangelo still desired to learn more. These two words should also be part of any Christian's life. No matter how long we have been a believer or studied scripture, we should always desire to learn more.

If we really think about it, all of us desire to learn more than we know now. We may desire to learn a new trade or technique to help in our career. Maybe, we desire to learn how to better parent our kids or love our spouse. Unfortunately, many in our world are more concerned about learning who will be kicked off American Idol than anything of eternal value. So the question isn't "do you want to learn" but rather "do you want to learn about Jesus?" It's in our knowledge of Him that we find the way of salvation, the way to peace and the way to an abundant life. Friend, as you crack open your Bible and search the scriptures, God will reveal Himself to you and you will never be the same. Are you ready to learn?

Life Lesson: God desires for us to be actively learning about Him.

Dear Father,
Thank You for Your Word and for making it available to me. Thank You for the men and women who died so that Your Word was kept safe throughout the years. Lord, give me a desire to read Your Word above everything else. Open my heart to Your Word and Your Word to my heart. Teach me so that I may be used for Your Kingdom. In Jesus' name, Amen.

OCTOBER 20
LEFTOVERS

Zephaniah 3:7
"I thought, 'Surely they will have reverence for me now! Surely they will listen to my warnings. Then I won't need to strike again, destroying their homes.' But no, they get up early to continue their evil deeds."
NLT

I really enjoy cooking...a lot. In fact, you could probably say I am a "foodie." I love the preparation, the smell of ingredients simmering on the stove and everything that comes with cooking; except maybe the clean up. Of course, often when you cook a large meal and everyone has had their fill, the leftovers are bagged up and hidden in the dark corners of the fridge or tossed to the dog. Friend, do you realize this is often true of our lives? We spend hours each week working, spending time with family and enjoying hobbies only to throw God the leftovers.

The truth is that God has given us the time we have, the money we spend and the abilities we enjoy and because of that, we should give back to Him. In fact, we can do that by simply asking Him for opportunities to serve Him and others throughout each day. So whether you are on the job or at the park, ask God to give you an opportunity to share the Gospel. As we actively pursue ways to glorify God and reach people, we will be giving God our best and in turn will find true joy.

Life Lesson: God deserves our best, not the rest.

Dear Father,
Thank You for the life You have given me and for the many blessings I enjoy. Lord, I pray that You will help me to use them for Your Kingdom. Please open doors for me to be able to share the Gospel with those around me and to help those in need. Lord, I don't want to simply give You leftovers. Help me give You my very best. In Jesus' name, Amen.

OCTOBER 21
I LOVE YOU IF YOU AGREE WITH ME

1 Corinthians 8:13
"So if what I eat causes another believer to sin, I will never eat meat again as long as I live-for I don't want to cause another believer to stumble."
NLT

Have you ever made a big deal out of something that was not a big deal? Every one of us has. As followers of Jesus, we have to choose to love people even when we think they are wrong or they think we are wrong. If we only walk in love when we agree, it's not really love is it? Are you willing to love someone beyond the point you agree into the scary land where you disagree?

I believe we should know our Bibles more, but more importantly, we should love God and people more. As a Bible teacher, I want people to understand solid doctrine but I know solid doctrine without love is useless. Walking in love, grace and unity are more important than trying to be right all the time.

John 17:21 "I pray that they will all be one, just as you and I are one - as you are in me, Father, and I am in you. (And why does Jesus tell us unity and love are important?) And may they be in us so that the world will believe you sent me." NLT

John 17:23 "I am in them and you are in me. May they experience such perfect unity (again Jesus ties unity to our ability or inability to fulfill our mission - the Great Commission - Matthew 28:18-20) that the world will know that you sent me and that you love them as much as you love me." NLT

Life Lesson: Unity is difficult and even painful and yet is needed to accomplish our mission of reaching the world.

Dear Father,
Help me to love people so much that I am more concerned with loving You and loving them than I am about being right. Please help me to encourage and protect the unity of the church by putting aside my personal preferences, tastes and traditions. Help me to love my brothers and sisters so much that I am careful not to stumble them. Help us to walk together to help people to believe in you as the Messiah. Please forgive me when I have not done this. In Jesus' name, Amen.

OCTOBER 22
SKILLED CRAFTSMAN

2 Chronicles 2:7

"Therefore send me at once a man skillful to work in gold and silver, in bronze and iron, in purple and crimson and blue, who has skill to engrave with the skillful men who are with me in Judah and Jerusalem, whom David my father provided."
NKJV

In 2 Chronicles 2, we find King Solomon preparing to build the Temple. In order to create this amazing structure, he enlists skilled laborers of all different trades to begin working on the Lord's house. Did you know the same is true even today? While we may not be building a physical temple, we are all working to build the Kingdom of God. To do this well, we must use the talents and gifts God has given us for His purpose.

Of course, I can hear some say "I don't have any gifts" or "I'm not skilled in anything." Friend, this is far from the truth. In fact, God's Word refutes that thought in Ephesians 2:10...

"For we are His workmanship, created in Christ Jesus for good works, which God prepared beforehand that we should walk in them." NKJV

You see, we are God's masterpiece and have been created by God to do good works for Him. In order to walk in those good works, He has gifted us each with certain talents. The exciting part is figuring out what these talents and abilities are and how we can use them to build His Kingdom. What's your skill? Are you ready to use it for the Lord?

Life Lesson: We are all skilled or gifted in an area or areas. Find your gifting and serve God with your whole heart.

Dear Father,
Thank You for making me. I praise You Lord for the abilities I have and the talents You have given me. Lord, help me to look for opportunities to use these special gifts for You. If there is anything keeping me from serving You with all my heart, please remove it. Fill me with Your Holy Spirit so that I will be fully equipped to help build Your Kingdom. In Jesus' name, Amen.

OCTOBER 23
AM I NOT AN APOSTLE?

1 Corinthians 9:1
"Am I not an apostle? Am I not free? Have I not seen Jesus Christ our Lord? Are you not my work in the Lord?"
NKJV

Apostle Paul... many of us hear that name and think of teacher, new testament writer and hard core missionary. As we read about his actions in the book of Acts and study his letters throughout the scriptures, we can easily see God's hand on His life. Yet, even this incredible man of God had to deal with people questioning his role as apostle and not just unbelievers, but believers who Paul himself had led to the Lord.

So, what are we to do when we begin to serve God only to find ourselves faced with discouraging words from those we thought we knew? Friend, we pray for them and then we continue walking with the Lord. It's in Christ that we find our encouragement and it's in Christ that we find strength during those battles. I'll go ahead and tell you now that serving God is not going to lessen the number of nay-sayers; it's going to bring more. Of course, while we may face harsh words from those around us, the sweetest words ever to be heard lay before us when Christ says, "well done good and faithful servant."

Life Lesson: The more good we do or impact or influence we have, the more people will speak ill of us.

Dear Father,
Thank You for my life and for the forgiveness I have through Jesus. Thank You for the opportunities I have to serve You and serve others. Lord, as I step out in faith and begin serving You, may I look to You for my encouragement regardless of what man says. Father, keep me focused on You no matter the circumstance. In Jesus' name, Amen.

OCTOBER 24
PEACE

Micah 5:4-5
"And He shall stand and feed His flock In the strength of the LORD, In the majesty of the name of the LORD His God; And they shall abide, For now He shall be great to the ends of the earth; and this One shall be peace."
NKJV

In Micah 5, we find one of many prophecies recorded in the Hebrew Scriptures pointing to the coming Messiah. Thousands of years later, we now know that Micah was true and that Jesus, the Messiah, was born just as had been foretold. We also know something else about Jesus, the One chosen by God to save mankind. In verse five Micah writes,

"And this One shall be peace." Micah 5:5

The One Micah is speaking of is Jesus Himself. He doesn't just offer peace between God and man, but He also is the very personification of peace. I don't know about you friend, but this is amazing to me. You see, this world is constantly searching for peace but the peace they search for is empty. Rather than seeking the One who is peace, they chase after false promises of peace through alcohol, drugs, relationships and even religion. The sad part is that the One who is peace, Jesus Christ, stands with open arms desiring to be peace to a world in desperate need of it. Friend, do you have peace? Or maybe I should ask, "Do you know the One who is peace?" You can today.

Life Lesson: Without Jesus we can do nothing.

Dear Father,
I know that I have sinned and because of my sin I do not have peace with You. Lord, please forgive me of my sins and cleanse me of all unrighteousness. Create in me a clean heart and fill me with Your Spirit so that I may know the One who is peace. I believe in Jesus and what He has done for me on the cross. Lord, change my life and use it for Your Kingdom. In Jesus' name, Amen.

OCTOBER 25
CLAY

Isaiah 29:16

"Surely you have things turned around! Shall the potter be esteemed as the clay; For shall the thing made say of him who made it, 'He did not make me'? Or shall the thing formed say of him who formed it, 'He has no understanding'?"
NKJV

Imagine...the God of the universe who spoke stars and galaxies into existence is the very one who formed you into the person you are today. Your eyes, nose, hands and feet were all created by the One who holds the oceans in the palm of His hands. I don't know about you friend, but that is a humbling image. What great comfort to know that the God of all things created me the way I am and yet, He still desires to mold and make me more and more like Jesus.

Of course, this process is tough and quite messy. There's a lot of molding, cutting and carving that seems painful at the time but in the Master's hands, we become a masterpiece. When we fully submit our lives to God, He is able to take hardened clay and bring new life to it by wetting it with His Word and Spirit. He then begins shaping us into the image of His Son by scooping out the excess clay that is weighing us down. He then prepares us for His service and writes on us His name because we now belong to the Master. Friend, if you find yourself enduring hardship or trials, know that the Father is molding you into a vessel that He can use. It may be difficult, but we can trust His hands because He loves us and knows what's best.

Life Lesson: We are the clay and God is the potter.

Dear Father,
Thank You for the forgiveness of sins through Jesus. Thank You for saving me and changing my life. Lord, I pray that You would take this broken ball of clay and make it new. Mold my life into what You desire. Help me to see the hardships in my life as the Master's hands shaping me more into the likeness of Jesus. Use my life for Your world and your glory. In Jesus' name, Amen.

OCTOBER 26
IF

Malachi 2:1-2
"And now, O priests, this commandment is for you. If you will not hear, and if you will not take it to heart, to give glory to My name," Says the LORD of hosts, "I will send a curse upon you, and I will curse your blessings. Yes, I have cursed them already, because you do not take it to heart." NKJV

"If"...That one word usually depicts a choice to be made or a condition that is being presented. For instance, if I decide to go to the beach, I cannot therefore go to the mountains too. If I break the speed limit, then I will find myself facing flashing lights in my rear view mirror. You see, the priests at the time of Malachi had chosen not to follow God's law and were offering blemished sacrifices. The priests had sinned and because of that sin God had to punish them, but not before using the word "if". God desired for them to turn from their sin and come back to Him. Sadly, they rejected the truth.

Friend, the same is true today as you read this. We have all offered blemished sacrifices to God because of our sin, but God is gracious and kind and He extends hope in the word "if". If we hear His Word and take that Word to heart, we will find life and peace. Of course this means the opposite is true. If we harden our heart to His Word and reject it, we will never find life or peace. Have you messed up? Have you fallen? Friend, God extends to you hope and promises that if you would hear His Word and take it to heart you will never be put to shame. He offers forgiveness and grace...if you chose to receive it.

Life Lesson: We need to be actively hearing, receiving and doing the will of God.

Dear Father,
I know that I have sinned against You. I also know that You offer me hope through Jesus. Lord, I hear Your word and desire to take it to heart and give my life to You. Change my life so that my sacrifices of praise may be worthy of such an amazing God. Thank You for life, peace and forgiveness. In Jesus' name, Amen.

OCTOBER 27
HARD WORK

1 Corinthians 9:9
"For it is written in the law of Moses, 'You shall not muzzle an ox while it treads out the grain.' Is it oxen God is concerned about?"
NKJV

Work is a good thing. God created work in the beginning before sin was part of the equation. On top of that, each one of us is gifted with talents and strengths that can be used for God. So that's said, "Are you ready?" God could place a giant billboard in the sky proclaiming Himself to the world, but He has chosen to use you and me. We are the people of God who get to share the story of God with a world in need of God.

"So how's it work?" Simple, get involved. Begin serving in your church. Look for opportunities all around you to share the love and words of Jesus. There will be times that it's hard but God will bless your hard work. Over time, you will look behind you to see a harvest of lives impacted by your diligence. Together, we can change the world for Christ. Let's Go.

Life Lesson: We should work hard and God blesses hard work.

Dear Father,
Thank You for salvation and Your many blessings. Give me a hunger to know Your Word and to share it with those around me. Open my eyes to opportunities to serve others and serve You whether in my church or around the corner. Fill me with Your Spirit and equip me for the work You have ready for me. In Jesus' name, Amen.

OCTOBER 28
THE VEIL

2 Chronicles 3:13-14
"The wings of these cherubim spanned twenty cubits overall. They stood on their feet, and they faced inward. And he made the veil of blue, purple, crimson, and fine linen, and wove cherubim into it."
NKJV

The temple of God was an amazing sight to behold. Filled with fine gold and ornate designs, it was a place where men could come stand in the presence of God. Then again, you would have to be part of the priesthood to enter the Holy of Holies and truly be in God's presence. For most everyone in Israel, they were only allowed partial access to God through His priests - but 2000 years ago everything changed.

Matthew 27:50-51 "And Jesus cried out again with a loud voice, and yielded up His spirit. Then, behold, the veil of the temple was torn in two from top to bottom; and the earth quaked, and the rocks were split," NKJV

The very veil that had been commanded by God for His temple was now being torn by God. It was His signal to us that He had made a way for us to approach Him without a priest. Friend, this is an amazing truth. The God of all creation has made a way for you and I to fellowship with Him. Because of Jesus' death and resurrection, we now have access to the Father through prayer. So have you spent time with Him today? Take to Him your sins, doubts, fears and troubles and know that He hears you and cares for you. My friend, the veil is gone! Let us approach the throne of grace with confidence.

Life Lesson: We have access to God only through the cross.

Dear Father,
Thank You for what You did on the cross. Lord, because of Jesus, I now have forgiveness of sins and access to You without need of pastor or priest. Help me to not take that for granted but to come to You in prayer on a daily basis so that I will be ready to do Your will. Use me Father to share this amazing truth with all those around me. In Jesus' Name, Amen.

OCTOBER 29
UNHINDERED

1 Corinthians 9:12
"If others are partakers of this right over you, are we not even more? Nevertheless we have not used this right, but endure all things lest we hinder the gospel of Christ."
NKJV

Paul had given up everything for the sake of the Gospel. He had been imprisoned, beaten, shipwrecked and snake-bit, but he still remained steadfast in declaring Christ crucified. Even in his letter to the church of Corinth, we see a man who is willing to continue the race even if all support falls out from underneath him. How could he do this? Simple, he knew the God he served.

When we step out in obedience to God, we don't always know what may happen next. He may lead us to share the Gospel with someone even though we don't know how they will respond. Sometimes, we may give to our church while not knowing how it will affect our budget for the week. Whatever the situation, there is one unchanging element - God. He is still the same God who provided for Paul despite the lack of those who gave. He's still the same God who protected Paul while adrift at sea. He is the same God who gave His own Son to die for our sins in the ultimate act of love. My friend, because He is God, we can step out in faith and experience a life like no other. Because He is God we have the freedom to serve Him with all our hearts.

Life Lesson: When we give our lives to God, only then do we discover maximum freedom.

Dear Father,
Thank You for all that You have done for me. Thank You for Jesus and the gift of salvation. Lord, because of that gift, I am now free to serve You with all my heart and soul. Remove the fear and doubt in my mind. Help me to give all of my life to You and use me for the work of Your Kingdom. In Jesus' name, Amen.

OCTOBER 30
A GREATER CLEANSING

2 Chronicles 4:6
"He also made ten lavers, and put five on the right side and five on the left, to wash in them; such things as they offered for the burnt offering they would wash in them, but the Sea was for the priests to wash in."
NKJV

With Israel being a desert community, anyone who walked to the temple would find themselves covered in dirt and sand. As they approached God's magnificent temple, they would find themselves facing containers of water which they were required to use in order to enter the temple. Even the priests who were serving inside the temple were required to bath in order to be in the presence of God. While this may seem trivial to many of us, God took it very seriously.

Exodus 30:21 "So they shall wash their hands and their feet, lest they die. And it shall be a statute forever to them—to him and his descendants throughout their generations." NKJV

While we may not have to take a bath to come to church, we still must be cleansed of our sins in order to stand before God one day. You see, in this life we fail and fall. We miss the mark of perfection and therefore are stained with the dirt and sand of our sins. The good news is that just as a bath was prepared for the priests, a greater cleansing has been prepared for all mankind. Jesus Christ came into this earth and died on the cross, taking our sins upon Himself. Because of this amazing act of love we may be cleansed of all our sin and stand before our Lord without fear. Because of Jesus, we can trust in the words of God that say, "Though your sins are like scarlet, they shall be as white as snow;" (Isaiah 1:18, NKJV).

Life Lesson: We should be washed in the Word of God.

Dear Father,
Thank You for the precious gift of salvation. Thank You for making a way for me to be cleansed of all my sins. Lord if I have sinned against you today, forgive me and help me live for You in all I do. Father, I stand on Your Truth in 1 John 1:9 that says if I confess my sins, You will cleanse me of all unrighteousness. Wash me clean and use me for Your Kingdom today. In Jesus' name, Amen.

OCTOBER 31
REWARDS

1 Corinthians 9:16-17
"For if I preach the gospel, I have nothing to boast of, for necessity is laid upon me; yes, woe is me if I do not preach the gospel! For if I do this willingly, I have a reward; but if against my will, I have been entrusted with a stewardship."
NKJV

Rewards - we all love them. Whether it's a paycheck at the end of the week or a medal at the end of a race, we all enjoy receiving a reward for our efforts. Friend, did you know that the Bible tells us that we will receive rewards for the good we do here on earth? While salvation is free and comes when we trust in Jesus for the forgiveness of our sins, once in heaven the Bible speaks of God rewarding those who served Him while here on earth.

Matthew 16:27 "For the Son of Man will come in the glory of His Father with His angels, and then He will reward each according to his works." NKJV

Imagine our Lord coming in all His glory and with Him rewards that will be given to those who served Him and helped build His Kingdom. Yes, we serve our King because He is worthy of our service. Yes, we show love to others because we love Him. Yet, we also serve Him in great expectation of the rewards He has prepared for us. So the question is, "Will you receive rewards?" Are you serving the Lord and therefore storing up treasures in heaven? You have all eternity to enjoy your rewards but only a short lifetime to earn them. It's either rewards or regrets - you get to decide now.

Life Lesson: We should desire spiritual rewards.

Dear Father,
Thank You that You have made a way for me to be saved. I praise You for Your grace and mercy. Lord, I also thank You that after all that You have done for me You allow me to earn rewards in Your Kingdom. Father, fill me with Your Spirit and guide me by Your Word so that I will use every opportunity to share the Gospel and store up treasures in heaven. In Jesus' name, Amen.

NOVEMBER 1
THE GOSPEL

1 Corinthians 9:22
"to the weak I became as weak, that I might win the weak. I have become all things to all men that I might by all means save some."
NKJV

The Gospel - those two words sum up the reason for all I do. If it were not for the Gospel, I would not know forgiveness. If it were not for the Gospel I would not have anything to teach on Sunday. If it were not for the Gospel, my life would have never changed and this world would be without hope. The fact is friend that the Gospel is real and it is indeed Good News. So why do we often let little things get in the way of this amazing news of Christ's love and forgiveness? Why do we allow petty opinions and secondary issues to crowd our eyes when the glory of God stands in our midst? Instead of condemning the world, why don't we begin changing it?

Let me ask it this way. Is it better to curse the darkness or light a candle? What's going to do the most good? Do you think the darkness is going to run from us if we tell it just how bad it is? No. Instead, we should walk into the darkness holding the light of Christ and allow His Word and His Spirit to change the lives around us. Yes, this means getting out of our comfort zone. It also means laying down opinions that are secondary to God's message of grace. If we can do that and speak with boldness the Gospel of Christ, this world will never be the same.

Life Lesson: We need to be willing to be inconvenienced for the sake of the Gospel. All who serve, give and pray will share in the rewards.

Dear Father,
Thank you for the Gospel and Your amazing love for a sinful people. God, help me look past myself and into the lives of those around me who need this good news. Give me opportunities to share the Gospel with all who will listen even if it means being uncomfortable. Father, fill me with Your Spirit that I may proclaim Your Truth boldly and with love. In Jesus' Name, Amen.

NOVEMBER 2
GOD'S TREASURE

2 Chronicles 5:1
"So all the work that Solomon had done for the house of the LORD was finished; and Solomon brought in the things which his father David had dedicated: the silver and the gold and all the furnishings. And he put them in the treasuries of the house of God."
NKJV

Solomon was one of the greatest kings of Israel and the one God chose to build His temple. Once finished, Solomon filled the treasuries with wealth unimaginable. While this was a blessing to the Lord, there is a treasure God values more than all of the world's riches. That treasure, my friend, is you.

You are the pearl of great price that our Savior bled and died for. God had all He could ever want in the heavenly realm, but He left it all so that humanity could be saved and spend eternity with Him. Why would He do it you ask? Simple, His love for you.

John 3:16 For God so loved the world that He gave His only begotten Son, that whoever believes in Him should not perish but have everlasting life." NKJV

Life Lesson: You are a valuable and precious treasure to God.

Dear Father,
Thank You for the salvation You offer through Jesus. While I know I have sinned, I also understand that You have died so that I can be forgiven. Change my heart and my life so that I may be used to share the Gospel with the world around me. In Jesus' name, Amen.

NOVEMBER 3
YES TO JESUS

Philippians 2:10-11
"that at the name of Jesus every knee should bow, of those in heaven, and of those on earth, and of those under the earth, and that every tongue should confess that Jesus Christ is Lord, to the glory of God the Father."
NKJV

Each day we are confronted by choices. Some of them are benign like whether I should eat chocolate or vanilla ice cream. Others are more important like who should I marry or where should I live? Each one of our choices affects our life in some way. Of course, there is a choice that is made that will not only affect your life but also your eternity. The choice is this...Jesus yes or Jesus no?

You see friend, you may have made every wrong decision there was to make in your life but there is hope in this choice. To say yes to Jesus is to open the gates of heaven and experience the joy that comes from being born again. He promises living water that quenches every thirst, bread of life that satisfies our very soul, and an abundant life in this world and the next. In short, to say yes to Jesus is to say yes to life. Unfortunately, the opposite is true. To say no to Jesus is to experience separation from the only source of hope you have. Surrender your life to the One who loves you and find rest for your soul. Friend, I pray you say yes to Jesus.

Life Lesson: We have a choice - Jesus yes or Jesus no - there is no third option.

Dear Father,
I know I have sinned and fallen short of Your perfect standard. I know that I deserve punishment, but I ask that You would forgive me. I believe that Jesus has died for my sins and because of His death and resurrection I can have a relationship with You for all eternity. Wash me clean and fill me with Your Spirit that I may live for You. Father God - I say yes to Jesus. In Jesus' name, Amen.

NOVEMBER 4
DAILY QUIET TIME

Micah 6:8
"He has shown you, O man, what is good; and what does the LORD require of you but to do justly, to love mercy, and to walk humbly with your God?"
NKJV

If anyone asked you what your daily walk with the Lord looked like, what would you say? Would you say that it's a 10 minute Bible read before running out the door? Maybe, you wake up early and spend a good half hour in reading and prayer or maybe you even spend an hour meditating on God's Word. Whatever your daily walk looks like, one thing is for certain—if you want to grow spiritually you must spend time with the Lord.

Often, we mention our 'daily quiet time' when we discuss our walk with the Lord. There are three things in that phrase that are critical to spiritual growth. First is the word 'daily'. Just like our bodies need daily nourishment, so does our spirit. Secondly, 'quiet' is also key because many times we must quiet ourselves and our surroundings in order to hear from the Lord. Finally, 'time' is also important. How much time you ask? That's something we each have to ask ourselves. Some days you may spend 15 minutes in quiet reflection while other times you will be able to enjoy an evening studying God's Word. The important thing is doing it so that you may know God more and be equipped to do His will. The Lord has an exciting adventure waiting for you and the directions are in your hand.

Life Lesson: To grow spiritually, spending time with God is vital.

Dear Father,
Thank You for the gift of Your Word. Fill me with Your Spirit and give me a desire to read Your Word on a daily basis. Help me to learn from it and then begin acting out the things I learn. Teach me Your ways and hide Your Word in my heart so that I may not sin against You. In Jesus' name, Amen.

NOVEMBER 5
HEAVENLY TREASURES

1 Corinthians 9:25
"And everyone who competes for the prize is temperate in all things. Now they do it to obtain a perishable crown, but we for an imperishable crown."
NKJV

Would you run a race for celery? As foolish as it sounds, in ancient times there were athletes who would work out and train just so they could cross the finish line for a crown of celery leaves. You may laugh, but the same happens to this day. Every few years, we watch as athletes from all over the world jump, swim, and run to gain a medal. Now I can hear some of you saying, "Well gold is a little different than celery." Is it? Friend, when this life is over and you are before the Lord, no medal or riches are going to matter. In fact, that gold medal you thought was something special is simply Heaven's asphalt.

If you are a follower of Jesus and know Him as Savior, then you are part of this race to the eternal finish line. It can be difficult at times but just like an athlete, you must train hard. The rewards are far greater than anything this earth may offer. As you step out in faith and begin serving and walking in obedience to His word, you begin storing up treasures in Heaven. So friend, are you storing up heavenly rewards? Did you know that your act of love, giving or word of Truth may impact the life of another human for eternity? This alone is worth the price paid, but God in His infinite love then credits our eternal account so that one day, He will present to us treasures beyond what we can think or imagine.

Life Lesson: We should live for eternal spiritual rewards. What we do in this life matters... forever.

Dear Father,
Thank You for Jesus and Your salvation that comes by grace through faith. Because of this free gift I have hope of Heaven and life abundant. Lord, help me to focus on the eternal things and live in obedience to You. Guide me as I seek to serve You and serve others and in turn store up heavenly rewards. May I be so heavenly minded that I impact this earth for all eternity. In Jesus' name, Amen.

NOVEMBER 6
SPIRITUAL MILK

1 Corinthians 10:3-4
"All of them ate the same spiritual food, and all of them drank the same spiritual water. For they drank from the spiritual rock that traveled with them, and that rock was Christ."
NKJV

Have you ever been around a newborn baby? They are beautiful and precious creations of God but if they do not get their milk, you better look out. Imagine if we, as Christians, craved God's Word like a newborn craves milk. That child does not want to sit and watch TV or discuss the latest news headline when they are hungry...they want to eat. This desire to fill their stomachs and find fulfillment is all consuming. Is this not how it should be with followers of Jesus?

1 Peter 2:2-3 "Like newborn babies, you must crave pure spiritual milk so that you will grow into a full experience of salvation. Cry out for this nourishment, now that you have had a taste of the Lord's kindness." NKJV

God has given us His Word and He is waiting for us to partake in it so that we may be nourished and grow in our relationship with Him. If we refuse to taste of God's goodness how can we expect to mature? This would be like staring at a fridge full of food and complaining that you are malnourished. God has done his part and has provided the Bible for us to read. We should consume every page with such passion that it leads to a life overrun with God's goodness and blessing. Only then will we be able to truly say, "I have tasted and seen that the Lord is good."

Life Lesson: The Bible, the Word of God, is our spiritual food and we should eat daily.

Dear Father,
Thank You for Your Word. Thank You for those who have given their lives so that I have access to the scriptures. Father, may I be like that newborn and crave Your Word. Lord help me to read it and to apply it to my life so that I may be a blessing to those around me. Fill me with Your Spirit and equip me for the good works You have prepared for me to do. In Jesus' Name, Amen.

NOVEMBER 7
SATISFACTION

Micah 7:1
"For I am like those who gather summer fruits, like those who glean vintage grapes; there is no cluster to eat of the first-ripe fruit which my soul desires."
NKJV

Each of us looks for something to satisfy our souls. In fact, companies and advertising agencies know this and have set out to convince you they have what you desire. The truth is that after all the colorful ads and convincing sales tactics, the product is temporary and will leave you right where you started - empty. The good news is that there is someone who loves us and what He offers will never fade away.

Micah 7:7 "Therefore I will look to the LORD; I will wait for the God of my salvation; My God will hear me." NKJV

You see friend, this world will offer you everything under the sun but what it cannot offer is lasting hope, forgiveness of sins and an abundant life both now and forever. This only comes through a relationship with Jesus Christ. He alone hung on the cross so that we could be freed of our sin. He alone rose from the grave, defeating death and securing our eternity. He alone can satisfy our soul. Like Micah, if you are searching for "fruit which my soul desires" then look no further than Jesus. Nothing on this earth can even compare to Him.

Life Lesson: We will not find solace for our emptiness from the world no matter how much we look.

Dear Father,
I am tired of looking to this world for satisfaction. Lord, I desire to know the fulfillment that comes from a relationship with Jesus. Father, forgive me of my sins and wash me clean of all unrighteousness. Fill me with Your Spirit and help me to seek You first above all things. In Jesus' name, Amen.

NOVEMBER 8
GOD'S SPEAKING

2 Chronicles 6:30
"...then hear from heaven Your dwelling place, and forgive, and give to everyone according to all his ways, whose heart You know (for You alone know the hearts of the sons of men),"
NKJV

Trials, hardships, frustrations—whatever they're called, we all deal with them at one time or another. The good news is that God desires to speak to us during those times. It could be that you are surrounded by circumstances that are difficult, or you may have made bad choices which have led to a bad situation. In those times friend, remember the words of Jesus Himself...

Matthew 11:28 "Come to Me, all you who labor and are heavy laden, and I will give you rest. Take My yoke upon you and learn from Me, for I am gentle and lowly in heart, and you will find rest for your souls." NKJV

Many times when life is going well, we can't hear the Lord, even when He is shouting to get our attention. It's often in those times of struggle that He whispers and we hear His voice loud and clear. If today you find yourself in the midst of hardships, seek the Lord. Use this time to seek forgiveness and cling to the grace of God. Cry out to God and He will hear from heaven and pour out His love upon you in abundance. When we do this, God makes the most of our pain and can bring something good from something bad.

Life Lesson: Whenever something in life goes wrong, use the moment to ask forgiveness and draw closer to the Lord.

Dear Father,
Thank You for the life You have given me. Lord, I pray that when this life gets difficult that I turn to You. Help me draw closer to You whether I am enjoying blessings or walking through trials. Father, may each day and circumstance be used to make me more like Jesus. Forgive me of my sins and fill me with Your Spirit so that I can be used to build Your Kingdom. In Jesus' name, Amen.

NOVEMBER 9
THOU SHALL NOT WHINE

1 Corinthians 10:5-6
"But with most of them God was not well pleased, for their bodies were scattered in the wilderness. Now these things became our examples, to the intent that we should not lust after evil things as they also lusted."
NKJV

Have you ever seen a child watch TV? They sit happily watching the characters they love dance across the screen. But, it's interesting to watch what happens when the show stops and the commercials come on. That once happy child turns into a loud, demanding whiner. "I must have it," they demand as they kick and scream when they are told "no." I wish this picture stopped at childhood. Sure... we've toned it down a bit, but how often do we find ourselves discontented and whining for the next job, house, car or spouse? This is not a new phenomenon by any means. In fact, Moses was threatened many times by a mob of angry whiners.

Numbers 11:5 "We remember the fish which we ate freely in Egypt, the cucumbers, the melons, the leeks, the onions, and the garlic; but now our whole being is dried up; there is nothing at all except this manna before our eyes!" NKJV

The children of Israel had been receiving supernatural food from Heaven and yet they were whining for something more. Friend, God has provided all eternity for us through Jesus. Because of Jesus' death and resurrection we can be forgiven. Because of His great love we can have our names written in the Lamb's Book of Life. With this Truth forever on our minds, how could we ever whine again? Instead, we should live content, thankful lives because the God of all creation loves us unconditionally.

Life Lesson: Thou shalt not whine.

Dear Father,
Thank You for the life You have given me. Lord, forgive me if I have whined or complained about life when You have blessed me in so many ways. Help me to see the amazing blessings all around me today and to share those blessings with others I meet. Fill me with Your Spirit and use me to reach others with the message of the Gospel. In Jesus' name, Amen.

NOVEMBER 10
LOVING WHAT GOD LOVES

Malachi 2:15

"But did He not make them one, Having a remnant of the Spirit? And why one? He seeks godly offspring. Therefore take heed to your spirit, And let none deal treacherously with the wife of his youth."
NKJV

What do you think of when you hear the word "marriage?" Do you imagine a Cinderella style ceremony followed by "happily ever after" or maybe you get the picture of the old "ball and chain." Our world paints many pictures of marriage, yet they fall short of what God intended. While marriage does involve a man and woman living life together and experiencing everything from kids to finances—it's so much more than that.

Ephesians 5:31-32 "For this reason a man shall leave his father and mother and be joined to his wife, and the two shall become one flesh." This is a great mystery, but I speak concerning Christ and the church." NKJV

In the beginning when God placed Adam and Eve together in the covenant of marriage, He was not just establishing an option for dealing with loneliness, but He was creating a beautiful picture of our future redemption. When a married couple stands together and says "I do" they are standing as an image of Jesus Christ and the church. This is why Malachi refers to marriage as "The LORD's holy institution which He loves." If that's the case—shouldn't we love it too?

Life Lesson: Marriage, at its root, is a picture of Jesus and the church.

Dear Father,
Thank You for marriage and all that is represents. Lord, help me to be a picture of Jesus and the church in the relationship with my spouse. Empty me of myself so that I will be a loving servant to them just as Jesus was to me. Help me to give of myself for the benefit of my spouse so that when the world looks at my marriage, they will see Jesus. Use me to reach others with the Gospel through my words and deeds. In Jesus' name, Amen.

NOVEMBER 11
A WAY OF ESCAPE

1 Corinthians 10:13
"No temptation has overtaken you except such as is common to man; but God is faithful, who will not allow you to be tempted beyond what you are able, but with the temptation will also make the way of escape, that you may be able to bear it."
NKJV

There it is, staring you down. It grabs hold of your attention and captivates your thoughts. It appears so harmless but in the end, it can be deadly. It is temptation, and every one of us has to face it. The good news is that if you have trusted in Jesus as your Savior, you don't have to face it alone. Because of Jesus' death and resurrection, we can be freed of our bondage to sin while also finding strength to resist it through God's Spirit. What an encouraging thought. When faced with temptation, God of all creation provides a way of escape or the strength to bear it.

Unfortunately, this does not mean we always take that way of escape. Like a kid standing over an open cookie jar, often we stand gazing into temptation and wonder why we were not able to resist. Friend, in those moments when we fail, we can come to God and experience His forgiveness and grace all over again. This is the beauty of the Gospel. Yes, we must resist sin and flee from temptation but when we do fall short, we have a loving God who desires to forgive.

Life Lesson: Take the way out of temptation when you have it.

Dear Father,
Thank You for loving me. I know that I have done wrong and have sinned against You. Father, please forgive me and fill me with Your Spirit so that I can fight temptation. Lord, when I find myself in a tempting situation, open my eyes to the way out so that I can escape. In Jesus' name, Amen.

NOVEMBER 12
GOD'S ROAR

Amos 1:2
"The LORD roars from Zion, and utters His voice from Jerusalem; the pastures of the shepherds mourn, and the top of Carmel withers."
NKJV

For the most part, many of us don't see people "roaring" in our day to day life. Unless you're part of a theatrical event, it would probably strike you as odd to hear someone roar. Of course in those moments of excitement, fear or confrontation, we may come close as we strive to portray the seriousness of our situation. In this passage, God is proclaiming judgment and is roaring from Jerusalem so that all will hear and understand the importance of His Word.

It's true that this message God is delivering is very serious, yet no less serious are the messages God delivers to us without roaring. Each week many of us read from God's Word, fellowship together and attend church services and during each week, God is trying to teach us. During those times, it is just as important to understand what God is saying. Anything that God shares with us that we take lightly and do not apply is harmful to our spiritual walk. What have you heard today that you can apply and use to grow in Christ? Did you read something in God's Word or hear from a friend a truth that could change your life? Friend, look for these gems of Truth everyday so that God does not have to roar to get our attention.

Life Lesson: All of God's Word is applicable to us. Taking it lightly would be folly.

Dear Father,
Thank You for Your Word and for the opportunity to read it and learn more about You. Give me a hunger for Your Word and help me to take the things I hear and read and apply them to my life so that I can be equipped to serve You. In Jesus' name, Amen.

NOVEMBER 13
COMMUNION

1 Corinthians 10:16
"The cup of blessing which we bless, is it not the communion of the blood of Christ? The bread which we break, is it not the communion of the body of Christ?"
NKJV

Communion is a blessed time for any believer. Each element presented is a picture of the ultimate sacrifice of our loving Savior. As we take the bread, we remember our Lord as He was beaten by soldiers and spit upon by those who hated Him. When we look at the cup, we catch a glimpse of the blood that was shed on the cross so that we could be forgiven. These two elements help followers of Christ to understand the penalty of their sins while rejoicing in a God who has made a way for them to be cleansed of all they've done wrong.

Luke 22:19-20 "And He took bread, gave thanks and broke it, and gave it to them, saying, "This is My body which is given for you; do this in remembrance of Me." Likewise He also took the cup after supper, saying, "This cup is the new covenant in My blood, which is shed for you." NKJV

In the garden of Gethsemane, Jesus accepted the cup that was placed before Him by the Father. It was the cup of our sins and the punishment that we deserved. Now in its place, Jesus offers us a new cup. The cup He offers is a cup of blessings, hope and eternal life. We may try to drink from other cups in this world, but only one leads to salvation. Drink deep my friend and taste and see that the Lord is good.

Life Lesson: Be careful what cup you drink from.

Dear Father,
Lord, I know that I have sinned against You. I realize that when You died on the cross You were taking the punishment that I deserved. Thank You for Your sacrifice. Forgive me for all the things that I have done wrong. I desire to drink deeply of Your cup - the cup of blessings. Each time I take communion, may I remember the sacrifice You made for me and may it lead me to tell others about Your amazing gift. In Jesus' name, Amen.

NOVEMBER 14
GOD IS GOOD ALL THE TIME

2 Chronicles 7:3
"When all the Israelites saw the fire coming down and the glory of the LORD above the temple, they knelt on the pavement with their faces to the ground, and they worshiped and gave thanks to the LORD, saying, "He is good; his love endures forever."
NKJV

Can you imagine being part of the congregation of Israel as God entered the Temple? Years of preparation and hard labor and the presence of God has come to rest with His people. What a glorious time. Imagine the celebration at this moment as the people began reflecting on all God had done for them. They may have thought back to the calling of a man named Abram in the land of Ur. Possibly, they cheered as they remembered their forefathers being brought out of Egypt and crossing the Red Sea. And as they stood in awe at this beautiful temple they may have cheered Solomon while remembering his father David. Truly, the people of Israel had much to celebrate but nothing was greater than the One who had brought them to this point.

Psalm 107:1-2 "Oh, give thanks to the Lord, for He is good! For His mercy endures forever. Let the redeemed of the Lord say so, Whom He has redeemed from the hand of the enemy," NKJV

The children of Israel had seen God's hand in every part of their nation's history and were led to praise the Lord for all that He has done. If you are reading this, you have been blessed with eyes to see and breath in your lungs. You have also been blessed with technology that allows you to email and read this newsletter. Of course, the greatest blessing of all came in the form of Jesus Christ laying down His life on the cross so that you could be forgiven. Because of this act of perfect love and grace we can stand with the children of Israel and proclaim that God is good and His love endures forever!

Life Lesson: God is good all the time.

Dear Father,
Thank You for Your amazing love. Thank You for dying on the cross for my sins, so that I could be forgiven. I believe that You have risen again and that one day, I will spend eternity with You in Heaven. Fill me with Your Spirit so that I may live for You. In Jesus' name, Amen.

NOVEMBER 15
THAT THEY MAY BE ONE

1 Corinthians 10:17
"For we, though many, are one bread and one body; for we all partake of that one bread."
NKJV

The body of Christ is truly amazing as millions of believers all over the world come together with a common goal of sharing the Gospel. When the church, the body of Christ, is functioning correctly, the world around it is blessed as people are fed, clothed and given the life-changing Truth of God's Word. Unfortunately, because of division, worldly pleasures or indifference, the church can lose sight of the lost as well as the One we are serving.

John 17:20-21 "I do not pray for these alone, but also for those who will believe in Me through their word; that they all may be one, as You, Father, are in Me, and I in You; that they also may be one in Us, that the world may believe that You sent Me." NKJV

Before Jesus was arrested, He prayed asking the Father to make all believers one as He and His Father are One. When Christians come together as the body of Christ, we come together with different likes and dislikes, personalities and social statuses. We may even have some secondary doctrinal differences but with all those differences, we have One unifying similarity. We have all been forgiven by a gracious God and we call Jesus Lord. With this as our banner, we can stand in unity as one body for the sake of the lost.

Life Lesson: There is a special relationship between people who are Christians.

Dear Father,
Thank You for the body of Christ. Thank You for loving brothers and sisters who are there to encourage and challenge me in my faith. Lord, I pray that You would help unite us as one so that we can be used in a powerful way to take Your Gospel to all the nations. In Jesus' name, Amen.

NOVEMBER 16
SKIMMING THE DROSS

Malachi 3:2
"But who can endure the day of His coming? And who can stand when He appears? For He is like a refiner's fire and like launderers' soap."
NKJV

Have you ever watched a goldsmith in action? It's an amazing thing to watch him heat up this precious metal and pour it into molds to harden so that it can be handled. But before he is able to pour it into a mold, he must first remove any impurities. These impurities, or dross, cannot be cut out of the gold or rubbed off. In order to remove the dross, the goldsmith must first heat the metal to incredible temperatures. Once this is done, the dross rises to the top and the goldsmith is able to scrape it off thus purifying the metal.

Friend, this is what our Father in heaven desires to do in each and every one of our lives. He desires to mold us and shape us more and more into the image of His Son, Jesus. To do that He must often lead us into His refiner's fire where He will skim our imperfections off the top. Most of the time this is not a pleasant process but we can trust that God has our best interest at heart. Like the ultimate goldsmith, God knows how much heat we can endure and how much handling we require. It's in His loving hands that we are refined so that like that precious metal, we reflect our Father's handiwork.

Life Lesson: God desires to act as refiner and purifier in our lives.

Dear Father,
Thank You for loving me. Thank you for your work in my life and for Your refiner's fire. While it may be difficult during those times of trial and purifying, I praise You because I know it is for my good. Lord, continue to skim the dross from my life so that I may be a shining example of Your love and grace. In Jesus' Name, Amen.

NOVEMBER 17
PERMISSIBLE BUT NOT BENEFICIAL

1 Corinthians 10:23
"You say, "I am allowed to do anything"—but not everything is good for you. You say, "I am allowed to do anything"—but not everything is beneficial."
NLT

People often think that Christianity is a list of do's and don'ts. While we should seek to walk in obedience to Christ, our salvation is not dependent on a list. Because we are saved by grace through faith, we have a freedom that the world does not understand. This freedom includes the right to make choices others may question and may include things the Bible does not directly speak about. Of course, even though we may have this freedom—I have to ask:

Is what I'm about to do going to help build my faith?

Is it going to share my faith or the Good News with unbelievers?

Is it going to encourage people?

If the answer is "no" to all of these things, then friend it may be best to steer clear. Because of what Christ has done for us, we have freedom to make various decisions, but we also have the responsibility to make sure our choices are Christ centered. As Paul mentioned in 1 Corinthians, "I'm allowed to do anything—but not everything is beneficial."

Life Lesson: Choose to spend time doing things that have a spiritual benefit.

Dear Father,
Thank You for Jesus and that salvation is not by works, but by grace. Lord, I pray that You would help me to be mindful of the choices I make so that they are centered on You. I am thankful for the freedom I have in Christ and pray that I can use that freedom for the benefit of others and the Gospel. In Jesus' name, Amen.

NOVEMBER 18
LEADERSHIP

Amos 2:1
"For three transgressions of Moab, and for four, I will not turn away its punishment, Because he burned the bones of the king of Edom to lime."
NKJV

As Israel was coming through the desert to the promised land, Balak, the king of Moab attempted to bribe God's prophet to curse God's people. Obviously, Balak was not a good leader as time and time again he dismissed God's words in order to forward his own kingdom. While Balak had the opportunity to submit to God, he chose not to and he and his people ended up suffering the consequences. Unlike the Moabites, it's important for the church to have godly leaders.

Leaders inside the church have a responsibility to remain faithful to scripture and stand firm on God's Word so that others will see this and be encouraged to do the same. In 1 Timothy, the Lord supplies qualifications for those who enter into leadership. These qualifications include being faithful to the body of Christ and their families. They must be self-controlled, peace loving and gentle. Living inside these guidelines, leaders are best equipped to guide others into a life dedicated to our Lord.

Life Lesson: Strong leadership in the church is important.

Dear Father,
Thank You for Your Word and for the godly leaders in my life. Father, I pray that you would continue to be with those in church leadership as they seek You. Give them wisdom and discernment as they teach, counsel and care for those in the body of Christ. Lord, protect them from the enemy and fill them with your Spirit. In Jesus' name, Amen.

NOVEMBER 19
TO THE GLORY OF GOD

1 Corinthians 10:31-32
"Therefore, whether you eat or drink, or whatever you do, do all to the glory of God. Give no offense, either to the Jews or to the Greeks or to the church of God,"
NKJV

Can you imagine what it would look like to do everything for the glory of God? Everything—not just worship on Sunday mornings, but every aspect of life dedicated to glorifying our Lord. As you step out of bed in the morning, your mind is praising the Lord for His mercies. As you eat, you are thanking God for the food He has provided. As you sit in a traffic jam, you are singing praises to God for your life and that opportunity to be still and know He is God. Yes, anything and everything can be a sweet offering to our Lord when we purpose in our hearts to glorify His Name.

Of course, some people may not appreciate your attitude or diligent work. But friend, it won't matter because you're doing it for the glory of God and not for the approval of others. Your purpose and meaning are to glorify our Lord and He is blessed as you serve Him with all your heart. So whatever you do in the course of your day, set your mind on glorifying God and watch as He uses you to be a blessing to others and a witness of His grace.

Life Lesson: Do all that you do for the glory of God.

Dear Father,
Thank You for Your amazing grace and the love You have shown me. Lord, fill me with Your Spirit and equip me to do everything for Your glory whether great or small. May my heart and mind be focused on You today and use me to share your goodness with a world in need. May my life bless You today. In Jesus' name, Amen.

NOVEMBER 20
NOW IS THE TIME TO WORSHIP

2 Chronicles 8:14

"And, according to the order of David his father, he appointed the divisions of the priests for their service, the Levites for their duties (to praise and serve before the priests) as the duty of each day required, and the gatekeepers by their divisions at each gate; for so David the man of God had commanded."

NKJV

Worship. That one word involves every part of our lives as a Christian. We can worship the Lord by the way we work at our job. We can enter into worship while caring for the kids or cleaning the house. No matter what we are doing we can do it unto the Lord as a sacrifice of praise.

Romans 12:1 "And so, dear brothers and sisters, I plead with you to give your bodies to God because of all he has done for you. Let them be a living and holy sacrifice—the kind he will find acceptable. This is truly the way to worship him." NLT

While it is true all aspects of our lives can be worship, there is a sweet blessing that comes as we lift our hands and voices to the Lord. Those times of praise and worship, whether surrounded by our church family or in a car alone, are refreshing to the soul as we focus on our King. When we take those moments to reflect on Jesus and sing praises to Him, it helps us refocus our attention on what is truly important. So on those days where life is hard and you find yourself struggling, crank up the stereo, iPod or radio and sing unto the Lord a new song. I guarantee you will be blessed in the process.

Life Lesson: We should make worship a part of every day God gives us.

Dear Father,
Thank You for Your love and for the opportunity to sing Your praises. Father, You are worthy of all my worship, and I pray that every aspect of my life is a beautiful sound to Your ears. Whether I'm singing to you or serving a neighbor, I pray that it will glorify Your name. In Jesus' name, Amen.

NOVEMBER 21
WHO DO YOU IMITATE?

1 Corinthians 11:1
"And you should imitate me, just as I imitate Christ."
NKJV

In 1 Corinthians 11, Paul is making a bold statement. He is calling the church at Corinth to pattern itself after him. Now, Paul is not saying he is the one they should worship but rather as he follows after Christ, he becomes a walking, talking example of what a Christian should look like. While we are ultimately following after Christ, we all need human examples of Christianity to help guide us in the right direction.

The Bible from Genesis to Revelation is filled with godly leaders who lead by example. Whether it was Moses leading God's people out of Egypt or Peter stepping out onto the waves, all were examples to those around them and continue to stand as godly examples today. While no human example is perfect, this doesn't mean we refuse to follow leadership. If a pastor, elder or deacon is following the Lord then look to them as an example and learn from them. There is a great blessing found in following after a man or woman of God, and as you imitate their life you may look behind you one day to see yourself being imitated.

Life Lesson: We need spiritual leaders; they are for our blessing and benefit.

Dear Father,
Thank You for the leaders in my life. Father, help me to learn from those around me who are seeking after You. As my pastor follows You, may I seek to imitate him and in turn become more like Christ. Lord, continue to be with those in leadership as they share your Word and minister to the body. In Jesus' name, Amen.

NOVEMBER 22
A FATHER'S LOVING CORRECTION

Haggai 1:10
"It's because of you that the heavens withhold the dew and the earth produces no crops."
NKJV

"This is going to hurt me more than it's going to hurt you." Most every child has heard that statement from their parents at least one time or another. While a child may not understand it at the time, no godly parent desires to punish their children. We desire to bless our children because we love them yet the Bible is clear that godly discipline is loving.

Hebrews 12:6 "For the Lord disciplines those he loves, and he punishes each one he accepts as his child." NLT

In the book of Haggai, we find God correcting His people. He is not doing it out of blind anger or to simply be mean. He is doing it out of a love for them and because He desires something greater in their life. Friend, the same is true for us today. God desires to bless us and to do amazing things in our lives, but we must be willing to submit to Him. In those times where we dig in our heels and begin throwing a tantrum, our heavenly Father will lovingly correct us so that we can grow in understanding and become more like Jesus. While these times of correction may be difficult, we can trust our Father and know that it is all for our good and His glory.

Life Lesson: God chooses to correct us for our sake and His glory.

Dear Father,
Thank You for Your grace and for the forgiveness of my sins. Lord, I pray that as I seek You that I would be submitted to Your correction. Help me to learn from Your loving hand and learn from those times I step away from You. Continue to mold me into the image of Your Son, Jesus. In Jesus', Amen.

NOVEMBER 23
BEWARE

Philippians 3:2
"Beware of dogs, beware of evil workers, beware of the mutilation!"
NKJV

Around 60AD, the church at Philippi began to preach a different message than what Jesus had taught. Jesus' message was that if we believe in Him, we will not perish but have everlasting life.

John 11:25-26 "Jesus said to her, "I am the resurrection and the life. He who believes in Me, though he may die, he shall live. And whoever lives and believes in Me shall never die. Do you believe this?" NKJV

To be forgiven of our sins, we just need to believe that Jesus' death on the cross is the only way to be forgiven. That's it. The church at Philippi began to say that people had to first become a Jew, be circumcised, and then they could become a follower of Jesus. That's not at all what Jesus said. Humanity often wants us to 'do something' before we can be made right with God. It's like putting our two cents in so to speak. Friend, that's what got us into trouble in the first place. Jesus has done everything needed so we can be forgiven of our sins. Beware of anyone who adds or takes away from the message of Jesus. It can be very harmful. There is nothing we can 'do' to make ourselves right with God. He is waiting with open arms for all who will call on Him.

Life Lesson: Anything beyond coming to Jesus in faith is works based mentality.

Dear Father,
Thank You for Your Son and doing everything necessary for me to have a relationship with You. Please give me opportunities to tell others that they can come to You just as they are. Thank You for caring for all of my needs and loving me so much. I do not ever want to put up obstacles for others to come to you. In Jesus' name, Amen.

NOVEMBER 24
NO THANKS?

Psalm 26:7

"That I may proclaim with the voice of thanksgiving, And tell of all Your wondrous works."0 NKJV

In the month of November, we, as a nation celebrate Thanksgiving. For one day the nation offers up thanks to... who or to what? It is important that as believers we offer up thanks not just one day a year but all the time. We do not offer up thanks to an unknown god but to a God that we know and Who knows us. We have so much to be thankful for - our God, our salvation, our forgiveness, our families, our church and the list goes on and on. Take the time everyday to thank God for all the many blessings He has so lovingly given you. While the world may celebrate Thanksgiving once a year, we can and should celebrate it every day.

Life Lesson: Thanksgiving to God should be an every day thing.

Dear Father,

Thank You for this gift of salvation. Thank You for Your love, grace and mercy. Thank You for my family, my friends and my church. You have given me so much to be thankful for, and, indeed I am. Lord, help me to overflow with this thanksgiving so that others will see and desire to know You. I pray this in Jesus' name. Amen.

NOVEMBER 25
TIME WELL SPENT

Amos 3:15
"'I will destroy the winter house along with the summer house; The houses of ivory shall perish, And the great houses shall have an end,' says the Lord."
NKJV

Wow, this sounds like a harsh word when you first read it. Let's remember the setting. The northern ten tribes of Israel in 750BC were worshiping false gods and idols. They were prospering as a nation, and they had built wonderful houses with excessive decor. They thought things were going well because of their wealth. Amos steps in with a message from God to tell them it will all be destroyed. They were living in luxury all for themselves, but they had forgotten the Lord. God is letting them know here that those things would not last. Don't miss the blessing here friend. Paul reminds us in Corinthians that everything we do in our selfish nature will not last. Those things we do for the glory of God will last for eternity.

1 Corinthians 3:11-15 "For no one can lay any foundation other than the one we already have Jesus Christ. Anyone who builds on that foundation may use a variety of materials-gold, silver, jewels, wood, hay, or straw. But on the judgment day, fire will reveal what kind of work each builder has done. The fire will show if a person's work has any value. If the work survives, that builder will receive a reward. But if the work is burned up, the builder will suffer great loss. The builder will be saved, but like someone barely escaping through a wall of flames." NLT

Let's be real, my house, cars, and the 'things' I will have accumulated during my life span will not make it into eternity. But the time I invest for the glory of God, not mine, will last forever. That is very good news.

Life Lesson: Every minute we live to please God is well spent.

Dear Father,
Thank You for loving me. I am grateful that I have an opportunity to live for You and will be rewarded. Please continue to give me the power and desire to live for Your Kingdom, not mine. In Jesus' name, Amen.

NOVEMBER 26
A FAIR QUARREL

1 Corinthians 11:16
"If anyone wants to be contentious about this, we have no other practice-nor do the churches of God."
NKJV

Hair-who would have thought that tiny strands of dead skin cells growing out of your head would cause so much trouble. While we may laugh at it today, not many years ago men with long hair would have been asked to leave a church or even had their salvation questioned. Of course, many of these same individuals speaking against long hair speak in full view of a picture of Jesus with long flowing locks. It may seem foolish but quarrels over things like this are painful to the body of Christ.

It's been over two-thousand years since Jesus walked this earth and throughout that time believers from every era have debated theological issues and deep moral questions. When we can agree on the essentials, we can have a loving discussion on secondary issues. The danger comes when discussions turn into a quarrel. Often this occurs when loving biblical understanding is laid aside and personal opinion takes over. As a follower of Christ, we should wrap our speech in love and be careful how we approach others on non-essential issues. We should stand for the Gospel with all our might and leave discussions about hair length to the barber.

Life Lesson: Do not get into quarrels or arguments about hair length or any other non-life or death arguments.

Dear Father,
Thank You for loving me. Lord, may I love others around me as You have loved me. Fill me with Your Spirit so that I may be a peace maker. Help me to stay away from quarrels and bickering on non-life or death issues. May I glorify You in all I do and say. In Jesus' name, Amen.

NOVEMBER 27
THE BLESSING OF GIVING

Malachi 3:8
"'Will a man rob God? Yet you have robbed Me! But you say, 'In what way have we robbed You?' In tithes and offerings."
NKJV

The idea of someone robbing God is pretty ridiculous. I can just imagine a criminal breaking the lock on the pearly gates and then trying to carry away chunks of the streets of gold - it's foolishness! This may be why the people of Israel reply with "In what way have we robbed You?" They didn't understand that it was not their action that led to theft but rather their inaction.

Even today, many inside the church misunderstand the importance of giving to the Lord. Giving of tithes and offerings is not just about supporting the church, but is a means to glorify God. When we step out in obedience and give to God our tithes we are declaring to Him that we love Him more than our money. As we give in faith, we are trusting in the One who says "try Me now in this." Then as we give cheerfully to our Lord, He responds by opening the windows of heaven and pouring out His amazing blessings upon our life.

Life Lesson: Giving is more about our heart than our money.

Dear Father,
Thank You for the blessings in my life. Forgive me for those times when I lose sight of Your goodness and rob You by not giving rightly. Help me to be a good steward of the money You have given me. May I glorify You and help equip the church by giving my tithes and offerings. In Jesus' name, Amen.

NOVEMBER 28
SO LONG SELF

1 Corinthians 11:21
"For some of you hurry to eat your own meal without sharing with others. As a result, some go hungry while others get drunk."
NKJV

In 1 Corinthians 11, Paul has to correct the church in Corinth for using the elements of communion for selfish gain. Rather than meditating on the bread as the body of Christ broken for them, they selfishly eat it without sharing. Instead of reflecting on the cup and the blood spilled for their sins, they were drinking to excess. Like a child with a toy, the church of Corinth had begun using that word so many toddlers use perfectly. "Mine!"

Philippians 2:3-4 "Let nothing be done through selfish ambition or conceit, but in lowliness of mind let each esteem others better than himself. 4 Let each of you look out not only for his own interests, but also for the interests of others." NKJV

As followers of Christ, we should be daily dying to ourselves and our "mine" mentality. Just as Christ left the riches of Heaven and all that was rightly His, we too should be willing to give up of ourselves for the sake of others. As we lose more of ourselves, we will find we have gained more of Christ.

Life Lesson: We should be growing less and less selfish.

Dear Father,
I thank You for Your amazing grace. Because of Your body which was broken and Your blood that was spilled, I have been forgiven. Lord, help me to be mindful of Your ultimate sacrifice. Since You were willing to come to earth and die for me, I should be willing to die to myself and serve others. In Jesus' name, Amen.

NOVEMBER 29
THE WAITING GAME

1 Corinthians 11:26
"For as often as you eat this bread and drink this cup, you proclaim the Lord's death till He comes."
NKJV

Have you ever had to wait in line for something you love? Maybe you waited to ride a roller-coaster at your favorite theme park or sat in line to be the first at a movie. You may even be someone who loves to get up at 2am so you can sit outside the store right before a big sale. Whatever the case, we all have experienced anticipation for something we love. You can even say that, as Christians, we are all living lives of expectation as we wait for the coming of our Lord.

Romans 8:18 "For I consider that the sufferings of this present time are not worthy to be compared with the glory which shall be revealed in us." NKJV

Imagine friend-the sufferings of this world including the pain, sickness and death that are all around us will one day be gone. While we wait here on earth and endure the hardships of a fallen world, Jesus Christ prepares our new home and will one day return to take us there. This is not fantasy or a mad man's dream. These are the very truths of God and they can be trusted. So no matter how long this line of earth may seem, continue to look up and be reminded that one day He is coming.

Life Lesson: We should always be thinking of and looking forward to the coming of our Lord.

Dear Father,
Thank You for your love and the hope I can have in Jesus. Forgive me of my sins and make me new. Fill me with Your Spirit so that I can share the hope of Heaven with everyone I meet. Use me today to change someone's eternity. In Jesus' name, Amen.

NOVEMBER 30
BLESSED TO BLESS

2 Chronicles 9:8
"Blessed be the LORD your God, who delighted in you, setting you on His throne to be king for the LORD your God! Because your God has loved Israel, to establish them forever, therefore He made you king over them, to do justice and righteousness."
NKJV

King Solomon was one of the greatest kings of Israel. During his reign, Israel experienced a great time of peace and prosperity. In 2 Chronicles 2, we see that Solomon asked the Lord for wisdom to rule the people and in response to this request; God blessed him with riches and honor like none other before or after. After this, Solomon's wisdom was known throughout the world and rulers like the queen of Sheba, came to hear his words and see his wealth.

Much like Solomon, God has blessed each and every one of us with something. It may not be the great power and wealth that Solomon had, but everything we have can be used for Him. When we use our time, money or words to be a blessing, we are living out the Gospel and bringing glory to God. Today, look for opportunities to bless others. As you do this, others around you will take notice and like the queen of Sheba will proclaim, "Blessed be the Lord your God."

Life Lesson: God blesses us so we can be a blessing to others.

Dear Father,
Thank You for the blessings in my life. I praise You for giving me so much and I pray that You would help me to use it for You. Open my eyes today for opportunities to bless others and glorify Your name. Continue to use me to reach others with the Gospel. In Jesus' name, Amen.

DECEMBER 1
SIN SNIFFING

1 Corinthians 11:28
"But let a man examine himself, and so let him eat of the bread and drink of the cup."
NKJV

While many people inside the church may believe that "sin sniffing" is a gift, I have yet to find it listed in scripture. Although there are times to lovingly correct a brother or sister, we should not be quick to condemn. Before we begin pointing our finger at someone else's problems, we need to first examine ourselves.

Matthew 7:5 "Hypocrite! First remove the plank from your own eye, and then you will see clearly to remove the speck from your brother's eye." NKJV

In scripture, Jesus draws an absurd but poignant picture of someone with a giant beam of wood in their eye striving to remove a speck of dust from their friend's eye. As we sit back and laugh at the imagery, the truth remains. Often, we believe we can ignore the sin in our life all the while condemning those who may be sinning in the same way. This leads to a life of hypocrisy and self deception. Instead, we should examine our own hearts and seek God for forgiveness. As we find freedom from our struggles, we will be fully equipped to care for our friends who need help removing the dust from their eye.

Life Lesson: We should examine ourselves, not others, for problems.

Dear Father,
Thank You for Your forgiveness and grace. Help me to examine myself everyday through Your Word and Your Spirit. Continue to shape me more into the image of Your Son so that I may help others. In Jesus' name, Amen.

DECEMBER 2
THINK ON THESE THINGS

2 Chronicles 10:16
"Now when all Israel saw that the king did not listen to them, the people answered the king, saying: "What share have we in David? We have no inheritance in the son of Jesse. Every man to your tents, O Israel! Now see to your own house, O David!"
NKJV

In our world of twenty-four hour news stations and action packed live reporting, it's easy to see and hear all the bad things happening in the world. If we compound this with our own personal struggles and pains, we will easily find ourselves anxious or worse yet, hopeless. In 2 Chronicles 10, the people of Israel are trying to come to grips with the splitting of their nation. As they watch their kingdom crumble, they chose to look at their circumstance rather than their God.

Philippians 4:8 "Finally, brethren, whatever things are true, whatever things are noble, whatever things are just, whatever things are pure, whatever things are lovely, whatever things are of good report, if there is any virtue and if there is anything praiseworthy-meditate on these things." NKJV

No matter where we are in life, we can always find something bad to focus on. Even in church, people clamber to hear the latest gossip or consume stories of doom and gloom. Friends, we need to flee from a constant diet of evil, impure talk. These things do nothing but cause division and pain. Instead, we should look to the author and finisher of our faith, Jesus Christ. As we set our eyes on Him we will find peace for our souls and life abundant.

Life Lesson: Follow that which leads you to Jesus.

Dear Father,
Thank You for Your forgiveness and grace. Help me to be discerning with what or who I listen to. May I always be mindful of Your goodness and grace. Father, use me to share whatever is good and right with others that are around me. In Jesus' name, Amen.

DECEMBER 3
THE GIFT GRAB

1 Corinthians 12:1
"Now concerning spiritual gifts, brethren, I do not want you to be ignorant:"
NKJV

"Oh yeah?-well watch this!" If you've ever heard that statement, you know that it usually does not end well. Anytime we strive to outdo someone or do something and we are not equipped, we fall on our face. During those times, we become painfully aware of our shortcomings. The good news is that God has blessed each of us with unique talents and spiritual gifts. When we walk in them rightly, we see amazing things happen.

Romans 12:4-5 "For as we have many members in one body, but all the members do not have the same function, so we, being many, are one body in Christ, and individually members of one another." NKJV

God knows what he is doing and He has given you a certain gift for a reason. You may desire a different one but trying to walk in a gift that you do not have will only lead to trouble. Instead, celebrate what God has given you and do it with all your heart, soul and strength. As you walk in your gifts, you will find God will use you to impact this world in a mighty way.

Life Lesson: Find out your gifts and walk in them, don't try to walk in someone else's gifts.

Dear Father,
Thank You for the spiritual gifts You have given me. Help me to not be jealous of others gifting but rather use my gift with all my heart. Fill me with Your Spirit and equip me to do everything You have called me to do. In Jesus' name, Amen.

DECEMBER 4
IT'S NOT YOU

1 Corinthians 12:4-6
"There are diversities of gifts, but the same Spirit. There are differences of ministries, but the same Lord. And there are diversities of activities, but it is the same God who works all in all."
NKJV

We all know that pride is a dangerous thing. It causes damage to others and leads to division and bitterness. But, do you know what is even worse than pride? Spiritual pride. You see friend, God has gifted each of us with spiritual gifts that we can use for the benefit of the body of Christ. Unfortunately, it can be easy to begin thinking it was our power to begin with.

Friend, just like salvation is a gift from God and not by works, the same is true with our gifts. We did not earn our gifts, and God does not show favoritism. Each spiritual gift is just that, a gift. It was given from a loving God who desires to equip you and me to share the Gospel with a hurting world. If we begin thinking we are the source of that power, we can be a hindrance to the Kingdom as well as our own spiritual growth.

Life Lesson: Your spiritual gifts do not come from you, they come from God.

Dear Father,

Thank You for the Holy Spirit. Thank You for His work in my life. Father, help me to continue to use the gifts You have given me for Your glory and not my own. I praise You for Your forgiveness and love and pray for opportunities to share Your Gospel with the world. In Jesus' name, Amen.

DECEMBER 5
READY OR NOT

2 Chronicles 11:12
"Also in every city he put shields and spears, and made them very strong, having Judah and Benjamin on his side."
NKJV

Are you ready? They're coming. No matter your age or status, as a follower of Christ, you will face battles. Sometimes these battles are unexpected and painful. Many times the battle will rage inside your heart and mind unknown to those around you. However they may come, don't be caught off guard. Instead, be ready to hold fast to the One who can help you endure.

Ephesians 6:10-11 "Finally, my brethren, be strong in the Lord and in the power of His might. Put on the whole armor of God, that you may be able to stand against the wiles of the devil." NKJV

Jesus Himself assured us that we would have trials, yet He did not leave it at that. Instead, He said, "take heart, because I have overcome the world. (John 16:33)." What an encouragement to know that we can take our stand against the enemy knowing that Christ has already insured his defeat. As we stand in Christ we will find strength for the battle and victory in the end.

Life Lesson: Be ready as a follower of Jesus to endure trials, tribulations and battles.

Dear Father,
I praise You for all that You have done for me. As I step out to serve You help me to be ready for the battles. May I look to You for strength and wisdom. Give me patience and help me to endure to the end. Teach me in the midst of the battle to trust in You. In Jesus' name, Amen.

DECEMBER 6
THE THRONE OF GRACE

Philippians 4:6-7
"Be anxious for nothing, but in everything by prayer and supplication, with thanksgiving, let your requests be made known to God; 7 and the peace of God, which surpasses all understanding, will guard your hearts and minds through Christ Jesus."
NKJV

Prayer is a mighty tool in the hands of a Christian. When we come to God in prayer, we step beyond ourselves and enter into conversation with the God of the universe. In the book of Hebrews, it states that we should "come boldly to the throne of grace." Imagine... weak and broken, we can come to God's throne with boldness knowing that He will hear us.

Unfortunately, many times we come to God with our wish lists and plans, all the while missing the greater blessing. As we come to God in prayer and lay before Him our thanks and petitions, we begin growing in our faith. As we share with Him our hearts desire, we find ourselves desiring His heart. Many times in prayer it is not our situation that is changed but rather it is ourselves. What joy to know that we can lift our voice to God and in return find hope, peace and a life forever changed.

Life Lesson: The goal of prayer is not to have God answer according to our desires, but for our hearts to be set to receive based on His desires.

Dear Father,
Thank You for loving me and allowing me to speak to You today. Because of Jesus, I am able to come to You directly and know that You are listening. Father, continue to change my heart and mind into that of Jesus. I lift up my family and friends who may not know You. Give me an opportunity to share the Gospel with them today. In Jesus' name, Amen.

DECEMBER 7
I WAS WRONG

2 Chronicles 12:6
"Then the leaders of Israel and the king humbled themselves and said, "The Lord is right in doing this to us!"
NKJV

Have you ever thanked God for discipline? I know it may sound odd to many of us. After all, I don't know of any children that are thankful for a spanking or for being grounded. Even though it may seem strange to us, discipline is a gift from God.

Hebrews 12:10 "For our earthly fathers disciplined us for a few years, doing the best they knew how. But God's discipline is always good for us, so that we might share in his holiness." NKJV

God's discipline is always best and can be a great benefit to us if we choose to see it that way. Unfortunately, many times when we find ourselves in hard situations of our own making, we look for others to blame. We say, "It was my mother's fault" or "I didn't have much as a child." We use these and many other excuses to keep us from saying what needs to be said - "I was wrong." You see friend, true repentance will not allow for blame to be placed on anyone but ourselves. Once we admit we have done wrong and come to God broken, we find forgiveness for our sins and rest for our souls.

Life Lesson: It is a gift from God to be able to say "I was wrong."

Dear Father,
I come to You broken today understanding that I am a sinner. I also thank You for Jesus and His death and resurrection. Because of His sacrifice for my sins I can be forgiven and know Your love. Help me not to blame others when I fall but to humbly come to You and find grace. In Jesus' name, Amen.

DECEMBER 8
THE HELPER

1 Corinthians 12:7
"But the manifestation of the Spirit is given to each one for the profit of all:"
NKJV

Can you imagine what it might have been like on the Day of Pentecost? Hearing a rushing wind, you look around to see tongues of fire upon each person assembled with you. Then as soon as you're filled with God's Spirit you begin speaking in other languages. As incredible as it all sounds, imagine what it might have been like hours before. Many of these men and women had seen or heard Jesus and knew of His resurrection. They also were aware of His great commission and were probably wondering how in the world they were supposed to go into all the world and share the Gospel. After all, they were a small group and it was a big world.

The good news is that God did not leave them there to strive in vain. They were not going to have to rely on their own strength to accomplish what Jesus had instructed them to do. In obedience to Christ, those men and women waited for the Helper, who came to them in power. Friend, that same Helper is available to you today. He is the Holy Spirit. When we ask Him to fill us with His Spirit, He will. Without Him, we'll find our efforts fall short, but when we are filled with His power, our lives can change the world.

Life Lesson: We need to be filled with the Holy Spirit to be witnesses, spread the Word and do the work of the ministry.

Dear Father,
Thank You for Jesus and the forgiveness of sins. I also thank You for the Helper Whom You have sent to equip me. Lord, today I pray that You would fill me with Your Holy Spirit so that I can be strengthened and empowered to serve You. Give me an opportunity to share Your love and Your Word with this hurting world. In Jesus Name, Amen

DECEMBER 9
WALKING OUT THE WORD

2 Chronicles 13:4
Abijah stood on Mount Zemaraim, in the hill country of Ephraim, and said, "Jeroboam and all Israel, listen to me!"
NKJV

In a world of Facebook and Twitter, everyone has something to say. Everything from mundane daily actions to personal confessions is placed online for everyone to read. While technology may have made this kind of personal self-expression more accessible, it has always been part of our nature to want to share with others. As followers of Christ, this is all the more true.

You see friend, the God of all creation has shown us His love by sending His Son to pay the price for our sin. It's this message of forgiveness and grace that we proclaim to a world in need. Not only that, but as we live out our lives dedicated to Christ, people will see the difference and desire to know the Truth. As we share God's Word and walk in obedience, we will find our lives impacting eternity in a far greater way than any status update we could make.

Life Lesson: We should be people of the Word and of our word.

Dear Father,
Thank You for Jesus and for the forgiveness of sins. I praise You for Your love and grace and pray that You would give me an opportunity today to share it with someone around me. Whether it's a kind word or an act of service, help me to live out Your Word in all that I do. In Jesus' name, Amen.

DECEMBER 10
FROM DEATH TO LIFE

1 Corinthians 12:9
"to another faith by the same Spirit, to another gifts of healings by the same Spirit,"
NKJV

What do you think about when you hear the words "healing" or "miracle"? Depending on how you grew up, these words may spark memories. Some may remember charismatic services involving miraculous signs and wonders while others may simply reject the notion that they even occur today. Regardless of what we have seen or heard, we must always remember to ask the question, "What does the Bible say?" You see friend, what we believe is not dependent on our opinion or upbringing, but fully relies on what God has revealed to us through His Word.

As we look into the perfect Word of the Lord, we see that He has given us His Spirit to help spread the Gospel and minister to one another. In 1 Corinthians 12, we see that Paul clearly states that the Holy Spirit can empower us with the gift of healings and miracles. While these can refer to many things, we must understand that we have the chance to be part of one of the greatest healings of all time. What is that you ask? Simply put, it's the dead coming to life. When we tell others the Gospel and they respond, they go from death to life, from condemnation to forgiveness, from being a child of the adversary to a child of the living God. Friend, maybe you've never experienced that supernatural healing. God desires to forgive your sins and make you new. All you have to do is come to Him. Are you ready for healing?

Life Lesson: God still heals. He heals us spiritually, physically and emotionally.

Dear Father,
I know that I have done wrong in my life and I ask that You forgive me. Lord, I believe that Jesus died on the cross for my sins and that He rose again. I come to You today and ask that You would create in me a clean heart and make me new. Fill me with Your Spirit and help me to walk with You every day of my life. I love You Lord. In Jesus' name, Amen.

DECEMBER 11
THE ULTIMATE DIRECTIONS

Zechariah 1:6
"Yet surely My words and My statutes, Which I commanded My servants the prophets, Did they not overtake your fathers?"
NKJV

Have you ever been on a trip to a brand new destination? You plan for months the things you're going to do and the areas you want to visit. Finally, the day comes and you head out the door with directions in hand and a joy in your heart. Of course, a few hours later that joy is gone as you realize those directions were not as foolproof as you had thought.

Friend, this world says that all roads lead to heaven and that truth is relative. While this may sound good to people, in practice it leads to frustration, bondage and separation from God. The good news is that God has revealed to us His Truth. His Truth is not dictated by man nor is it blown around by every fad or current event. His Truth is the rock, and we can place our lives on it and find peace for our souls. Maybe today you awoke to a life in turmoil and an uncertain future. Well, I am here to tell you that God has a future and hope for you. You can find out all about it in the Bible. It's a story of love, grace and forgiveness. It's also the ultimate guide book and much better than any directions you'd find online.

Life Lesson: The revelation of God's Truth can be that hope which sets you free.

Dear Father,
Today, I woke up with questions, fears and uncertainty. Lord, give me a heart for Your Word. Help me to read it daily so that I can answer the questions of life and overcome my doubts and fears. Guide my life so that it is a reflection of You. Thank You for Your love and forgiveness, use me today. In Jesus Name, Amen.

DECEMBER 12
IT'S MINE!

Philippians 4:19
"And my God shall supply all your needs according to His riches in glory by Christ Jesus."
NKJV

"It's mine!" For any parent, those words are all too familiar. Every child at some point or another will grab something they want whether it is rightly theirs or not and scream "mine!" While as adults we may not grab a car in the parking lot and scream "mine," we still struggle against the sin of coveting. Often the things we have are not enough and even when we are blessed, we miss the opportunity to be a blessing in return.

Psalm 24:1 "The earth is the LORD's, and all its fullness, The world and those who dwell therein." NKJV

In scripture, we find a great truth that helps us overcome this mine syndrome. This basic truth is that nothing we have is ours to begin with. All our money, time, health and family are simply on loan from God. In a moment's notice, He could take it all, but instead He allows us to manage them. When we dedicate these things to Him and give of our finances and other resources for His Kingdom, we become a conduit of blessings for others. Friend, once we realize that none of what we have is ours, we find freedom from coveting and dissatisfaction. Instead, we find contentment and joy as we give our lives away for our Lord.

Life Lesson: Understanding the source of our blessings prepares us to be used as a vessel to bless others.

Dear Father,
Thank You for all that You have done for me. Because of Jesus, I have forgiveness. Because of Your continued mercy and grace, I am blessed with life and daily bread. Help me to be a blessing to others today as I channel the blessings I have to others. In Jesus' name, Amen.

DECEMBER 13
RELIGIOUS NOISE

1 Corinthians 12:12
"For as the body is one and has many members, but all the members of that one body, being many, are one body, so also is Christ."
NKJV

Can you imagine the chaos that would occur if your body decided to attack itself? What if your arm was mad at your foot for not saying "hi" in the hallway, or your liver decided to quit simply because it was jealous of the mouth? While it may seem ridiculous to imagine, this sad scenario occurs every week in churches all over the world. The body of Christ, formed to demonstrate the love and forgiveness of Jesus, turns on itself out of selfishness and pride. Friend, it doesn't need to be this way and it shouldn't be this way. Paul writes...

1 Corinthians 13 "Though I speak with the tongues of men and of angels, but have not love, I have become sounding brass or a clanging cymbal." NKJV

This chapter is dedicated to promoting love as the ultimate spiritual fruit. Do you prophesy and understand great mysteries? Great, but do you love? Are you able to speak with tongues of angels? Awesome, but do you love? You see, no matter what gift we are given, if we are not acting in love towards one another, we are nothing more than religious noise. Instead of useless noise, let's sing out a sweet song of forgiveness and love. That is a tune sure to impact the world for Christ.

Life Lesson: No matter how gifted we are or what our giftings are, if we don't have love, we are just religious noise.

Dear Father,
Thank You for the spiritual gifts You have given me and those around me. Father, help us to use those gifts for Your glory and not our own selfish gain. Teach us to love like You love. Fill us with Your Holy Spirit so that our love for one another will cause the world to take notice and turn to You. In Jesus name, Amen.

DECEMBER 14
HIS PERFECT LOVE

Malachi 4:2

"But for you who fear my name, the Sun of Righteousness will rise with healing in his wings. And you will go free, leaping with joy like calves let out to pasture."
NLT

The prophets of the Hebrew Scriptures often centered on a common theme of the coming judgment for the people of Israel. In the book of Malachi, it is no different. This final book of the Old Testament brings a very real promise of coming judgment, yet in the midst of this proclamation is a message of hope and blessings. You see, the reality is that our sin is worthy of God's judgment. We have broken His laws and deserve punishment...but God does not leave us there. Instead, He stepped down out of heaven in the form of Jesus Christ and made a way for us to be saved from this punishment.

When Jesus died on the cross 2000 years ago, He proclaimed to the whole world His love for mankind. Now because of this amazing love, we can find hope and a future in a relationship with Jesus. When we realize our sin and turn to God for forgiveness, He opens His arms wide desiring to shower us with His grace and mercy. This is the God of the Bible, both perfect in judgment and perfect in love. Do you know Him? If so, rejoice my friend because the coming of the Lord brings healing and joy! If not, then come to Him today and find rest for your weary soul and love for all eternity.

Life Lesson: The day of the Lord brings healing & joy to those who fear the Lord.

Dear Father,
I know that I have sinned against You and I pray that You would forgive me of my sins. I believe that Jesus died on the cross and rose again so that I could be forgiven. Fill me with Your Holy Spirit and help me to live a life dedicated to You. Thank You for Your love and grace. In Jesus' name, Amen.

DECEMBER 15
CARBON COPY

1 Corinthians 12:15-16

"If the foot should say, "Because I am not a hand, I am not of the body," is it therefore not of the body? And if the ear should say, "Because I am not an eye, I am not of the body," is it therefore not of the body?"
NKJV

If you've been alive for any amount of time, you've probably witnessed the strange things people will do to be 'unique'. Between hairstyles, clothes or body art, people want to be noticed for their differences. Because of this attitude, many people claim that the church leads to nothing but the same old same old. Well friend, I'm here to tell you that any church that is living biblically will not be a factory of sameness.

In fact, God's Word describes the body of Christ as different people with unique talents and abilities coming together with a single purpose in mind. Just as God created the vast array of flowers that brighten our world, He has created each and every one of us with special gifts that can be used for His glory. What a beautiful picture of unity with diversity. So instead of seeking out differences to hold against each other, let us use our differences in an effort to build God's Kingdom. As the world looks on and sees us walk in loving unity, they will wonder how and we can simply say, "Jesus."

Life Lesson: Christian unity does not mean uniformity or "sameness".

Dear Father,
Thank You for the special gifts and abilities You have given to me. Father, I pray that You give me and my church a heart of unity. Help us to use our differences for Your Kingdom and not to allow the enemy to cause division. May my heart and mind be set on You and the Gospel. In Jesus' name, Amen.

DECEMBER 16
CONTAGIOUS

2 Chronicles 14:11
"Then Asa cried out to the Lord his God, "O Lord, no one but you can help the powerless against the mighty! Help us, O Lord our God, for we trust in you alone. It is in your name that we have come against this vast horde. O Lord, you are our God; do not let mere men prevail against you!" NKJV

In life, we are all faced with difficulties and trials. Whether it is a struggle within us or a struggle with another person, we often can find ourselves beat up and deflated. This is why it is vital for any believer to surround themselves with people who are courageous at heart. These are men and women who know the obstacles but are not stopped by them. Friends, who may be challenged by life but their faith in God overpowers their fear.

All too often we can find ourselves surrounded by those who seem more apt to throw a pity party than a pep rally. In these times, we need to seek out those who will be an encouragement and strength during our times of weakness. As we fellowship with Christians who are empowered by their faith and set on fire through the Spirit, we will find ourselves igniting with hope and courage. A steady diet of courageous fellowship leads to a life that is blessed and growing. This is the life Christ came to give us-an abundant life.

Life Lesson: Courage and faith are contagious.

Dear Father,
Thank You for Your love for me and the hope I have in You. Help me to seek out those who can encourage me in my walk with You. May I surround myself with those who love You and are full of faith so that I may be better equipped to serve others and Glorify Your name. In Jesus' name, Amen.

DECEMBER 17
EXTREME LOVE

Amos 4:9

"I blasted you with blight and mildew. When your gardens increased, Your vineyards, Your fig trees, And your olive trees, The locust devoured them; Yet you have not returned to Me," Says the LORD."
NKJV

Often in the Hebrew Scriptures, we read of the judgments of God and gasp as we see Israel and other nations suffering under the Lord's power. While the judgments of God are difficult, we must understand that all through the Old Testament God is showing grace and mercy. In the prophets, He calls for people to turn from their wicked ways and He will forgive them. You see friend, while God's discipline can often seem extreme, His love is just as potent.

Romans 5:8 "But God demonstrates His own love towards us, in that while we were still sinners, Christ died for us." NKJV

Extreme love-that is what the God of all creation has shown towards us. While we were steeped in sin and suffering under the weight of condemnation, He stepped out of Heaven and gave His life for ours. The punishment that we deserved was placed upon Jesus on the cross. Each strike of the nails that pierced his hands was done so that we could know forgiveness. Each cruel word and slash of the whip on Jesus' body happened so that we could spend eternity with Him. All we have to do is come to Jesus seeking forgiveness and trusting in Him for salvation. As we do, we take part in the greatest love anyone could ever know.

Life Lesson: God goes to extreme measures to reveal His love for us.

Dear Father,
I know that I have done wrong. Today, I come to You and ask that You would forgive me of all my sins. I confess that Jesus is Lord and I believe that He died for my sins and was raised from the grave three days later. Lord, make me a new creation and fill me with Your Spirit so that I can live for You. In Jesus' name, Amen.

DECEMBER 18
WE NEED EACH OTHER

1 Corinthians 12:21
"And the eye cannot say to the hand, "I have no need of you"; nor again the head to the feet, "I have no need of you."
NKJV

This week chances are real good that you've been to the grocery store. Without really thinking about it, each week we go to the store to get food then drive home all the while taking for granted that the store will be there the next time we run out. But what if...it wasn't? What if the stores closed or ran out of food? Now, I'm not saying this to cause alarm, but I am trying to paint a picture of just how dependent we are on one another.

Each one of our lives impacts those around us and this fact is even greater inside the church. You see friend, God created the body of Christ to function together. Without the feet, there would be no walking and without the eyes, there would be no seeing. God did not make us to work apart but rather together as one. Yes, we all have different pasts, pains and problems but God is greater than that. With His Spirit in each of us, we can find the power to work together for the sake of His Kingdom.

Life Lesson: We need God and we need each other.

Dear Father,
Thank You for the church. Thank You for those in the church who are united under the name of Jesus to love one another and to help each other. Father, I pray that You would help me take my eyes off myself and to focus them on you. As I do that I will find strength and unity as the body of Christ. In Jesus' name, Amen.

DECEMBER 19
DENY YOURSELF

1 Corinthians 12:24-25
"but our presentable parts have no need. But God composed the body, having given greater honor to that part which lacks it, that there should be no schism in the body, but that the members should have the same care for one another."
NKJV

It was there in the garden, when Eve looked at the fruit and saw that it was good. It was found in the face of Cain after His brother's sacrifice was accepted and not his. It was also seen around the cross as religious leaders mocked Jesus. What was it? It was selfishness. Friend, selfishness is the root of so much sin and suffering around us. Think about it. What causes one man to steal from another? It's a selfish desire for what's not his own. What leads a man or woman to commit adultery? It's a self-focused desire and want, with no consideration of their spouse. What would cause people inside the church to fight or divide? You guessed it... it is selfishness.

In Luke 9:23, Jesus states something extremely contrary to our nature. He says "If anyone desires to come after Me, let him deny himself, and take up his cross and follow Me." Deny ourselves. It's easier said than done but, with the power of God's Spirit, it is possible. Imagine if each person in the church would seek to bless the other. Imagine if instead of spreading gossip, we all spread encouragement. What if instead of condemnation, we practiced mercy. You see, in order for the body of Christ to function as a whole, it cannot be divided. This means nailing our selfishness to the cross and leaving it there. When that happens, our church, our community and even our world will never be the same.

Life Lesson: The Bible points out that division is rooted in selfishness.

Dear Father,
Thank You for Your love for me and for making me part of the church. Father, help me to be a blessing to the body and not a hindrance. Teach me to share encouragement and love with those I meet. Give me the power to deny myself and live my life dedicated to serving and loving others. In Jesus' name, Amen.

DECEMBER 20
YOUR FINEST HOUR

1 Corinthians 12:27
"Now you are the body of Christ, and members individually."
NKJV

We have all heard the expression, "there is no 'I' in teamwork" and this is even truer for the church. Like a team that has made it to the Super Bowl, we should stand united in Christ working together for one unified purpose - to proclaim the Gospel to the world. This is a lofty goal, yet it is one that our coach has called us to. Christ has given us the directive and now we must follow through, as a team.

Romans 12:15 "Rejoice with those who rejoice, and weep with those who weep." NKJV

Like a team, the church must support each player as they gain ground for the Kingdom. If one member is in pain, the rest should grieve for them then do what they can to help. If there is a big play and one person is blessed, we all rejoice with glad hearts. There is no room for selfishness or jealousy in the family of God. These things lead to bitterness, deceit, and division. Remember, this is not about us. If we think that this life is about us, then we miss out on God's amazing blessings and the team suffers. It's about our Lord and it's about others. In front of us is the field of life and the God of all creation has empowered us to gain ground for His Kingdom. It's bigger than you and I, yet God has called us to the line of scrimmage. Are you ready? This could be your finest hour.

Life Lesson: We are in Christ and a part of something bigger and more important than just ourselves.

Dear Father,
Thank You for life and for inviting me to be part of this adventure with You. Thank You for the gifts you've given me. Lord, I pray that You use them for Your Kingdom. Help me to get rid of any selfishness and to put others first. In Jesus' name, Amen.

DECEMBER 21
GIFT OF OBEDIENCE

Hosea 1:2
When the LORD began to speak by Hosea, the LORD said to Hosea: "Go; take yourself a wife of harlotry and children of harlotry, for the land has committed great harlotry By departing from the LORD."
NKJV

We often hear Christians say things like "The Lord just wants me to be happy" or "God wouldn't ask me to do anything that I can't handle." The truth is that God often asks His people to do what seems impossible. It is also clear that happiness rarely has anything to do with His commands. Hosea was told by God to take a wife that would cause him much pain. Abraham was told to sacrifice his only son, whom he called 'laughter' and loved dearly. Mary, who was called most blessed among women, was required to stand by and watch her son die on the cross. These three, and many others in the Bible, were asked by God to do what we would think impossible for them; things that would bring pain and suffering. They had different circumstances, and different struggles, but the one thing they shared was obedience.

Matthew 16:24-25 "Then Jesus said to His disciples, 'If anyone desires to come after Me, let him deny himself, and take up his cross, and follow Me. For whoever desires to save his life will lose it, but whoever loses his life for My sake will find it.'" NKJV

Jesus went through incredible suffering and pain to free us from the bondage of sin. He did not die just so we could be happy. He did not give His life, so that we could simply pursue our own selfish desires. He died to set us free, and to give us the model of how to live free. What He taught the disciples through His words and by His example is that our calling in this life is to lay down our own lives for the sake of others.

Life Lesson: Following Christ is hard, but it's the least we can offer Him for the price He paid.

Dear Father,
Thank You for loving me so much that You were willing to die a horrible death and suffer the humiliation of my sins. Lord, I choose to follow You, wherever You lead me, because I love You. Jesus, help me to walk in obedience. Give me Your strength, Your power and Your Love, so that I can willingly lay down my life for others. I pray this in Jesus' name, Amen.

DECEMBER 22
GRUDGE MATCH

Obadiah 1:3
"The pride of your heart has deceived you, You who dwell in the clefts of the rock, Whose habitation is high; You who say in your heart, 'Who will bring me down to the ground?'"
NKJV

In the book of Obadiah, the prophet is proclaiming judgment on the nation of Edom. This nation and God's people of Israel have a history full of conflict starting at the birth of Jacob and Esau. For hundreds of years what began with deception on the part of Jacob continued with violence as Israel and Edom locked horns in an extended bout of sibling rivalry. If Edom had forgiven Israel and turned to the Lord, they would have found freedom rather than bondage to their bitterness.

While you may not be fighting with another nation, maybe you are harboring resentment towards a friend or family member who wronged you. Now, like Esau, you desire revenge and will stop at nothing to get it. Holding a grudge may make us feel empowered, but it does nothing but rob us of joy. When we step outside ourselves and forgive others as God has forgiven us, we find freedom from our cage of contempt. Forgiveness of others also opens the floodgates of God's forgiveness in our own lives so that we may find rest for our souls and the perfect joy of the Lord.

Life Lesson: We need to practice active forgiveness.

Dear Father,
Thank You for forgiving me of my sins. Help me to forgive others as You have forgiven me. If I am holding any grudges or bitterness, show me so that I can practice active forgiveness. In Jesus' name, Amen.

DECEMBER 23
DANGER! DANGER!

1 Timothy 1:3-4
"As I urged you when I went into Macedonia-remain in Ephesus that you may charge some that they teach no other doctrine, 4 nor give heed to fables and endless genealogies, which cause disputes rather than godly edification which is in faith."
NKJV

In the body of Christ, we must be careful to guard ourselves against divisiveness and false doctrine. These things will penetrate the body and can lead to sin as well as a misunderstanding of God's Word. Often, those who come representing a "new way" or a "higher understanding" are deceived. Their train of thought is dependent upon human wisdom or even an evil motive. This is why many times throughout the scriptures the apostles warn against false teachers and bad doctrines.

Often, bad teaching comes from those who want to do it their own way. They are not content with God's Word as the final authority so they twist it or reject it all together. Friend, this is dangerous. If we are to truly understand life, we need to look to the One who gave life. If we desire to know about this world, we must hold tight to the words of God who formed it. Most importantly, if we are to know how we can find forgiveness and eternal life, we have no other option than to embrace the Truth found in the Bible. When we live by God's Words and not our own, we will find hope for this life and unending joy in the next.

Life Lesson: There is danger to living our lives by our own standards rather than God's.

Dear Father,
Thank You for the Bible. What a blessing it is to be able to read the very words of God. Father guard my heart against false teaching and help me to stand firm on the Truth of Your Word. Hide Your Word in my heart so that I will not sin against You and use me to share Your Word with others. In Jesus' name, Amen.

DECEMBER 24
CHRISTMAS

Luke 2:7
And she brought forth her firstborn Son, and wrapped Him in swaddling cloths, and laid Him in a manger, because there was no room for them in the inn.
NKJV

It is the season where we celebrate the birth of our Lord Jesus Christ; when God became Man. His reception was not a glorious one by any standard. Our Lord and Savior, the Creator of the universe, was born in a barn and lain in a feeding trough because there was no room for Him in the inn. Before we judge the people of that day for not making room for Him, ask yourself, are you making room for Him? Are you making time to spend with Him, time for fellowship with others who know Him, to worship Him and to learn of Him from the Bible? Or is there a sign written on your heart and life that says 'no room'. My prayer for you in the busyness of this Christmas season and in the coming year is that you would make room for Him in your life and in your heart.

Life Lesson: Make room for Jesus.

Dear Father,
Thank You for loving us so much that You would come as one of us, not in ritual and splendor - though You could have, but You came in simplicity and humility. Lord, if there is any way that I have failed to make room for You in my heart and life, I ask You to forgive me and to show me. I pray this in Jesus' name, Amen.

DECEMBER 25
MERRY CHRISTMAS

Isaiah 9:6
"For unto us a Child is born, unto us a Son is given; And the government will be upon His shoulder. And His name will be called Wonderful, Counselor, Mighty God, Everlasting Father, Prince of Peace."
NKJV

To my extended family, I wish you all the joy that Jesus brings with the deep meaning of the season. In the middle of this busy holiday season, it is important for us to remember that Jesus is not only the reason for this season but He is the reason for all seasons. This Christmas, as you gather gifts for family and friends, may you remember the One whose grace-gift is greater, Jesus. May we cross the bridge to a deeper and more meaningful life as together, we change the world. Let your light shine. I wish you a very Merry Christmas.

Luke 2:13-14 "And suddenly there was with the angel a multitude of the heavenly host praising God and saying: "Glory to God in the highest, And on earth peace, goodwill toward men!"

Life Lesson: Keep the focus on Jesus.

Dear Father,
Thank You for the opportunity Christmas brings to worship You through selfless acts of love and giving. I want to keep Jesus the focus and bear light that others might see the way to the Prince of Peace. Please give me opportunity to be that light of love in the lives of many. I pray this in Jesus' name. Amen.

DECEMBER 26
WHAT IS LOVE?

1 Corinthians 13:3
"And though I bestow all my goods to feed the poor, and though I give my body to be burned, but have not love, it profits me nothing."
NKJV

Love - that one word possesses great power. When a couple first releases that word into their vocabulary, it changes the dynamic of their relationship. On the other hand, when someone you care for tells you they no longer love you, it could impact your life for years. Unfortunately, this word has many times been misunderstood. Our world sees love as a souped up version of lust but that's not what God created love to be and neither is it the example He has shown us.

1 John 4:16 "Beloved, let us love one another, for love is of God; and everyone who loves is born of God and knows God."

Love is not morality or religion. It's not something else to put on your to-do list. Rather, love is our motivation and it is seen perfectly in our Lord. In short, love is Jesus. In every second of His life on earth, Jesus was love and demonstrated that love. From his healing of the sick and feeding the hungry, to His correction of the Pharisees, Jesus' end goal was love. You could do all the good deeds in the world, but without love they would be like a string of zero's - meaning nothing. Jesus loved others because He loved the Father. The same is true with us. As we love our Heavenly Father, we will be able to love others; even those who we feel may not be that lovable.

Life Lesson: Love is the perfection of human character.

Dear Father,
Thank You for Your love. Because of Your love for me, I have forgiveness of sins and hope of heaven. Father, fill me with Your Spirit and help me to love like You love. Make me more like Jesus so that I can share Your grace and mercy with those around me. Use me today to show love. In Jesus' name, Amen.

DECEMBER 27
TRUE POWER

1 Timothy 1:12-13
"And I thank Christ Jesus our Lord who has enabled me, because He counted me faithful, putting me into the ministry, although I was formerly a blasphemer, a persecutor, and an insolent man; but I obtained mercy because I did it ignorantly in unbelief."
NKJV

"Why would God use me?" "I've done terrible things in my past so how can I minister to others?" We've all been there and have stood on the edge of a ministry opportunity facing doubts and fears. "What if they don't believe me?" "I don't have a degree in theology...what do I know?" All these questions and thoughts cloud our perspective and leave us unmoved and powerless — unless we grab hold of the Truth.

2 Corinthians 3: "It is not that we think we are qualified to do anything on our own. Our qualification comes from God." NLT

Yes, we are weak vessels. Yes, we may stumble at times, but our power does not lie inside ourselves. Our power comes from the One who created Heaven and Earth. The power that raised Jesus from the dead is the same power that fills us as followers of Christ. It is God who equips us and strengthens us for ministry. Whether you are a full time pastor or a volunteer at the church, God is the One equipping you to impact lives for eternity. Admit your weaknesses and then step out in faith trusting the power of the One who has saved you. In Him, you will find victory over fear and power to reach a lost and dying world with the Gospel.

Life Lesson: When the Lord calls you into ministry, He alone equips you.

Dear Father,
Thank You for the salvation found in Jesus Christ. I praise You for the forgiveness of sins and the new life. Father, help me to overcome my fears or doubts. Empower me to step out in faith into ministry wherever I am today. Use me to reach this lost world for Christ. In Jesus' name, Amen.

DECEMBER 28
LUV IS A VERB

1 Corinthians 13:6
"[Love] does not rejoice in iniquity, but rejoices in the truth."
NKJV

Many years ago a popular Christian group wrote a song titled, "Luv is a Verb." While their spelling may have been off, the truth of the song was not. Love is not simply a feeling or intellectual process but an active expression. This view of love seen in scripture is purposeful and benevolent. It actively engages others, thinking of them above ourselves. Biblical love is not hindered by anything but seeks with passion to be shared with anyone and everyone.

How is this possible? How can we even begin to love in a way that looks for opportunities rather than excuses? Simply put, we plug into the source of love. Friend, the God of all creation left everything in heaven for you and me. He stepped from the throne of God and wrapped Himself in our weak flesh in order to die on our behalf. That kind of love is life changing. That kind of love will fuel our lives so that we too can love like our Savior. Today, seek out an opportunity to love. Whether it's a kind word, act of service or a merciful response, let's love like Jesus. That kind of love will never be stopped - no matter how you spell it.

Life Lesson: Love will find a way. A lack of love will find an excuse.

Dear Father,
I praise You for the amazing love You have shown me. Help me to grasp this love so that I will be equipped to love others in the same way. Strip me of any excuses and use me to reach others with the love of Jesus. In His name, Amen.

DECEMBER 29
APATHY IS NOT AN OPTION

Obadiah 1:11

"In the day that you stood on the other side-In the day that strangers carried captive his forces, When foreigners entered his gates And cast lots for Jerusalem— Even you *were* as one of them." NKJV

Apathy, detachment, disinterest, disregard—no matter what you call it, it's not an option as a follower of Jesus. In the book of Obadiah, God proclaims judgment on Edom because they stood by and watched Israel be destroyed and taken into captivity. They saw their brother in need yet did nothing. Contrast this to Jesus who was active in our redemption.

Philippians 2:7-8 "7 but made Himself of no reputation, taking the form of a bondservant, and coming in the likeness of men. 8 And being found in appearance as a man, He humbled Himself and became obedient to the point of death, even the death of the cross." NKJV

Jesus intentionally left His throne and the glory of Heaven to walk among the pain and suffering of world. He then purposefully gave up His life so that we could know forgiveness. He could have stayed in Heaven, but because of His great love for us and in obedience to the Father, Jesus acted. As followers of Christ, may we be active in loving, caring and sharing with others. Who knows what a small act of kindness or encouraging word could do to change a life. The world is waiting— let's go!

Life Lesson: Apathy is not an option as a follower of Christ.

Dear Father,
Thank You for Jesus and His love and obedience. Because of His active role in my redemption, I can know forgiveness and grace. In the same way that You were intentional in the salvation of man, may I be intentional in ministering to those around me. Fill me with Your Spirit and equip me to be a light in this dark world. In Jesus' name, Amen.

DECEMBER 30
NEVER-ENDING LOVE

1 Corinthians 13:8
"Love never fails. But whether there are prophecies, they will fail; whether there are tongues, they will cease; whether there is knowledge, it will vanish away."
NKJV

One day all that we know here on Earth will be changed. When Christ appears in all His glory, Heaven will come to Earth and our lives, homes, bodies and relationships will change forever. Yet, there is one thing that will never change. That thing is love. When we see Christ face to face, we will no longer need faith. As we glimpse the realities of heaven all around us, we will no longer cling to hope of a better day. But love will never disappear. The love that created the world and gave life to humanity will still sustain the saints in heaven. The love that walked out of heaven and went to the cross is the same love that prepared a place for us for all eternity. And, the same love that strengthens us in this life is the same love that welcomes us into the next. This love never fails, never wavers and never grows weary. This love is the love of God.

1 John 4:19 "We love Him because He first loved us." NKJV

Because this love will always remain, let us begin loving even now. We will spend eternity with our brothers and sisters in Christ, so why not love them now? As we love each other with the love given to us through Christ, the world will see it and desire the same. When they do, we can point them to the never-ending source of love, Jesus.

Life Lesson: Love releases the power of the Spirit in our lives and in our churches.

Dear Father,
Thank You for the love You have shown me. Help me to love others in the same way You have loved me. Use me today to share the love of God with someone I see. In Jesus' name, Amen.

DECEMBER 31
THAT HE GAVE

John 3:16-17

"For God so loved the world that He gave His only begotten Son, that whoever believes in Him should not perish but have everlasting life. For God did not send His Son into the world to condemn the world, but that the world through Him might be saved."

NKJV

What's the first thing you think of when you hear the word 'Christmas'? Is it a tree decorated with lights and tinsel? Maybe it's those brightly colored gifts or a special Christmas tradition you remember as a kid. Many of us may think of Christ lying in a manger surrounded by Mary, Joseph and shepherds. While we all have different perspectives on Christmas, there is one thing that Christmas brings to light that can change our lives-forever. It's this, "For God so loved the world that He gave..."

The Maker of all creation gave to us. He did not give to us because we were worth it or because we had something to offer. He gave because He loved. The moment God became flesh was the most perfect act of love in history. Jesus left the glories of heaven and the throne of His Father and came into the tiny town of Bethlehem as a baby. With this act, God declared to all of humanity, "You are not alone." Friend, Jesus did not come into Bethlehem bringing condemnation. He came so that He could give His life so that our sins could be forgiven. This is the greatest gift you will ever receive, but like all gifts you must open it first.

Life Lesson: Jesus came to save and forgive anyone who believes in Him, not to condemn them.

Dear Father,

Thank You for Christmas. Thank You for sending Jesus into our world so that we can have hope. I understand that it's because of His life, death, and resurrection that I can be forgiven of all that I've done. Father, help me to keep this as my focus this Christmas and give me the boldness to share this good news with family and friends this holiday. In Jesus' name, Amen.

TOPICAL INDEX

NOTES

❖❖
❖

APRIL 4th

1. Charles Spurgeon quoted in Robert J. Morgan, *Stories, Illustrations, & Quotes* (Nashville, TN: Thomas Nelson, Inc., 2000).

MAY 17th

1. Aiden Wilson Tozer. BrainyQuote.com. Xplore Inc, 2011. 10 June. 2011. www.brainyquote.com/quotes/quotes/a/aidenwilso153976.html

JUNE 2nd

1. Charles Spurgeon. *Morning and Evening* (New Kensington, PA: Whitaker House, 2001)

JULY 23rd

1. C.T. Studd quoted in Warren Wiersbe, *On Being a Servant of God* (Grand Rapids, MI: Baker Publishing Group, 2007).

SEPTEMBER 18th

1. Jeff Foxworthy. *You Might Be a Redneck if...This is the Biggest Book You've Ever Read* (Nashville, TN: Thomas Nelson, 2004).

SEPTEMBER 30th

1. Wopler, David (Producer), Stuart, Mel (Director). 1971. Willy Wonka & the Chocolate Factory (Motion picture). USA: Bavaria Film Studios.

FREE DAILY E-VOTIONALS

Please sign up for my daily devotional thoughts (e-votionals) and periodic updates at:

Cross*the*Bridge.com

Treat yourself to captivating devotions overflowing with relevant wisdom, inspiration, power and hope! You can receive my encouraging and helpful thoughts free in your email inbox every morning. All you need to do is to sign up at www.crossthebridge.com. It's easy, only takes a minute and can help you for a lifetime. Please do it now and tomorrow morning, you can start receiving the help and guidance you need.

Join the thousands who've already discovered a deeper, stronger walk with Jesus and strengthened faith for everyday living with daily e-votionals.

Incorporate them in your family devotions or enjoy them as personal quiet times with God.

These e-votionals can be used as a great way to encourage anyone to devote daily time with God. All it takes is a moment to change your day, your life and your world. So go ahead to crossthebridge.com and sign up today. I look forward to sharing with you tomorrow morning!

Living to tell what He died to say,

Pastor David McGee

Change your day,
Change your life.
Change your life,
Change your world.
Change your world,
…or leave no trace that you were ever here.

Sign up now & change your day!

crossthebridge®
with **David McGee**

THINK ABOUT LIFE. THINK ABOUT JESUS

Cross the Bridge Ministries

You're invited to partner with Cross the Bridge Ministries to bring hope and healing to lives by using T.V., radio and Internet. We help those who don't know Jesus to know Him and to help those who do know Him to go deeper than they have ever been before. Help us to equip people to Cross the Bridge from death to life and from spectator Christianity to a joy-filled life dedicated to serving God. Become a Bridge Builder by committing to give a monthly gift to this ministry. We pray every Wednesday for our Bridge Builders and bless them with unique gifts and offers. Please call 877-458-5508. People are standing by right now or visit www.crossthebridge.com and click on BridgeBuilders.

Visit www.CrosstheBridge.com to find valuable edifying and encouraging information such as:

- Archives of Pastor David's radio program and teaching.
- The growing list of broadcasting stations and schedules.
- Daily e-Votionals.
- "God's Plan" section to encourage your daily walk with God.
- Downloads of audio and video.
- Online eStore with faith building resources for you and your family in your adventure with Him.
- You will also find a link to Pastor David's home church, The Bridge.

The Bridge is a vibrant congregation located in the heart of the Triad near Winston-Salem, NC. Come visit us for worship and teaching God's Word. Schedules are available online, so join us in person or via our live streaming iCampus. Visit www.aboutthebridge.com where you will learn more about Pastor David and the church.

Please check us out online, give us a call or write us a letter.

Most importantly, we want you to submit prayer requests online so we can specifically pray for those you care about that need Salvation.

CrosstheBridge.com
Cross the Bridge Ministries
P.O. Box 12515
Winston-Salem, NC 27117

1-877-458-5508

ABOUT the AUTHOR

❖

D avid McGee has led an interesting life. He was born a deaf-mute. Doctors discovered a birth defect that kept him from speaking. He was 95 percent deaf. He was healed through nine surgeries and four years of speech therapy. David worked as a professional rock musician, a remodeling company owner, a recording studio owner, and a traveling Christian teacher/musician. Now he is the senior pastor of a vibrant fellowship. His story is certainly a unique and exciting one.

In 2002, David moved from his small home Bible study into the public sphere. That once-small fellowship of fifteen people has exploded to over two thousand in weekly attendance with an incredible facility and a dynamic and growing media ministry. He has since launched a satellite church and plans to launch several more. David's teachings are broadcast around the world on TV, radio, and the Internet in an ever-increasing outreach to people. David has appeared on numerous television and radio shows, making appearances on ABC, CBS, CBN, FOX, NBC, TCT and TBN.

David continues to serve as the senior pastor of The Bridge, near Winston-Salem, NC and recently moved his congregation from a 36,000 square foot facility to an incredible 80,000 square foot location! He is also the pastor and speaker for the media outreach, Cross the Bridge Ministries. In 2010 alone, over 100,000 people attended David McGee's local, satellite and i-campus church services at The Bridge. Cross the Bridge supports 53 missionaries, provides for the housing and needs of 50 orphans, airs on over 430 radio stations nationally, produced 287 television programs and broadcasts through online television programs world-wide daily. The Cross the Bridge website has reached a record 18.8 million hits, with people all over the world discovering the online teaching tools, the plan of salvation, David McGee's blog, and the ministry is continuing to explode onto the Christian media landscape.

His verse-by-verse teaching through the Bible is marked by powerful personal insights, humorous comments, and in-depth knowledge of the Hebrew language and customs. This style of teaching deeply impacts the lives of those who come in contact with David and his ministry. One of the things that make this ministry so unique is David's love for God, for people, and for the Bible. In a time when biblical literacy has fallen to an all-time low, David makes the Bible fun, exciting, and personally meaningful. He is seen as cutting edge and culturally relevant, yet biblically solid.

It is the passion of this man and this ministry to communicate the timeless truths of the Bible to a lost, dying, and confused world. In addition to exploding media attention and increasing DVD and CD sales, David has expanded his ministry team. He has released, *Cross the Bridge to Life: Discover Your Adventure, and now Cross the Bridge Every Day*. He will be unveiling his next book soon!

"And they were astonished beyond measure, saying, "'He has done all things well. He makes both the deaf to hear and the mute to speak."
—Mark 7:37 NKJV

FOR MORE ON DAVID MCGEE'S TESTIMONY, VISIT DAVIDMCGEE.ORG

FOR MORE RESOURCES
BY DAVID MCGEE

Thank you for buying this book. *In appreciation of your support of this life-changing ministry, we'd like to bless you with a 10% discount offer for all items you purchase exclusively from our eStore:*
www.CrosstheBridge.com
Please visit the site often because we are always adding new ways to help you in your adventure.

Use this 10% Discount Code with your next online purchase:
CTBEVRYDY
(Discounts available for a limited time.)

Cross the Bridge to Life: Discover Your Adventure
As you journey through this book, get ready to be challenged, refreshed, inspired, and equipped to start enjoying the blessed life God destined for you.
Retail: $9.99; *Your Cost: $8.99* (with discount code)

Passover Seder
David McGee guides you through nearly 3 hours of the Passover Seder meal, revealing the prophetic significance and fulfillment of each step in the process. Every believer in Jesus must experience this special DVD teaching!
Retail: $29.99; *Your Cost: $26.99* (with discount code)

Israel: The Bible and You
Join David McGee as he teaches from one of the largest archaeological sites in Israel, Beit She'an. Pastor David has led numerous large group tours to Israel, and he has a deep understanding of Israel and the Hebrew language. Discover amazingly how God's relationship with Israel in the Bible and throughout history can help you to better understand your covenant relationship with Him. What you learn and discover in "Israel, the Bible and You', may change your life.
Retail: $14.99; *Your Cost: $13.49* (with discount code)

Israel: The Journey Home
Join Pastor David McGee as he takes the journey home exploring the rich history of Israel and the Bible. See the actual locations of events you may have read about in the Bible and listen as David makes the book come alive in a way you will never forget.
Retail: $29.99; *Your Cost: $26.99* (with discount code)

MP3 of the Book of Romans

David McGee teaches through the book of Romans covering each verse with incredible Biblical and historical insight. With his vast knowledge and personal insight, David provides practical application for our daily lives in every teaching.
Retail: $69.99; *Your Cost: $62.99* (with discount code)

Romans from Rome

Join David McGee from Rome, Italy as he guides you through scriptures and the historical settings of Rome. Discover and hear teachings on Rome and its connection to Christianity at the time of Christ, Paul and today.
Retail: $14.99; Your Cost: $13.49 (with discount code)

Music Theory 101 & 201

Music Theory 101 & 102 from our Worship Conference led by Pastor David McGee. David is the Senior Pastor of The Bridge as well a professional musician involved in performing, recording and producing music.
Retail: *$14.99; Your Cost: $13.49* (with discount code)

Bridge Builders DVD

In the church today, only a small percentage of people tell others about the wonderful forgiveness they have found. Armed with God's Word and a passion for the lost, David McGee equips you with the tools needed to overcome your fear and become a bridge builder to Jesus.
DVD Retail: $14.99; **Your Cost: $13.49** (with discount code)
CD Retail: $4.99; Your Cost: $4.49 (with discount code)

"All for One" CD

Enjoy this enthusiastic contemporary worship CD recorded by David McGee and The Bridge Worship Band. Includes 5 of David's original compositions!
Retail: $9.99; *Your Cost: $8.99* (with discount code)

"The Journey" CD

Journey through this very personal and re-flective collection of songs written by David McGee. Enjoy these songs as they are performed dynamically and passionately to the Lord.
Retail: $9.99; *Your Cost: $8.99* (with discount code)

"The Offering: Songs of David" CD

Dedicated to God the Father, Son and Holy Spirit, David McGee pours out his heart to God as he records this contemporary worship CD with personal application, uplifting style and enthusiasm.
Retail: $9.99; *Your Cost: $8.99* (with discount code)

NOTE: ALL PRICES EFFECTIVE AS OF THE DATE OF PUBLICATION & SUBJECT TO CHANGE WITHOUT NOTICE.